Charles Hastings Collette

Saint Augustine

A Sketch of his Life and Writings as Affecting the Controversy with Rome

Charles Hastings Collette

Saint Augustine
A Sketch of his Life and Writings as Affecting the Controversy with Rome

ISBN/EAN: 9783337336448

Printed in Europe, USA, Canada, Australia, Japan

Cover: Foto ©Lupo / pixelio.de

More available books at **www.hansebooks.com**

SAINT AUGUSTINE

(AURELIUS AUGUSTINUS, EPISCOPUS HIPPONIENSIS).

A.D. 387–430.

A SKETCH

OF HIS LIFE AND WRITINGS

AS AFFECTING THE CONTROVERSY WITH ROME.

BY

CHARLES HASTINGS COLLETTE.

" Let not these words be heard between us, ' I say,' or ' you say,' but rather let us hear 'Thus saith the Lord ;' for there are certain books of our Lord, in whose authority both sides acquiesce ; there let us seek our Church, there let us judge our cause. Take away, therefore, all those things which each alleges against the other, and which are derived from any other source than the canonical books of the Holy Scriptures. But, perhaps, some will ask, why take away such authorities? Because I would have the Holy Church proved, not by human documents, but by the WORD OF GOD."—AUGUSTINE. *De Unitate Ecclesiæ*, c. 4, Tom. vii. p. 625. Lugduni, 1562.

LONDON:
W. H. ALLEN & CO., 13, WATERLOO PLACE, S.W.
1883.

PREFACE.

"The main object in discussion should be not to refute error, but to establish truth."—
DR. J. H. NEWMAN.

AUGUSTINE shines among the early Christian writers as a star of the greatest magnitude; "not only," as Sir W. Hamilton has observed, "in the character of the most illustrious of the Christian Fathers, but as one of the profoundest thinkers of antiquity." And Alban Butler, in the "Lives of the Saints," says that "the name of the great Augustine raises in all minds the most exalted idea, and commands the most profound respect." Du Pin, the Roman Catholic historian, in his "History of Ecclesiastical Writers," adds to his biography:—"The name only of St. Augustine is the greatest commendation that can be given him; and whatever may be said after that can serve only to lessen the opinion men have conceived of his rare merit and his great piety." He has been proclaimed by the Roman Church as a Doctor and Teacher, and a Saint in heaven; and an annual festival is set apart for his commemoration, and Romanists struggle hard on every available occasion to induce us to believe that he was a member of the Roman branch of "the Catholic Church." It becomes, therefore, a matter of interesting inquiry, what were the opinions of Augustine on the various subjects in controversy between the Reformed and the Roman Church. I have endeavoured to work out this view of the question in a practical manner, not so much "to refute error, but to establish truth." Independent of that consideration, the extracts from the writings of Augustine, which I have transferred to the following pages, will, I trust, afford subjects for profitable meditation.

To enter into a detailed criticism of the voluminous works of Augustine would be far beyond the scope and object of the present sketch, for who could improve on the elaborate and learned review so ably executed by Du Pin in the history above referred to? I may, however, with advantage, borrow the following paragraph with which he continues his criticism:—

"Though we have given a sufficient account both of St. Augustine's character and genius, in speaking of his works; yet it is convenient to say something of them here in general. He was a man of great extent, great exactness, and great force of mind. His reasonings were very strong. His ordinary method is to lay down extensive principles, from which he draws an infinite number of consequences; so that all the points of his doctrine have a great connection one with another. He argued more upon most of the mysteries of our religion than any author before him. He starts several questions never thought of before, and resolves many of them by the mere strength of his wit. He often left the notions of his predecessors to follow a path wholly new, whether in expounding the Scriptures, or in opinions of divinity. That may be said of him, as to divinity, what Cicero said of himself, as to philosophy—that he was *magnus opiniator*; that is, that he advanced several opinions that were only probable. But St. Augustine doth it modestly, and with much prudence, without pretending to oblige others to embrace his opinions without examination; whereas, when the question is about the doctrine of the Church, he proposes and maintains it stoutly, and as strongly opposes its opposers. He had much less learning than wit; for he understood not the languages, neither had he read the ancients much. He wrote with greater facility and clearness, than politeness and elegancy. Though he had taught rhetoric, yet either he was not master of the eloquence of the orators, or he neglected it; nay, his expressions are not always pure; for he often uses improper and barbarous words. He often uses little strokes of wit, and plays with words. He repeats the same things, and insists upon the same arguments in hundreds of places. He dwells long upon the same thought; to which he gives several turns, and enlarges frequently upon commonplaces. He treated of infinite numbers of things, by laying down principles; and framed (if we may so say) the body of divinity for all the Latin Fathers that came after him. They have not only taken out of his books the principles they make use of, but often they have only copied them. The Councils have borrowed his words to express their decisions. In short, Peter Lombard, in the twelfth century, going about to compose an epitome of the whole body of divinity, did little else but collect passages out of St. Augustine. And though Thomas Aquinas, and other schoolmen, followed another method; yet, for the most part, they have stuck to St. Augustine's principles, whereupon they erected their theological opinions."

In every case, with respect to my citations, I have added precise references to the editions purported to be quoted, but the difficulties of my task increased as I progressed in my investigations in endeavouring to separate the genuine from the spurious writings of Augustine, on which so many questions have been raised. I have, however, restricted my extracts to writings generally admitted as genuine by Roman Catholic writers; but even some of these, which I have quoted, have been questioned. I have not been able to satisfactorily account for the fact that the numerous Sermons attributed to Augustine—if delivered at public services of the Church—are in

Latin. In his "Confessions" Augustine tells us that as a student he took a great dislike to Greek, but the study of the Latin language was a pleasing task to him, which he speedily acquired. This presupposes that Latin was not his native tongue, and of consequence not the vernacular of his country. In that view it is highly improbable that the Sermons were ever delivered as such. That may account for the doubt which has been raised as to the genuineness of many of those now attributed to Augustine. In fact, the question arising on the authenticity of the writings of this, and many others of the early Christian Fathers of the Church, must be extremely perplexing to a conscientious member of the Roman Church, since by his Creed he is precluded from placing any interpretation on any text of Scripture unless the Fathers are unanimous on that particular interpretation, rendering that branch of his Rule of Faith practically a dead letter. Setting aside other insurmountable difficulties, how is he to arrive at what is a genuine production of any particular Father?

But we have another difficulty to encounter, namely, the manner in which Romish writers themselves treat these same Fathers when they apparently go counter to their modern theories. Several instances I have given in the sequel as applied to the writings of Augustine. On this view of the subject I cannot do better than quote the opinions expressed by Dr. J. H. NEWMAN, now a Cardinal in the Roman Church, extracted from his "Lectures on the Prophetical Office of the Church" (2nd Edition):—

"Whatever principles they profess in theory, resembling or coincident with our own, yet when they come to particulars, when they have to prove this or that article of their Creed, they supersede the appeal to Scripture and Antiquity by the pretence of the Infallibility of the Church, thus solving the whole question by a summary and final interpretation both of Antiquity and of Scripture" (p. 60).

"They [the Romanists] extol the Fathers as a whole, and disparage them individually; they call them one by one Doctors of the Church, yet they explain away one by one their arguments, judgment, and testimony. They refuse to combine their separate and coincident statements; they take each by himself, and settle with the first before they go on to the next. And thus their boasted reliance on the Fathers comes at length to this,—to identify Catholicity with the Decrees of Councils, and to admit those Councils only which the Pope has confirmed" (p. 71).

"Romanist, heretic, and infidel unite with one another in denying the orthodoxy of the first centuries" (p. 74).

"The Fathers are only so far of use in the eyes of Romanists as they prove the Roman doctrines, and in no sense are allowed to interfere with the conclusions which their Church has adopted; they are of authority when they seem to agree with Rome, of none if they differ" (p. 53).

"How useless then is it to contend with Romanists, as if they practically agreed to our foundations, however much they pretend to it! Ours is Antiquity, theirs the existing Church" (p. 85).

"According to the avowed or implied conviction of their most eminent Divines, there is much actually to censure in the writings of the Fathers, much that is positively hostile to the Roman system" (p. 97).

"Enough has been said to show the hopelessness of our prospects in the controversy with Rome. We have her own avowal that the Fathers ought to be followed, and again that she does not follow them; what more can we require than her witness against herself which is here supplied us? If such inconsistency is not at once fatal to her claims, which it would seem to be, at least it is a most encouraging omen in our contest with her" (p. 99).

"As far as it is Catholic and Scriptural, it [Romanism] appeals to the Fathers; as far as it is a corruption, it finds it necessary to supersede them" (p. 124).

The various subjects on which I have treated might have been considerably elaborated and strengthened by additional quotations from the writings of Augustine, at the expense of the patience of the reader; but sufficient proofs, I trust, have been advanced to establish, as a fact, that the "Catholic Faith," as taught by Augustine, was wholly different from the theological system as now professed by the Roman Church, as promulgated by the Decrees of the Trent Council and the Creed of Pope Pius IV., including the more modern additions of the Immaculate Conception of the Blessed Virgin Mary, and the Supremacy and alleged Personal Infallibility, "in faith and morals," of the local Bishop of Rome.

Augustine of the fifth century, the subject of the present sketch, has often been confounded with Augustine—or Austin the Monk—of the seventh century, who sought to subjugate British Christians to the dominion of the Bishop of Rome. Nevertheless, as a fact beyond dispute, not one single dogma covered by the Pian Creed, and the subsequent additions above alluded to, including the "Supremacy," formed part of the faith of the Roman Church of that period, or of the Christian dogmas alleged to have been then planted in this country. These were all additions of successive subsequent periods.

CONTENTS.

	PAGE
PREFACE	iii
CHAPTER I.—BIOGRAPHICAL	1
,, II.—AUGUSTINE AS AN AUTHORITY IN CONTROVERSIES	7
,, III.—ROME'S EXPURGATORY INDEX AND AUGUSTINE	20
,, IV.—ON THE ALLEGED SUPREMACY OF THE BISHOP OF ROME	26
,, V.—SCRIPTURE AND TRADITION	44
,, VI.—TRANSUBSTANTIATION	60
,, VII.—INVOCATION OF SAINTS	66
,, VIII.—PURGATORY	76
,, IX.—IMAGES	84
,, X.—THE SACRAMENTAL SACERDOTAL SYSTEM	91
,, XI.—BELLARMINE AND AUGUSTINE	99
,, XII.—CARDINAL WISEMAN AND AUGUSTINE	105
,, XIII.—DR. JOHN MILNER AND AUGUSTINE	115
,, XIV.—"THE FAITH OF CATHOLICS" AND AUGUSTINE	126
CONCLUSION	136
APPENDIX A.—EXTRACTS FROM AUGUSTINE'S "CITY OF GOD" ON MIRACLES	138
,, B.—EXTRACTS FROM THE ROMISH MAGAZINE, "THE RAMBLER," ON PERSECUTIONS	141

SAINT AUGUSTINE.

"Mira sunt quæ dicitis, nova sunt quæ dicitis, falsa sunt quæ dicitis. Mira stupemus, nova convenimus, falsa convincimus."*—August., Cont. Julianum, Lib. iii. c. 3.

CHAPTER I.

BIOGRAPHICAL.

OF all the Fathers of the Church AUGUSTINE is reputed, and justly so, one of the most illustrious. Milner, in his "History of Christianity,"† gives the following testimony as to his genius:—" Of the several Christian writers since the Apostles, Augustine has maintained the most prominent and extensive influence. . . . By the extraordinary adaptation of his genius to his own age, the comprehensive grandeur of his views, the intense earnestness of his character, his inexhaustible activity, the vigour, warmth, and perspicuity of his style, had a right to command the homage of Western Christendom. He was at once the first universal, and the purest and most powerful of the Latin Christian writers. . . . . He retained the fervour and energy of the African style, with much purer and perspicuous Latinity. His ardent imagination was tempered by reasoning powers which grappled with every subject." A late writer has thus summed up the general estimate of Augustine:—"Augustine's position in history has been a singular one. Most prophets and teachers of that high rank have been honoured by a large measure of the world's hatred and abuse. But it has been his lot to receive, through all the ages, a nearly unanimous acclaim of admiration. Romish Church historians, like Dupin, tell us of 'his holiness and his virtues, known and admired by all the world;' or, like Butler, in his Lives of the Saints, remark that 'the name of the great Augustine raises in all minds the most exalted idea, and commands the most profound respect.' As to Protestant writers, it is not at

---

* " Your assertions are wonderful, are novel, are false. At the wonderful we marvel; the novel we answer; the false we refute."

† London, 1840. Vol. iii. Book iii. cap. x. pp. 263, 371.

all surprising that, with Mosheim, they speak of him as a man 'whose fame is spread throughout the Christian world;' or, like the late Dean Milman, describe him as 'the one great authority in Latin theology;' or, like the Church historian, Robertson, as 'a teacher of wider and more lasting influence than any since the apostles;' or, like Dean Waddington, as 'the most celebrated among the ancient Christian fathers.' But the most recent writer, and not least competent judge, Dr. Merivale, Dean of Ely, may be allowed to sum up all former testimonies, when he describes this great theologian as—'He who is regarded by common consent as the greatest of the Christian Fathers, the most illustrious, I may say, of all Christian thinkers; the most learned, for his time the most enlightened—let me add, the most spiritually-minded, of the early Church—St. Augustine.'"

Augustine is professed to be held in the highest estimation by members of the Roman Church. The compilers of the "Roman Breviary"* inform us that:—"Augustine wrote so much, and that with such godliness and understanding, that he is to be held among the very chiefest of them by whom the teachings of Christianity have been shown forth. He is one of the first of those whom later theologians have followed in method and in argument." He has been raised to the distinguished position of "Saintship," and takes his place in the Roman Calendar as one of the canonized. His festival is celebrated on the 28th August. One of the requisites previous to canonization is proof that miracles have been wrought by or through the candidate proposed for celestial honours, either during this life or after death. In the "Roman Breviary," which otherwise contains an elaborate profusion of miracles attributed to various (so-called) "Saints," none are there recorded as having been performed by or through Augustine; nor do we find any mention throughout his voluminous works that he exercised any such power. In his celebrated work on "The City of God," at the beginning of the eighth chapter of the second book, he said:—"I can say miracles were necessary before the world believed, that it might believe; but whosoever now doth require a wonder that he may believe, is himself a wonder that believeth not when all the world believeth."†

At what time, or under what circumstances, Augustine was declared to have attained that exalted rank does not appear. Although he repudiated the authority of the Bishop of Rome, and actually died in what would now be called heresy, and if living would subject himself to the ban of Rome's excommunication, his works teeming with, as we shall presently see, heretical teaching, Augustine is

---

* See Dublin Edition, 1846. Pars Æstiva, p. 603.
† The reader is referred to the remarks in cap. XIII. *infra*.

nevertheless considered an object worthy of prayer as a Mediator before God, and his merits are pleaded on behalf of men.*

Augustine was born at Tagaste, a town of Numidia, in Africa, on the 13th Nov., A.D. 354. His father, Patricius, a citizen of that place, embraced Christianity late in life. He was poor, but a member of the Town Council. His mother, Monnica, was a Christian woman, remarkable for her piety and for her devotion to her son.

The early days of Augustine were by no means encouraging to his parents. His father sent him to Madaura, to advance him in classical learning, but he not only showed no inclination for study, but was what we should call in the present day " a fast young man." This we learn from his " Confessions," which he wrote in the forty-first year of his age. He there tells us that he " shunned the school as a plague ; he loved nothing but gaming and public stews ; he stole all he could from his father ; he invented a thousand lies to avoid the rod, which they were obliged to make use of to punish his licentiousness."†

At the age of sixteen he was removed from Madaura and sent to Carthage to study rhetoric. Here he made great progress in the sciences ; but, alas ! he gave himself up to debauchery and other vices,‡ and notwithstanding the earnest remonstrances of his mother, he persisted in his career of vice. He tells us that he " looked upon her admonitions as such womanish advice that he was ashamed to follow it."§ This life of dissipation he continued to indulge in, even up to the time of his baptism, which took place in his thirty-third year.

While at Carthage Augustine perfected himself in rhetoric and other sciences. When he returned to Tagaste he became a teacher of rhetoric, and gained for himself considerable applause for the uncommon abilities he displayed. The study of the Scriptures was not suited to so unhealthy a mind ; he was disgusted with their simplicity, devoting himself rather to the study of Pagan writers. He was a great admirer of their eloquence. In this frame of mind it is not surprising that we find him joining the Manicheans, a heretical sect founded by one Manes in the third century, who taught most pernicious doctrines, alike repugnant to reason and Holy Scripture. Augustine, however, did not embrace all their opinions. It was a happy event for the cause of Christianity that so zealous and powerful an advocate and reasoner, one who understood so well the arts of controversy, eventually abandoned the Manichean heresy. His restless energy, and perhaps his ambition,

---

* The " Roman Breviary," in the Festival of Augustine, has the following prayer :— " O right excellent Teacher, Light of the Holy Church, Blessed Augustine, lover of the Divine Law, pray for us to the Son of God."—Pars Æstiva, p. 603. Dublin Edition, 1846.

† " Confessions," Lib. i. c. xix.

‡ Ibid. Lib. ii. c. ii. § Ibid. Lib. ii. c. iii.

certainly his love of argument by profession, might have induced him to become a leader of the sect, and in his more mature years to frame such a system as might have become formidable to the orthodox bishops and clergy, as well as a stumbling-block to the laity, all of whom had sufficient to try their constancy in the persecutions of the age. While, on the other hand, the intimate knowledge he had acquired of the practical working of these very heresies led him, by God's mercy, to be one of their most determined and effective opponents. He continued a follower of the Manichean sect for nine years, and unhappily led many, during that period, to embrace their errors.

Augustine went back to Carthage A.D. 380, where he also taught rhetoric with continued success and reputation to himself. He was accompanied by his mother, who devoted herself to the apparently hopeless task of weaning him from his vices. His ambition led him to go to Rome, A.D. 383, where he hoped to find a new field for the display of his learning and abilities. His father was then dead, but he was maintained by an intimate friend, Romanian. He left Carthage without communicating with either his mother or his patron, lest they should thwart him in his designs. At Rome he taught rhetoric with as much success and applause as at Carthage; but, after a short stay of only a few months, he left the city in disgust at the fraudulent conduct of the students. By the introduction of Symmachus, Prefect of Rome, he was appointed, A.D. 383, Professor of Rhetoric at Milan. Here also he was much esteemed, and was received with great kindness by the Bishop of that city, the illustrious AMBROSE. He was first induced to attend his lectures from curiosity, having heard a high report of his eloquence. His mother followed him to Milan, and she continued to bestow on him her maternal tenderness and advice. It pleased God that this double influence should convert his heart. In his "Confessions" Augustine thus describes the first Christian influence on his mind:—

"There at Milan I waited on Ambrose, the Bishop, a man renowned for piety throughout the world, and who then ministered the bread of life to the people with much zeal and eloquence. The man of God received me like a father, and I conceived an affection for him, not as a teacher, but as a man kind to me; and I studiously attended his lectures, only with a curious desire of discovering whether fame had done justice to his eloquence or not. But salvation is far from sinners such as I then was; and yet I was gradually approaching it, and knew it not. By degrees I was brought to attend to the doctrines of the Bishop. A number of difficulties raised upon the Scriptures by the Manichees found in the exposition of Ambrose a satisfactory solution. My mother was now come to me, courageous through piety, following me by land and sea, and trusting confidently in Thee through all perils. She found me very hopeless with respect to the discovery of truth. However, when I told her my present situation, she answered that she believed in Christ that before she left this world she would see me a sound believer."*

Augustine was now led to study the Scriptures; and by the aid of his mother's prayers, tears, and entreaties, and the wholesome society and influence of his friends, Alypius and Simplician, and of the venerable Ambrose, it pleased God to give him a new life.† He ceased to teach rhetoric, and was baptized by Ambrose on Easter Eve, in the year 387. His illegitimate son, Adeodatus (a strange name this—*A-deo-datus*—to give to such an offspring) was baptized at the same time. Augustine appears also to have been greatly influenced by reading the life of the Hermit Antonius. He further describes the immediate incidents which led to his conversion. He tells us that he retired to a quiet spot, accompanied by his friend Alypius, and there in tears he bewailed his former iniquities, beseeching God's grace to assist him in his repentance, when he heard " from a neighbouring house a voice, as of a boy or girl, chanting or oft repeating the words *Tolle et lege, tolle et lege*— 'Take up and read.' " He received this, he says, as an invitation to take up the Holy Scriptures, which he did, and he opened the book, and his eyes fell on the text (Romans xiii. 13, 14), " Not in revelling and drunkenness, not in chambering and wantonness, not in strife and jealousy: but put ye on the Lord Jesus Christ, and take no thought for the flesh to fulfil the lusts thereof."

This incident seems to have directed his future course of action, leading to a new and Christian life. His mother, however, did not long survive to joy over the final conversion of her son—the single aim and object of her life. She died at Ostia, on the Tiber, on her journey home to Africa with her son; and in the ninth book of his "Confessions" Augustine has left a brief, but touching, tribute to her memory. He was ordained priest A D. 391 by Valerius, Bishop of Hippo, having spent the three previous years in retirement and study, when he wrote, among other works, his book on "True Religion."

In the year 395 Augustine became coadjutor to his Bishop, and was in that year consecrated Bishop of Hippo, which see he occupied for the space of thirty years, and died A.D. 430, in the seventy-sixth year of his age, during which period he devoted himself with untiring zeal and energy in combating the various heresies which threatened almost the existence of Christianity—

---

* "Confessions," Lib. v. c. xiii. xiv., Lib. vi. c. i.

† In the early part of his "Confessions" Augustine thus refers to his having received the truth through the ministry of Ambrose :—" My Faith, O Lord, calls on Thee: the faith which Thou hath breathed into me by the incarnation of Thy Son, through the ministry of Thy Preacher." ("Confessions," Lib. i. c. i.)

believers suffering at the same time under the cruel persecutions of the invaders who had laid desolate the vast provinces of the Roman Empire, and who, in 429, under the ferocious Genseric, devastated the north of Africa. Hippo, Augustine's native town, was one of the few cities which still afforded a refuge for the persecuted provinces. This venerable Bishop and soldier of Christ refused, though more than seventy years old, to abandon his post. In the third month of the siege he was released by death, and escaped the horrors of the capture, the cruelties of the conqueror, and a witness to the desolation of the Church. We are informed by the compilers of the Roman Breviary that "his body was carried to Sardinia, but Luitprand, King of the Lombards, afterwards bought it for a great price, and took it to Ticino, where it is honourably buried." At the present day the tomb of Augustine is exhibited in the Cathedral Church of Pavia, a town in Lombardy, on the River Ticino, where it is pretended his body still reposes.*

This great and good man, whose youth was spent in debauchery and vice, died, there can be no doubt, a true servant of Christ; and his own life he has himself described with much dramatic fidelity in his "Confessions."

The works of Augustine have gained for him immortal honour. Among these we may particularly mention "The City of God," a remarkable production of human intellect and industry; while his (so called) "Retractations," written late in life, shows him to have had a mind superior to earthly vanity, since in this he had the courage to acknowledge errors into which he had fallen in his previous writings. His "Confessions" are also remarkable as being, perhaps, the only work of the kind of the early Christians, giving the reasons which led so powerful an intellect to quit the more seductive paths of Pagan philosophy. It illustrates the successive workings of a reasoning mind, which induced him ultimately to embrace the simplicity of the Gospel, and to lead a holy life, inseparable from the practice of true Christianity.

His principal efforts were directed against heresies. He enumerates eighty-eight distinct heresies which distracted the Church.†
Again, the unauthorized novelties and superstitions introduced by recent converts to Christianity formed the subject of many of his protests, but apparently not with the same zeal which led him to combat the heresies of his day. "Approve of these things," he said, "I cannot; reprove them more freely I dare not."‡

---

* Addison, in his interesting travels in Italy in 1699, refers to this subject. He states:—"That the Canons Regular, who held half of the same church in their hands, would by no means allow it to be the body of the Saint, nor is it yet recognized by the Pope." (London, 1726, pp. 24, 25.)

† Lib. de Hæres. Tom. viii. p. 3, Bened. Edit.

‡ Epist. ad Januar. Tom. iv. p. 142.

The best edition of the works of Augustine is that printed at Paris, under care of the Benedictine Monks of St. Maur, 1679–1700.* If all that is attributed to him were genuine, we should have [fifteen in] eleven folio volumes the produce of his indefatigable pen. Among these, however, some are admitted to be decidedly spurious, others doubtful, and many of the genuine writings have been interpolated. Dr. James, in his learned "Treatise of the Corruptions of Scripture, Councils, and Fathers by Prelates, Pastors, and Pillars of the Church of Rome for the Maintenance of Popery,"† has cited sixty different works attributed to Augustine which have been admitted by learned Romish theologians to be either doubtful or decidedly spurious, but which are nevertheless repeatedly quoted as genuine by less scrupulous writers, in order to maintain the authority of some modern Romish dogma, under the sanction of so illustrious a Prelate as was Augustine. It is a lamentable fact that the garbled and interpolated passages, and the decidedly spurious writings attributed to Augustine are those principally quoted by Roman Catholic controversialists in order to give a colour of antiquity to their modern dogmas.

∗ *From the manner in which I have treated my subject, taking the citations of different champions of Romanism, some few repetitions will be found. Under the circumstances such repetitions can scarcely be avoided.*

CHAPTER II.

AUGUSTINE AS AN AUTHORITY IN CONTROVERSIES.

Controversy, on questions of religious belief, which turn principally on points of dogma, is at all times unsatisfactory. The trite proverb is too true, that the disputant convinced against his will claims the right, notwithstanding, to retain, and does retain, his original convictions. When, however, a great and esteemed theologian and Christian Bishop, such, for example, as the illustrious Bishop of Hippo of the fourth century, is claimed as a Doctor and Teacher, and as belonging to one particular communion of Christians, it becomes a legitimate, and, to a certain extent, an interesting subject for investigation, how far that exclusive claim can be justified by the only test afforded us—namely, by an impartial examination of his writings.

* I have quoted largely also from the 1562 edition (Lugduni), being greatly assisted by the admirable and careful selection made by Mr. Keary in his "Handbook of the Fathers."
† London, 1843, pp. 45-67. Du Pin enumerates about 330 sermons as "spurious." Nouvelle Biblioth., Tom. v. p. 218, col. 1. Paris, 1690.

Augustine being claimed as a canonized Saint of the Roman Church, the question at once suggests itself: "Did St. Augustine hold and teach the distinctive principles of Rome's dogmatic theology of the present day?" A lay member of the Roman Church, who is required to accept everything relating to his religion upon trust, and without inquiry, will doubtless consider the proposition self-evident from the fact that the individual in question is claimed as a canonized Saint, and a Doctor and Teacher of his Church. He misquotes, or rather, misapplies the oft-repeated saying attributed to Augustine : "Roma locuta, causa finita est "—" Rome having spoken, the question is settled." We, however, of the Reformed Churches, look higher for our guidance on such matters. We follow the wise counsel of Paul, to " Prove all things, and hold fast that which is good." With us, therefore, the proposition raises a fair subject for consideration.

Members of the Roman Church generally affect the greatest reverence for the Fathers. Their Church, in her Creed known as Pope Pius IV.'s Creed, lays down a precise rule for their guidance— namely, that no one shall advance any particular interpretation of Scripture unless that particular interpretation *is supported by the unanimous agreement of the Fathers.**

Another principle insisted on and repeatedly asserted in the decrees of the Council of Trent is, that their doctrines, as defined by that Council, have remained unchanged since the time of the Apostles; and have, as thus defined by them, been universally taught by the Fathers, and through them been held unchangeably by the Church. Their doctrines, they assert, are proved from Scripture and Tradition. The former the *written* word of God, the latter the word of God not committed to writing by the Apostles, but revealed to them by Christ, and handed down by them by word of mouth. It is frankly admitted that there are doctrines taught by the Roman Church, as matters of faith, which are not found in Scripture. The late Cardinal Wiseman in his Lectures says—" I have more than once commented on the incorrectness of that method of arguing, which demands that we prove every one of our doctrines individually from the Scriptures. I occupied myself, during my first course of lectures, in demonstrating the Catholic principle of faith that the Church of Christ was constituted by Him the depository of His truths, and that although many were recorded in His Holy Word, still many were committed to traditional keeping."† He here refers to a statement made in his third lecture‡ with reference to these Traditions of his Church, where his definitions are clear and

---

* Concil. Trid. apud Bullas, p. 311. Romæ, 1564.
† "Lectures on the Principal Doctrines and Practices of the Catholic Church." 1851. Lect. xi. vol. ii. p. 53.
‡ Ibid. vol. i. p. 61.

concise :—"*Tradition*, or the doctrine delivered down, and the *unwritten* Word of God, are one and the same thing. But it must not be thought that Catholics conceive there is a certain mass of vague and floating opinions which may, at the option of the Pope, or of a Council, or of the whole Church, be turned into Articles of Faith. Neither is it implied by the term *unwritten Word*, that these Articles of Faith, or Traditions, are nowhere recorded. Because, on the contrary, suppose a difficulty to arise regarding any doctrine so that men should differ, and not know what precisely to believe, and that the Church thought it prudent or necessary to define what is to be held, the method pursued would be to examine most accurately the writings of the Fathers of the Church to ascertain what in different countries and in different ages was by them held ; and then collecting the suffrages of all the world and all times—not, indeed, to create a new article of faith—but to define what has always been the faith of the Catholic Church." To the same effect did Cardinal Bellarmine as distinctly, but in fewer words, declare that :— "Although these Traditions are not written in the Scriptures, they are, nevertheless, written in the monuments of the ancients, and in the ecclesiastical books."* We need not wait to comment on the hopeless—nay, we venture to assert, the impossible—task here set before us. The inquirer after the truth must first ascertain which are the genuine works of the Fathers, and then he has to satisfy himself what is a genuine Tradition to constitute it an Article of Faith. But this hopeless task, nevertheless, exemplifies the importance professed to be given to the written testimony of the Fathers in all questions of disputed doctrine. In the "Faith of Catholics"† we are informed that "Antiquity is the badge of our Faith. In any other view, as the Catholic Creed in all its Articles is clearly defined, and is as unchangeable as it has been unchanged," . . . . "the Creed or religious belief of Catholics is not confined to Scripture, but it is that which our Saviour taught, and His Apostles delivered, before the sacred books of the New Testament had any existence. During the course of His mission, and after His resurrection, the Apostles had been instructed by their Divine Master, fully and explicitly we cannot doubt, in all things that it was necessary for them to know." We are not informed which are the dogmas thus alleged to have been communicated to the Apostles, which they did not afterwards commit to writing. As a fact, we in vain search in the writings of Apostles, or of (what are called) the Apostolic Fathers – or even of the Christian "Fathers" for four hundred years —for any sanction or authority whatever to lead us to believe that any one single Article of the Roman Church—added to the old Creed—has been handed down as an Apostolic Tradition ; and it

---

* Bell. de Verbo Dei non Scripto, Lib. iv c. 12.
† Introduction, pp. vii-xi. vol. i. Edit. 1846.

may be boldly asserted that not one of these additional Articles, now made necessary to salvation, to be believed as an Article of Christian Faith, is to be found in the voluminous writings of Augustine. Nevertheless, the Fathers are claimed as Rome's exclusive property. We, on the other hand, examine their writings for what they are worth, as a Counsel would a Witness; and, as a general rule, we admit them as bearing testimony to the common belief of the Church of their day. In perusing their writings, we are not required implicitly to admit all that they taught. We accept them only so far as they conform to Scriptural teaching. Augustine himself invites us to examine his writings by this rule. He says:—
"That which in my books you think to be undoubtedly true, unless thou provest it to be true indeed, hold it not."* Again, he said:—
"We give not such weight to the writings of men, be they never so worthy and Catholic, as to the Canonical Scriptures, yet yielding that reverence that is due unto them. We may mislike and refuse something in their writings, if we find they have thought otherwise than the truth may bear; and such am I in the writings of others, and such I would wish others to be in mine."†

Again he protested in these emphatic words:—"If, concerning Christ or His Church, or concerning any other thing which belongs to the Faith or to our life, I will not say if we, for we are not to be compared with him who said, 'But if we,' and immediately added, 'or an angel from heaven, declare to you any gospel besides that which we have received *in the legal* and Evangelical Scriptures, let him be accursed.'"‡

Augustine's reverence for the Scriptures, and his estimation of their authority, are clearly shown in the following declaration:—
"Let not these words be heard between us—'I say,' or 'you say;' but rather let us hear—'thus saith the Lord;' for there are certain books of our Lord in whose authority both sides acquiesce; there let us seek our Church, there let us judge our cause. Take away, therefore, all those things which each alleges against the other, and which are derived from any other source than the *canonical* books of the Holy Scriptures.§ But perhaps some will ask, Why take away such authorities? Because I would have the Holy

---

* August. de Prom. Lib. iii. de Trinit., p. 55, Tom. xi. Edit. Basil.
† August. ad Fortunat. Epist. Tom. ii. p. 502. Paris, 1679.
‡ Lib. iii. Cont. Lit. Petil. c. vii. Tom. ix. p. 302. Bened. Edit.
§ I shall have to consider, in its proper place, the question of Augustine's alleged acceptance of the 47th Canon of the Council of Carthage, containing, in the list of the Canon of Scripture, the Apocrypha, as is erroneously alleged. For the present I content myself with referring to the following works of Augustine, wherein he specially rejects the whole of the Apocrypha from the sacred Canon of Scripture:—De Mirab. Sacræ Script. Lib. ii. c. 34, p. 26, Tom. iii. Pt. i. Paris, 1686; De Civ. Dei, Lib. xviii. c. 36, p. 519, Tom. vii Paris, 1685; Cont. Secundam Ep. Gaud. Lib. i. c. 31, p. 821, Edit. Basil.

Church proved, not by human documents, but by the WORD OF GOD."*

And this is the rule by which we desire that our Reformed Church should be judged. "Holy Scripture containeth all things necessary to salvation; so that whatsoever is not read therein, nor may be proved thereby, is not to be required of any man that it should be believed as an Article of Faith, or be thought requisite or necessary to salvation."

There is, therefore, this marked difference between the members of the Reformed Church and the members of the Roman Church in estimating the doctrine and teaching of Augustine, or any other of the early Christian writers. We hold all that they taught when it agrees with Scriptural teaching, and reject—as invited by Augustine himself — whatever is contrary or repugnant thereto; while Romanists, on the other hand, arbitrarily reject all that does not agree with the teaching of their Church, as embodied in the decrees of the Trent Council and their Pian Creed, irrespective of Scriptural authority. Nevertheless, while they reject such parts of Augustine's writings as are repugnant to modern Romish dogmas, they still claim him as an orthodox Doctor and teacher, because, as Möhler interprets him: "herein he showed himself a good Catholic, that he himself gives us permission to examine his private opinions and to retain only what is sound." This is true; but Augustine did not submit his works to the authority of "THE CHURCH" which, in modern parlance, means the Pope and Bishops and the "Congregation of the Index," who claim the right of prohibiting or purging supposed erroneous sentiments; but he defers to the judgment of each individual reader, lay or clerical. We shall see that the rejected opinions of Augustine are exactly those which are thoroughly Scriptural, and such as militate especially against Romish excrescences on "the faith once delivered to the Saints."

Augustine was one of the most prolific writers of the early Church; and notwithstanding modern objections, the greatest weight is at times professedly attached to all he wrote. Of his writings Jerome, a Presbyter, and claimed also as a Saint of the Roman Church, a contemporary of Augustine, observed, in his 172nd Epistle:—"Whatever could be said respecting sacred Scripture, or derived from its source by the most profound intellect, has been said by thee." And even in modern times we find Maldonat, a Jesuit writer, express the opinion—though at times inconsistent with himself, as we shall presently see—that:—"St. Augustine is an author of that esteem, that were his opinion neither proved by Scripture nor reason, nor any other author, yet the sole reverence of his person deserves sufficient authority by itself."† So important, indeed, were

* De Unit. Eccl. c. iv. Tom. vii. p. 625. Lugduni, 1562.
† Mald. in John. vi. No. 69, p. 1171. Lugduni, 1615.

the opinions of Augustine considered, that the whole of the Romish Church, in the seventeenth century, was thrown into confusion, more particularly in France, arising from a dispute whether certain doctrines on grace and justification, alleged to have been taught by him, were or were not in his works. A most deadly feud arose on the subject between the two contending sects of Romanists, who were called respectively Jansenists and Jesuits, the Augustinians and Dominicans siding with the former. It was Dr. Newman (now Cardinal), in one of his lively moods, who wrote:—" I venture to say, that if you wish to get a good view of the unity, consistency, solidity, and reality of [Roman] Catholic teaching, your best way is to get up the controversy on *Grace* and the Immaculate Conception."*

Cornelius Jansen, Professor of Divinity at the College of Louvain, and afterwards Bishop of Ypres, after twenty years of close study of the works of Augustine, wrote his celebrated work entitled " Augustinus Cornelii Jansenii," which, when it appeared, some time after his death, convulsed the whole of France ; the contest between the opposing sects lasted nearly seventy years ; the propositions respecting the mystery of Divine grace, supposed to have been derived by Jansen from Augustine, and alleged to be in the " Augustinus," being violently opposed by the Jesuits.

The controversy had arisen previous to the days of Jansen, and was maintained for many years with the greatest acrimony on both sides. The question which raged between the Dominicans and Jesuits had been referred to Pope Clement VIII. He entrusted the investigation to a committee of learned divines, who, after several years' deliberation, reported in favour of the Dominicans and Augustinians, whose opinions they declared were more in accordance with Scripture and the Fathers than those advanced by Molina, the champion of the Jesuits. Clement died in the year 1605, before his decision was given. Paul V. laboured on the questions, but he also died before his infallible wisdom could be brought to decide the dispute. Jansen's book was, nevertheless, through the influence of the Jesuits, condemned by the Inquisitors in 1641 ; and Urban VIII., in the year following, anathematized it by a solemn Bull. The Jansenists, however, treated that Bull with contempt. Ultimately, Innocent X., by Bull dated 31st May, 1653,† in five leading propositions condemned the doctrines of the Jansenists, and of consequence the teaching of Augustine on the disputed points, as heretical.‡

There can, however, be no doubt that an impartial reader will agree that Jansen followed the doctrines taught by Augustine; and

---
* Newman on " Anglican Difficulties," p. 225, 1850.
† See Bullarium Romanum, Tom. vi. p. 456.
‡ See Mosheim's Eccl. Hist. Cent. xvii. c. i. sec. ii. part i. § xlii.

we cannot but admire the inconsistency of Rome condemning, on the one hand, the doctrines of the Augustinians and Dominicans, as maintained by Jansen and as taught by Calvin, and lauding and canonizing Augustine on the other. The Council of Trent condemned the doctrine of "Free-will" as taught by Calvin; and yet nothing is more clear than that the teaching of Calvin and Augustine was one on "Free-will" as well as "Predestination," as explained by Jansen. This has been clearly proved by Canon Mozley in his admirable book, "The Augustinian Doctrine." Milner, in his "History of Christianity," remarks:—"In later days Augustinian theology formed much of the doctrinal system of Luther; it was worked up into a still more rigid and uncompromising system by the severe intellect of Calvin, and it was remoulded into the Roman Catholic doctrine of Jansen. The popular theology of most of the Protestant sects is but a modified Augustinianism."* And the learned Priest Erasmus said that some condemned those things in Luther's writings which in St. Augustine's and St. Bernard's works passed for orthodox and pious.†

The followers of Thomas Aquinas, into whom it was said that the soul of Augustine had migrated, and the Dominicans, taught much the same doctrine on "Free-will" as did Augustine and the Jansenists; and yet they would have deemed it a libel to be classed with Calvinists. "If one might be suffered," said the learned Bayle, "to judge of another's thoughts, here would be great room for saying that Doctors are, in this case, great comedians, and only acting a part; and that they cannot but be sensible that the Council of Trent either condemned a mere chimera, which never entered into the thoughts of the Calvinists, or else that it condemned, at the same time, both St. Augustine and the 'physical predestination;' so that, when they boast of having St. Augustine's faith, and never to have varied in the doctrine, it is only meant to preserve a decorum and to save the system from destruction, which a sincere confession of the truth must necessarily occasion."

The Jansenistic and Calvinistic doctrines were, in fact, so identical with those taught by Augustine that the Church of Rome found herself in some perplexity. She could not repudiate so great a name, which she had glorified; but there were those who had more zeal than discretion, who went to the source of offence—namely, Augustine himself, and attacked him. Among others we may mention John Adam, the French Jesuit and preacher of the seventeenth century.‡ When John Adam was reproached for his boldness he very justly retorted:—"I fear nothing; no one can attack my

---

* Vol. iii. p. 246, Edit. 1840.
† Erasm. Epist. ad Albert. Episcop. et Princ. Mogunt. Cardin. Tom. iii. p. 514. Lugd. Bat. 1703
‡ See Bayle's Dictionary, title "John Adam," Notes C, D, L. London, 1734.

sermons, nor my book about 'Grace,' without undertaking at the same time to support Calvin." And in our day we have Dr. Möhler, who, in his "Symbolik" (i.-v. 42) (a work recommended by the late Cardinal Wiseman, in his Introduction to his Moorfield Lectures), and on the authority of the Fathers, says:—" No Church Father, even the most eminent, ever succeeded in imposing his own peculiar views on the Church. Augustine is a remarkable illustration of this. What writer ever acquired a higher authority than he? Yet his theory of *original sin* and *grace* was not that of the Church; and herein precisely he shows himself a good Catholic, that he himself gives us the permission to examine his private opinions, and to retain only what is sound." This is an artful evasion of a palpable difficulty, ingeniously conceived by a most subtle controversialist.

It may not be considered out of place to insert here a few of the many maxims uttered by Augustine on the doctrine of "justification by faith":—

"All our good merits are only wrought in us by grace; and when God crowns our merits, He crowns nothing but His own gifts."*

"If it were not given gratuitously, but was a rendering of one's due, there would be no grace."†

"Righteousness is not by the law, nor by the possibility of our nature, but by faith, and the gift of God through our Lord Jesus Christ."‡

"'For who makes thee to differ, and what hast thou that thou hast not received?' (1 Cor. iv. 7.) Our merits therefore do not cause us to differ, but grace. For if it be merit, it is a debt; and if it be a debt, it is not gratuitous; and if it be not gratuitous, it is not grace."§

"Have just men, then, no merits? Certainly they have, because they are righteous. But they were not made righteous by merits. For they are made righteous when they are justified; but, as the apostle says, they are justified freely by his grace."‖

There are not wanting numerous other examples where Roman Catholics have from time to time been compelled to reject the authority of Augustine when he appears to have condemned, by anticipation, as it were, their favourite dogmas. To give a few instances of the many that might be adduced, Augustine said:— "The works which are done without faith, though they seem good, are turned into sin."¶ Such a sentiment cuts at the very root of Rome's favourite teaching on merits and works of supererogation, on which so much depends, especially "Indulgences," and, to a certain

---

* Ad Sextinus, Epist. 194, Tom. ii. Edit. 1691.   † Epist. 105.
‡ To Innocent, Letter 177, Tom. ii. p. 626. Edit. as above.
§ Sermon 293, on the Birth of John the Baptist, Tom. v. p. 1182.
‖ To Sextinus, Letter 194, Tom. ii. Ed. as above.
¶ Aug. Cont. duas Ep. Pelag. ad Bonif. Lib. iii. c. 5, Tom. xvi. p. 457. Paris, 1690.

extent, Purgatory. The same Maldonat above quoted opposes Augustine, and says:—"We may not defend that opinion which the Council of Trent did of late justly condemn—'*Omnia infidelium opera esse peccata.*' ('All works done without faith are sinful.') —although the great Father, St. Augustine, seems to be of that opinion."* Again, when Augustine said that the "Rock" referred to in the text Matt. xvi. 18 was CHRIST,† Stapleton, a celebrated champion of Romanism, replied that:—"It was a human error, caused by a diversity of the Greek and Latin tongues, which either he (Augustine) was ignorant of or did not mark."‡ And, referring to the same interpretation, Cardinal Bellarmine said that Augustine "was deceived only by ignorance of the Hebrew tongue."§ And when Augustine is found to interpret the words of Christ, "This is my body,"‖ figuratively, by saying that Christ spoke these words when he gave a *sign* of His body, their champion, Thomas Harding, D.D., apologizes for these words thus:—"St. Augustine, fighting against the Manichees, oftentimes useth not his own sense and meaning, but those things which by some means, howsoever it were, might seem to give him advantage against them, so he might put them to the rout."¶ How truly characteristic is this! Here is a Roman Catholic who does not hesitate to admit that it is justifiable to put a false and alleged heretical interpretation on a text of Scripture for the purpose of obtaining a temporary victory over an opponent. When Augustine, commenting on the words in St. Luke's Gospel, "I will not henceforth drink of the *fruit of the vine*," says: "They are to be understood of the sacramental cup,"** and, consequently, it remained *wine* after consecration, Bellarmine replies that:—"He did not well consider that text, which appears by this, that he passed it over lightly."†† And upon the same subject, where Augustine said:—"The Israelites ate of the same spiritual meat, but not the same corporal, which we eat; for they ate manna, we another meat, but both the same *spiritual* meat."‡‡ Maldonat found this to be too Calvinistic, as he termed it; that is, it denied Transubstantiation, so he explained:—"I am verily persuaded that if Augustine had been living in these days, and had seen the Calvinists so interpret St. Paul, he would have been of another mind, especially being such an utter enemy of heretics."§§

---

* Mald. Com. in Matt. vii. 18, p. 171. Lugd. 1615.
† Ang. De. Verb. Dom. Serm. xiii. Tom. iii. p. 822. Paris, 1680.
‡ Stapleton, Princip. Doct. Lib. vi. c. 3. Edit. Antvp. 1596.
§ Bell. Disp. Lib. 1, de Pont. c. x. sec. 32. Prag. 1721.
‖ August. Cont. Adim. c. xii. p. 124, Tom. viii. Paris, 1688.
¶ See Jewel, Art. xii. p. 346. London, 1609.
** Aug. de Consens. Evang. Lib. iii. c. 1, p 99, Tom. iii. pt. 2. Paris, 1680.
†† Dico Augustinum non expendisse hunc locum diligenter. (Bell. de Euchar. Lib i. c. xi. sect. 61. Prag. 1721.)
‡‡ August. in Johann. Tract. 26, Tom. iii. p. 1934. Paris, Bened. Edit.
§§ Maldonat in John. vi. n. 50, p. 1476. Lugd. 1615.

That is to say, Augustine would have written against his own conviction for the sake of expediency!

We know that modern Roman controversialists allege that the daily sacrifice spoken of by the Prophet Malachi was a prophecy pointing to the sacrifice of the Mass, whereas Augustine, following the interpretation given by Justin Martyr, Clement of Alexandria, Hilary, and others, interpreted the prophecy as simply meaning the "prayers and praises of saints."* Azorius, a noted Romanist, takes Augustine to task for this, and says boldly:—"We oppose against him the general consent of the other Fathers and the testimony of the Council of Trent."† Again, Augustine said:—"I know certain worshippers of tombs and pictures whom the Church condemns."‡ Bellarmine objects by saying that:—"This book was written in the beginning of his first conversion to the Catholic faith."§ And in like manner Augustine, in his 119th "Epistle ad Januarium," cap. xi., said:—"No image of God ought to be worshipped," &c. Bellarmine gives the same reply, and adds that:—"On better information, Augustine changed his mind." He nowhere, however, tells us where we are to find such retractation! And, once again. The text 1 Cor. iii. 13, wherein Paul says that fire shall try every man's work of what sort it is, is quoted by Romanists to prove their doctrine of Purgatory. Now, Augustine upsets this theory by stating that:—"By this fire is meant the fire of tribulation in this life."‖ Bellarmine thus summarily disposes of him by saying:—"This opinion of his we have rejected."¶

But perhaps the most extraordinary piece of assurance in this line was perpetrated by Fulbertus, Bishop of Chartres. In the year 1608 was published in Paris the works of this Bishop, "pertaining as well to the *refuting of the heresies* of his time as to clearing of the history of the French." In page 168 we find quoted, word for word, a passage from Augustine's commentary on the words of our Lord in the 6th chapter of St. John's Gospel;** the interpretation given by Augustine is directly attributed to heretics! The passage is as follows:—"Unless ye eat the flesh of the Son of Man and drink His blood, ye have no life in you. Now, this seems to command a crime, or horrid thing, therefore it is a figure, *will the heretic say*, commanding us to communicate in the passion of our Lord, and sweetly and profitably to treasure up in our memory that the flesh was crucified and wounded for us."

The passage is thus given in the original, being Augustine's

---

* August. Lib. ii. Cont. Lit. Pet. c. 86, p. 272, Tom. ix. Paris, 1688.
† Azor. Inst. Moral. part 1, Lib. x. c. xi.
‡ August. de Mor. Eccl. Lib i. c. 34. p., 713, Tom. i. Paris, 1679.
§ Bell. de Imag. Lib. ii. c. 16, sect. 6. Prag. 1721.
‖ August. de Fide et Oper. c. 16.
¶ Bell. de Purg. Lib. i. c. 5, sect. 36. Prag. 1721.
** De Doctrina Christ. Lib. iii. c. 16, p. 66. Lugd. 1562.

exact words, except "dicet hæreticus":—"Nisi manducaveritis, inquit, carnem Filii hominis, et sanguinem biberitis, non habebitis vitam in vobis. Facinus vel flagitium videtur jubere. Figura ergo est, *dicet hæreticus*, præcipiens passioni Domini esse communicandum tantum, et suaviter atque utiliter recondendum in memoria quod pro nobis caro ejus crucifixa et vulnerata sit."

So, according to this Bishop of Chartres, Augustine was a heretic for giving this figurative interpretation to our Lord's words!

And so we might proceed to weary the reader by citing additional examples.*

The above fully justifies what Dr. (now Cardinal) Newman said, when a Minister in the Church of England, in his "Lectures on the Prophetical Office of the Church,"† on the use Romanists make of the Fathers as it may suit their purpose. "The Fathers," he said, "are only so far of use in the eyes of Romanists as they prove the Roman doctrines, and in no sense are allowed to interfere with the conclusions which their Church has adopted; they are of authority when they seem to agree with Rome, of none when they differ."

As an apt illustration of this jealousy of the Fathers, Cardinal Hosius, a learned Polish Bishop, said:—"Often, when I was at Rome, I used to deplore this misery of ours, and so much the more because, when I was desirous of purchasing works of the four principal Doctors of the Church [St. Ambrose, St. Augustine, St. Athanasius, St. Chrysostom], I was informed by the bookseller that he was not allowed to sell them—because there was an *Edict* of the *Pope* to the contrary."‡

Another summary way of overcoming difficulties presented by the writings of Augustine, adopted by the Roman Church, is to order passages repugnant to her modern theories to be expurgated or expunged from his works. We find these expurgated passages conveniently classified in their Expurgatory Indices, under different headings. I have in the next chapter given a series of examples, selected from many others, set forth in the Madrid (1667) Edition.

This process of Ecclesiastical Vandalism is boldly admitted by the compilers of the "Belgian Expurgatory Index," published at Antwerp, 1571. In page 5 we read:—"We bear with many errors in the old Catholic writers; we extenuate them; we excuse them; and by inventing some devised shift, we oftentimes deny them, and

---

* See Sir H. Lynde's "Via Devia," sect. xii.
† London, 1837, p. 83. See Appendix A.
‡ Quoted by Dr. Wordsworth in his "Sequel to Letters to M. Goudon," 2nd Edit. p. 102. London, 1848.

feign some commodious sense for them, when they are objected to in disputations or conflicts with our adversaries." In fact, the Expurgatory Indices of the Roman Church are the clearest and most damning witnesses against her modern innovations. Had Augustine lived to see this process of expurgation, he would have exclaimed, in the words of his great master, Ambrose, " They may well blot out our letters ; but our faith they shall never abolish." (Orat. i., Cont. Arian.)

But some of their crew took even a bolder step by publishing the works of Augustine, from which they excluded everything which, in their estimation, savoured of heresy, and repugnant to—what they were pleased to call—the Catholic faith.

David Clement, in his "Bibliothèque Curieuse Historique et Critique,"* refers to this corrupted edition in the following words: "The editor warns us, as an honest man, that he has removed everything which might infect Catholics with heresy, or cause them to turn from the orthodox faith." And several examples of manipulating of the text are cited. The same fact is recorded by Le Clerc in his "Bibliothèque Universelle."† Referring to the same edition (Venice, 1570) he says: "They inserted in the title, that they had exercised great care to cause to be expunged everything that might possibly infect the souls of the faithful with any evil of heresy, or to draw them from the Catholic and orthodox faith *curavimus removeri illa omnia quæ fidelium mentes hæreticâ pravitate possent inficere, aut a Catholica orthodoxa fide deviare.*" Thus fully confirming the extract given in the note below.

In the preface to the reader to the index of prohibited books, Geneva 1629 we read the following passage :—" St. Augustine was lately printed at Venice (1570), in which edition, as we have restored many places according to the ancient copies, so likewise we have taken care to remove all those things which might either infect the minds of the faithful with heresies, or cause them to wander from the Catholic faith."‡

Augustine was accordingly purged, as they frankly admitted §

Another mode of dealing with Augustine and his views is to misquote his very words.

The facility with which the uninitiated may be misled is exempli-

---

* Göttingen, 1741, Tom. ii. pp. 268-272.
† Tom. v. p. 272. Amsterdam, 1687.
‡ Augustinus nuper Venetiis excusus in quo, præter multorum locorum restitutionem secundum collationem veterum exemplarium, curavimus removeri illa omnia quæ fidelium mentes hæreticâ pravitate possent inficere, aut a Catholica orthodoxa fide deviare. Præfat. Ind. Lib. prohibit. ad Lectorem, Genevæ impress. an. 1629.
§ "In hunc modum est repurgatus, ut in libri inscripsione testantur qui editioni præfuerunt." James, "On the Corruption of Scriptures, &c.," p. 6.

fied in a quotation, purporting to be the exact words of St. Augustine, cited in the first and second editions of "The Faith of Catholics," being extracts from the writings of the "Fathers," edited by two priests of the Roman Church, Kirk and Berington, a work purporting to be compiled with the greatest care, and which forms a text-book for Roman Catholic controversialists generally. "On the authority of the Church" (of course they mean the Roman Church), we have in the second and revised edition, 1830, p. 25, a passage from Augustine's book "Contra Crescon.", and the reference given is Lib. i. T. vii. p. 168, Edit. Paris, 1614:—

"This Church, moreover, the divine authority commends, and, as *it* cannot deceive us, he who fears to be imposed on, under the obscurity of the present question [re-baptism], will consult the Church, which, without any ambiguity, the Scriptures establish."

An ordinary reader would conclude that "the divine authority" here is "the Church," that the "it" which cannot deceive is the same Church; whereas the phrase translated "the divine authority" is "*Scripturarum ipsarum authoritas*"—" the authority of the *Scriptures* themselves:" and that rendered "as *it* cannot deceive us" is "*quoniam sancta Scriptura fallere non potest*"—"because *Holy Scripture* cannot deceive."*

It should be noted that, on the subject under discussion, "re-baptism," Augustine in the same place distinctly admits that there is no Scriptural authority. It is natural, therefore, to refer to the practice of the Church, "established by the Scriptures;" but that is no reason why Messrs. Kirk and Berington should make it appear, by omitting the reference to the Scriptures, that the authority of the Church supersedes that of the Scriptures, which is the modern Roman theory so well appreciated by Dr. J. H. Newman, before he fell away, as shown in the following passage in his "Prophetical Office" of the Church (p. 60, 2nd Edition).

"Whatever principles they profess in theory, resembling or coincident with our own, yet when they come to particulars, when they have to prove this or that article of their Creed, they supersede the appeal to Scripture and Antiquity by the pretence of the Infallibility of the Church, thus solving the whole question by a summary and final interpretation both of Antiquity and of Scripture."

It is a matter for wonderment that in the face of all these facts Augustine should be still claimed as a great light of the Roman Church.

The above sketch amounts merely to negative evidence, as expos-

---

* See, in addition to the editions above cited, Edit. Antwerp, 1577, Tom. vii. p. 168; Benedict. Edit., 1679, Tom. ix. p. 407; Elit. Paris, 1531, Tom. vii. p. 46; Elit. Basil., 1642, Tom. vii. p. 219. And see Pope's Roman Misquotations, pp. 46 and 188. London, 1840.

ing the fallacy of such a claim. A careful examination of Augustine's writings themselves will enable us to arrive at a more decisive opinion, how far this illustrious Bishop taught the modern theories which form the substance of the present Creed of the Roman Church. Such an examination, as we shall presently see, will prove him, measured by such a standard, to be a heretic. I shall, however, first draw attention to Rome's Expurgatory Index, and show how Augustine has been treated by "the Sacred Congregation," entrusted with the supervision of literature in general, and theological literature in particular.

CHAPTER III.

ROME'S EXPURGATORY INDEX AND AUGUSTINE.

The following is an arrangement, in a tabular form, of some of the leading sentiments of Augustine which are to be found in various parts of his writings, and have been condemned as heretical, and, as such, have been placed in Rome's Expurgatory Index, with a command that none of the editions referred to, in which the extracts are found, are to be tolerated until the passages objected to have been expunged.

The second title-page of the volume from which I quote is as follows:—

"Indices Librorum Prohibitorum et expurgandorum novissimi Hispanicus et Romanus. Anno MDCLXVII." MADRITI. Folio.

The condemned passages cover eleven closely-printed pages in double columns, from page 54 to page 64, both inclusive. Five entire columns are taken up with censures on editors of, and commentators on, Augustine's works.

The editions that are specially condemned are:—

Paris; per Claudium Chevallonium, 1531.
Basileæ; ex off. Frobenianum, 1556.
Basileæ; apud Ambrosium, &c., 1570.
Lugduni, 1586.
Paris; apud Ambrosium; Girault, 1543.
And two other Paris editions, 1516, 1685.

The Benedictine Paris Edition, 1679-1700, was not then published.

Were I to transcribe all the condemned passages on *Grace, Justification, Merits, Good Works, Faith,* and *Free will,* they would cover many pages. This fact alone is sufficient proof how widely the Roman Church differs from the teaching of Augustine on the doctrines on which the Reformation was principally based.

There are many other subjects than those I have selected which are condemned as heretical in Augustine's works, but I have limited my extracts to the more immediate questions in controversy. The following, however, are amply sufficient for our present purpose:—

"Out of thine own mouth will I judge thee."—Luke xix. 22.

The Alleged Heresies of Augustine.

1. God alone is to be adored.

1. Solus Deus adorandus. (P. 56, col. 2.)

2. Angels neither good nor bad are to be worshipped.

2. Angeli, nec boni, nec mali colendi. (P. 56, col. 2.)

3. The adoration of angels is prohibited.

3. Angelos adorantes prohibentur. (*Ibid.*)

4. That angels cannot be our mediators.

4. Angelos non posse esse mediatores nostros. (P. 59, col. 2.)

5. How saints are to be honoured, not adored.

5. Sancti quomodo honorandi, non adorandi. (P. 57, col. 2.)

6. Saints are unwilling to be adored.

6. Sancti nolunt adorari. (P. 57, col. 2.)

7. Created beings are not to be adored on account of having represented in a figure certain holy things.

7. Creaturæ adorandæ non sunt, propterea quod saucta quædam figurarunt. (P. 57, col. 2.)

8. Created beings are not to be worshipped nor adored.

8. Creaturæ non colendæ neque adorandæ. (P. 61, col. 1.)

9. There are no mediators between us and God.

9. Non sunt mediatores inter nos et Deos. (P. 60, col. 1.)

10. Strike out what follows after "the worship of saints," that we do indeed celebrate their memory, but do not invoke them.

10. Litera S. post sanctorum cultus, &c., *dele*. " quod sequitur et quod memoriam quidem illorum celleremus, non invocamus." (P. 61, col. 1.)

11. The dead have no concern for the living.

11. Mortuis nulla cura de vivis. (P. 59, col. 1.)

12. No help of mercy can be rendered to the dead.

12. Mortuis nullum auxilium misericordiæ præberi potest. (P. 59, col. 1.)

13. Saints are to be loved and imitated, but are not to be worshipped.

13. Sancti amandi et imitandi, non colendi sunt. (P. 59, col. 2.)

14. Saints are to be honoured with imitation, but not with adoration.

14. Sancti honorandi imitatione, non adoratione.

15. We neither build temples to saints, nor offer sacrifices to them.

16. We do not honour saints by oblations.

17. John left a forewarning against the invocation of saints.

18. The holy dead, after this life, cannot help.

19. The saints are not mediators between God and man.

20. Prayer, unless preceded by a good life, is not heard.

21. Temples are not to be built to angels.

22. It is not lawful to build temples to saints.

23. It is a sacrilege to build temples to created beings.

24. The adorers of images are censured.

25. The use of images is prohibited.

26. Against the worshippers of images.

27. It is wicked for Christians to place images of God in churches.

28. There is no use in images.

29. The invention of images has brought with it many evils.

30. Against those who say, I do not worship images, but through them I address my petitions to that which I ought to worship.

31. Even the Pagans detest the use of images.

32. Scriptures condemn images.

33. The worship of images is pestilent.

15. Sanctis, nec templa statuimus, nec sacrificia.

16. Sanctos non honoramus oblationibus.

17. Sanctorum invocationem præcavit Joannes.

18. Sancti mortui post hanc vitam subvenire non possunt.

19. Sancti non sunt mediatores inter Deum et hominem. (P. 59, cols. 1 and 2.)

20. Oratio, nisi bona vita præcedat, non exauditur. (P. 59, col. 1.)

21. Templa angelis non sunt construenda.

22. Sanctis ædificare templa non licet.

23. Templa creaturis ædificare sacrilegium est. (P. 59, col. 1.)

24. Imaginum adoratores taxantur.

25. Imaginum usus prohibitus.

26. Contra cultores imaginum. (P. 58, col. 2.)

27. Simulachrum Dei in templis ponere nefas est Christianis.

28. In Simulachris nulla utilitas.

29. Simulachrorum inventio multa mala attulit.

30. Contra eos, qui dicunt, simulachra non colo, sed per se ea id quid colere debeo adhortor. (P. 59, col. 2.)

31. Simulachrorum usus etiam detestantur Pagani.

32. Simulachra reprehendit Scriptura. (P. 59, col. 2.)

Simulachrorum pestilens cultus. (P. 61, col. 1.)

---

34. Mary even in Christ's Passion doubted concerning him.

34. Maria etiam in Christi passione, de ipso dubitavit.

35. It is by no means to be believed that one Joachim was the father of Mary.

36. Mary bore and did not bear the Son of God.

37. *Mary was mother of Christ's Humanity, not of his Divinity.*

35. Mariæ patrem fuisse quemdam Joachim minime credendum.

36. Maria genuit, et non genuit Filium Dei. (P. 58, col. 2.)

37. Maria fuit mater humanitatis Christi, non Diviuitatis. (P. 61, col. 1.)

---

38. The authority of the Scriptures and not of Councils is to be relied on.

39. Let him who is without the authority of the Scriptures follow the Church.

40. Nothing is to be added to Christ's words.

41. The book of Maccabees is apocryphal.

42. That the legends of the saints are apocryphal.

38. Non Conciliorum sed Scripturarum auctoritati imitandum est.

39. Ecclesiam sequatur qui Scripturarum auctoritatem non habet. (P. 58, col. 1.)

40. Christi verbis nihil addendum. (P. 60, col. 1.)

41. Machabœorum liber apocryphal. (P. 58, col. 2.)

42. Sanctorum legendas apocryphas. (P. 59, col. 2.)

---

43. God crowns His own gifts, not our merits.

44. Salvation is of grace, not of free-will.

45. Grace and merit are opposed to each other.

46. We are saved by grace, not by works.

47. Our justification is through faith, and what is the justification of faith.

48. In man there is no merit.

49. Our merits are only God's gifts.

50. Works do not go before justification.

51. Without charity no one performs any good work.

52. Faith is void without good works.

43. Dona sua, non merita nostra, coronat Deus. (P. 56, col. 2.)

44. Ex gratia salus, non libero arbitrio. (P. 56, col. 2.)

45. Gratia et meritum pugnant. (P. 56, col. 2.)

46. Gratia salvamur, non operibus. (P. 57, col. 1.)

47. Justitia nostra ex fide est, et quæ sit justitia fidei. (P. 57, col. 1.)

48. Meritum hominis nullum. (P. 57, col. 1.)

49. Merita nostra non sunt nisi Dei dona. (P. 57, col. 1.)

50. Opera non præcedunt justificationem. (P. 57, col. 1.)

51. Sine charitate nemo quidcunquam boni facit. (P. 57, col. 2.)

52. Fides nulla est sine bonis operibus. (P. 58, col. 1.)

53. We are justified through faith alone.

54. Faith alone delivers from condemnation.

55. There is no merit of ours, but it is God's only.

56. We are not saved by merits, but condemned by merits.

57. By our merits we do not merit eternal life.

58. Good works done without faith are wicked.

53. Per solam fidem justificamur. (P. 58, col. 1.)

54. Fides sola damnatione liberat. (P. 58, col. 2.)

55. Meritum nostrum nullum est, sed unius Dei. (P. 58, col. 2.)

56. Meritis non salvamur, sed meritis damnamur. (P. 58, col. 2.)

57. Meritis nostris vitam æternam non meremur. (P. 58, col. 2.)

58. Bona opera extra fidem facta impia sunt. (P. 60, col. 1.)

---

59. Confession is not necessary to salvation.

60. Confession is to be made in the nearest church, if there is no priest at hand.

61. God forgives sins before confession passes the lips.

62. Remission of sins can be given by means of the Church; but only by the Lord can the sinner be quickened to life.

59. Confessio non est necessaria ad salutem. (P. 61, col. 1.)

60. Confessio proximo fano facienda, si non adsit sacerdos. (P. 58, col. 1.)

61. Prius quam confessio ad os veniat Deus peccata dimittit. (P. 58, col. 1.)

62. Absolutio peccatorum per Ecclesiam dari potest, suscitari autem peccator, nisi à Domino, non potest. (P. 57, col. 2.)

---

63. Sacrament] strike out "from the side of Christ flowed two sacraments."

64. The two sacraments of Christians are Baptism and the Eucharist.

63. Sacramentum] *dele.* "Ex latere Christi manarunt duo sacramenta." (P. 57, col. 1.)

64. Sacramenta duo Christianorum Baptismus et Eucharistia. (P. 58, col. 1.)

---

65. The body and blood of Christ] strike out, "Christ gave the sign of his body."

66. Eucharist] strike out, "What Christ propounded with relation to eating his flesh, is to be understood spiritually."

67. The Sacrament of Bread] strike out, "Christ is Bread from the Kingdom of God, and is eaten by faith."

65. Corpus et sanguis Christi] *dele.* "Corporis sui signum dedit Christus." (P. 56, col. 2.)

66. Eucharistia] *dele.* "Quæ de carne sua manducanda Christus proposuit, spiritualiter sunt intelligenda." (P. 56, col. 2.)

67. Panis Sacramentum] *dele.* "Panis de Regno Dei Christus, et fide comeditur." (P. 57, col. 1.)

68. Spiritual Bread is either the Eucharist or the word of God.	68. Panis spiritualis, vel est Eucharistia, vel verbum Dei. (P. 57, col. 2.)
69. The flesh of Christ profiteth nothing.	69. Caro Christi nihil prodest. (P. 57, col. 2.)
70. The body of Christ is a mystical sacrifice.	70. Corpus Christi mysticum est sacrificium. (P. 57, col. 2.)
71. Christ called it his body when he gave a figure of his body.	71. Corpus suum dixit Christus, cum figuram daret corporis sui. (P. 58, col. 1.)
72. In the Eucharist the Lord delivered a figure of his body and blood.	72. In Eucharistia figuram corporis, et sanguinis sui tradidit Dominus. (P. 58, col. 1.)
73. The Eucharist for children under both species.	73. Eucharistia parvulis sub utraque specie. (P. 58, col. 1.)
74. That the Eucharist is not a sacrifice, but a memorial of a sacrifice.	74. Eucharistiam non esse sacrificium, sed sacrificii memoriam. (P. 58, col. 1.)
75. Christ commended to his disciples a figure of his body and blood.	75. Corporis et sanguinis figuram discipulis Christus commendavit. (P. 60, col. 1.)
76. The Sacrament of the Eucharist, although visible, should nevertheless be understood in an invisible and spiritual manner.	76. Sacramentum Eucharistiæ, etsi visibile sit, invisibiliter tamen, et spiritualiter debet intellegi. (P. 60, col. 2.)

---

77. Whether there be a purgatorial fire after this life Augustine doubts.	77. Purgatorius ignis post hanc vitam, an sit, dubitat Augustinus. (P. 59, col. 1.)
78. It is not incredible that there is a purgatory after this life, but whether it be so may be a question.	78. Purgatorium post hanc esse vitam incredible non est, sed utrum sit, quæri potest. (P. 59, col. 1.)
79. In a future state there is none other than condemnation or reward.	79. In futuro sæculo nihil aliud, quam condemnatio, aut remuneratio est. (P. 59, col. 1.)
80. That purgatory is not to be found in the Scriptures.	80. Purgatorium non inveniri in Scripturis. (P. 59, col. 1.)

---

81. Peter never claimed for himself a primacy.	81. Petrus Primatum sibi nunquam vindicavit. (P. 59, col. 1.)

"Suo sibi gladio hunc jugulo."—Terence, *Adelph.*, v. 8.
We thus foil them with their own weapons.

CHAPTER IV.

ON THE ALLEGED SUPREMACY OF THE BISHOP OF ROME.

WHEN we discuss the claim of the Bishop of Rome to a supremacy over all Christian Churches, we are gravely informed by Cardinal Bellarmine that we are discussing the very sum and substance of Christianity. He said : *—" For what is the subject in dispute when we discuss the Primacy of the Pontiff? In a few words, it is the sum and substance of Christianity; whether the Church ought any longer to maintain its existence, or to dissolve and so fall into ruin. What is the difference between asking whether it is expedient to remove the foundation from a building, the shepherd from his flock, the general from his army, the sun from the stars, the head from the body, and asking whether it is expedient that the building should fall, the flock be scattered, the army routed, the stars darkened, the body prostrate?" And a late seceder to the Roman Church, appreciating the importance of the subject, declared his " conviction that the whole question between the Roman Church and the Church of England, as well as the Eastern Church, turns on the Papal Supremacy, as at present claimed, *being of Divine right or not.*" †

This theory was formally promulgated by the *ex-cathedrâ* Bull *Unam Sanctam*, issued by Pope Boniface VIII., in which he stated : —" We declare, we say, *we define*, that it is necessary for the salvation of every human creature that he should be subject to the Roman Pontiff."‡

We are informed by Bishop Fessler, who acted as Secretary-General of the Vatican Council, that by reason of the Pope using the word " definimus," " we define," so far as that clause is concerned, it was an *ex-cathedrâ* definition on a matter of faith ; and by the late Vatican decree, vesting Infallibility in the Pope personally, it becomes of consequence an *article of faith.* §

The same rule was subsequently adopted by a so-called General Council, and is therefore doubly binding on every member of the Roman Church.‖

" This right of the Popes," Bellarmine further tells us, " has its

---

* " De quâ re agitur, cum de primatu Pontificis agitur ? Brevissime dicam, de summâ re Christianâ, &c." In Lib. de Sum. Pont. in Præfat. sec. ii. Edit. Prag. 1721.

† The Rev. Mr. Allies' " See of St. Peter," 2nd Edit. Preface, p. iii. Dublin, 1855.

‡ Corpus Juris Can. Extrav. Com., Lib. i. Tit. 8, c. i. ; Tom. ii. p. 1159, Edit. Lipsiæ, 1839.

§ " The True and False Infallibility of the Popes," translated by Ambrose St. John, 2nd Edit. p. 67. London, 1875.

‖ Fifth Lateran Labb. et Coss. Concil., Tom. xiv. col. 313. Paris, 1671.

foundation in the fact that St. Peter established his seat at Rome *by Divine command*, and that he occupied it till his death."*

When the Pope is crowned, the following form is used at the present day :—" Receive this tiara, embellished with three crowns, and never forget, when you have it on, that you are the Father of Princes and Kings, and Ruler of the world, and on earth the Vicar of Jesus Christ our Saviour."† Picard, quoting the words of Innocent III., the original of which he gives in a note, says that this Pope asserted that the Church, the bride of the Vicar of Christ, conferred on him in the marriage a full power over the temporal and spiritual; that the Mitre is the sign of Spiritual, the Crown is of the Temporal; that one and the other teach to all Christians that he is King of Kings, and Lord of Lords.‡

I need only add that the present Roman Creed makes it imperative to believe that the Roman Church is the Mother and Mistress of all churches, and that true obedience is exacted to the Bishop of Rome, as the alleged successor of St. Peter, the Prince of the Apostles and Vicar of Jesus Christ.§

To a member of the Roman Church, therefore, the importance is apparent of being able to answer in the affirmative that Augustine recognized in the Bishop of Rome any such supremacy.

The period which our inquiry legitimately covers is from the time when Augustine first embraced the Christian religion until his death. We have seen that he was baptized by Bishop Ambrose, at Milan, in the year 387, after which he returned to his native country, Africa, where he was ordained Priest A.D. 391, and made Bishop of Hippo A.D 395, and died A.D. 430.

It may be here convenient to name the contemporary Bishops of Rome :—

> Siricius, from A.D. 385 to A.D. 398.
> Anastasius I., from A.D. 399 to A.D. 402.
> Innocent I., from A.D. 402 to A.D. 417.
> Zosimus, from A.D. 417 to A.D. 418.
> Boniface I., from A.D. 418 to A.D. 422.
> Celestine I., from A.D. 422 to A.D. 432.

It is not my intention to enter on an investigation of the subject of Peter's alleged occupation, as Bishop, of the See of Rome, or even his alleged visit to that city. The supposed presence of Peter at Rome has been so often discussed (the result being that there is no reliable evidence whatever in support of the Papal view), that I am spared a re-examination of the subject. Indeed, neither the alleged

---
* De Rom. Pont., Lib. ii. c. i.
† See Paris "Univers," 1 July, 1846, and Picard's "Cérémonies Religieuses, &c.," Part ii. Tom. i. Amsterdam, 1723 ; title, "A Fifth Adoration of the Pope."
‡ Picard, as above, p. 51, "Rex Regum et Dominus Dominantium."
§ Concil. Trid. apud Bullas, p. 311. Romæ, 1564.

Episcopacy of Peter, nor his alleged visit to Rome, are matters of faith in the Roman Church; the propositions may therefore be rejected without our being charged with heresy. Further, Peter Dens, in his "Theologia," a text-book of authority, informs us that:—"It is *probably* a matter of faith that a modern Pontiff is the Vicar of Christ, but not a matter of *obligatory* faith. It is, however, to be noted," he continues, "that a modern Pontiff being the successor of Peter and the Vicar of Christ *is not a matter of obligatory faith*, for *that* is not sufficiently propounded by [or set before] the whole Church with the necessity of believing it."* And as such speculations were never suggested in the days of St. Augustine, we will take for granted the propositions thus laid down by Peter Dens, and reject them as a matter of faith. What we have to consider is, have we any evidence to lead us to suppose that Augustine accepted any such proposition as the supremacy of the Bishop of Rome, by *Divine right* or otherwise, as successor of St. Peter?

As an historical fact, recorded by Irenæus, Bishop of Lyons A.D. 190 (the first ecclesiastical writer who refers to the subject), Peter and Paul, while they were going about founding and constructing churches, together ordained LINUS as the *first* Bishop of Rome;† but so little could even this bit of tradition be relied on, that his contemporary, Tertullian, tells us that the same two Apostles appointed CLEMENT, not Linus, the *first* Bishop of that See.‡ Neither, however, ever mentions that Peter himself was the *first* Bishop of Rome.

The claim of Supremacy by Divine appointment being, nevertheless, maintained up to the present day,§ I may be excused if I digress for a while from my immediate subject, in order to trace the history of this usurped Supremacy.

We have seen that Cardinal Bellarmine said that the theory of the Pope's Supremacy is the "sum and substance of Christianity." He added: "The Supremacy of the Bishop of Rome may be proved by fifteen several names or titles, as, namely, 'Prince of Priests,' the 'High Priest,' the 'Vicar of Christ,' the 'Universal Bishop,'" and the like.‖ As a fact, however, none of these titles was given to the Bishop of Rome, exclusively, for a period of six hundred years.

The title of "Universal Bishop" was first assumed by John, Bishop of Constantinople. Pelagius II., Bishop of Rome A.D. 590,

---

* Dens' Theologia, Vol. ii. pp. 19-22. Dublin, 1832.
† Adv. Hæres., Lib. iii. c. 3, p. 171, fol. Geneva, 1570.
‡ De Præscrip. Hæret., c. 32, Tom. ii. p. 40. Halæ Magd., 1770.
§ Every Bull or Brief of the Popes from the days of Hildebrand (Gregory VII.) to the late Vatican decree proclaiming the Pope's Personal Infallibility, maintains the title to Supremacy on the alleged appointment of Peter as Vicar of Christ, and the Bishops of Rome as his alleged Successors.
‖ De Rom. Pont., Lib. ii. c. 31, sec. i.

at once denounced the assumption of this title as an unlawful usurpation, and protested that none of his predecessors had assumed "such a profane appellation."* His successor, Gregory I., declared the title to be a "name of vanity," a "new and profane appellation," a "name of blasphemy, in which the honour of all priests is taken away, while it is arrogated madly to himself by a single individual."†

And, again, the same Bishop said: "No one of my predecessors ever consented to use this so profane appellation; for if a single patriarch be styled *Universal*, the name of Patriarch is taken from the others. But far, very far, be it from a Christian mind, that any person should wish to snatch himself a title, whence he may seem, in any even the smallest degree, to diminish the honour of his brethren."‡

"To consent to the adoption of that wicked appellation is nothing less than to apostatize from the faith."§

"I indeed confidently assert," he further said, "that whosoever either calls himself, or desires to be called, *Universal Priest*, that person, in his vain elation, is the precursor of Antichrist, because, through his pride, he exalts himself above others." ||

This title, then, so late as the year 601, was repudiated by the Bishop of Rome; but, notwithstanding the above denunciation, it was assumed by Boniface III. A.D. 607, second in succession to Gregory I., under the following circumstances:—Phocas having obtained the empire by the murder of the Emperor Mauricius, his predecessor, with his wife and five children, made common cause with Boniface III. against Cyriacus, Bishop of Constantinople, who refused to countenance his murderous and traitorous deeds. The compact was, that Boniface should recognise Phocas as lawful Emperor, and the latter should recognise the Church of Rome to be the head of all churches, and the Bishop of that See as Sovereign and *Universal Bishop*. This spiritual title was thus given and confirmed to the Bishop of Rome by Imperial edict, not by Divine right. It is under this title that the succeeding Bishops of Rome hold their *spiritual primacy*.

The title "Vicar of Christ" was never applied to a Bishop of Rome exclusively before the Council of Florence, 1439; and, even then, it was expressly stated to be so applied "reserving the rights of the Bishop of Constantinople." The spiritual power was to be exercised only "according as it is contained in the acts of General Councils and in the Holy Canons."¶ We find this title in Cyprian's

* Pap. Pelag. II., Ep. viii. Labb. et Coss., Tom. v. cols. 949, 950. Paris, 1671.
† Pap. Greg. I., Ep. Lib. iv. Ep. xx. Opera, Tom. ii. p. 748. Benedict. Edit. 1705.
‡ Ibid., Lib. v. Ep. xxv. Tom. ii. p. 771.
§ Ibid., p. 742.
|| Ep. xxiii. Tom. ii. p. 881, and Labb. et Coss., Tom. v. col. 1027. Paris, 1671.
¶ Labb. et Coss., Tom. xii. col. 154. Paris, 1671.

12th Epistle; but it is applied to all bishops. So also it was used in the Synod of Compiègne, under Gregory IV., A.D. 833:—"It is convenient that all Christians should know what kind of office that of bishop is—who, it is plain, are the Vicars of Christ, and keep the keys of the kingdom of heaven."* And so at the Synod of Melun, under Sergius II., A.D. 845:—"And although all of us are unworthy, yet we are 'the Vicars of Christ, and successors of the Apostles.'"†

Further, for one thousand years after Christ the title "Pope" was not the exclusive privilege of the Bishop of Rome. Hildebrand (Gregory VII.) was the first who declared that this title should be exclusively applied to the Bishop of Rome.‡

It is thus clear that the titles "Supreme" or "Universal Bishop," "Vicar of Christ," or even "Pope," were not assumed as the exclusive right of the Bishop of Rome in the days of Augustine.

The Temporal Power of the Popes was not assumed until the year 741, when it was conferred by the usurper Pepin on Zachary, the result of an unholy compact between them. And here again we have the solemn protest of Gelasius I., Bishop of Rome A.D. 492. The treatise *De Anathematis Vinculo*, "On the Bond or Tie of the Anathema," attributed to Gelasius, is one of four tracts which are to be found under his name in all the orthodox editions of the Councils, such as Labbeus and Mansi, Binius and others. In this tract Gelasius lays down a clear distinction as then existing between the temporal and the spiritual jurisdiction of bishops and emperors or kings. He states that anciently the royalty and priesthood were often united in one and the same person, among the Jews as well as the Gentiles; but that since the coming of Christ these two dignities, and the different powers that attend them, have been vested in different persons; and from thence he concludes that neither ought to encroach on the other, but that the temporal power entire should be left to princes, and the spiritual to priests; it being no less foreign to the institution of Christ for a priest to usurp the functions of sovereignty than it is for a sovereign to usurp those of the priesthood.§ This is a very clear statement, and could never have been made by a Bishop of Rome had he held the modern notions of the present possessor of the Papal See, who declares that the temporal is inseparable from and is necessary to the spiritual rule.

But to return to Augustine. He imbibed his first principles of Christianity from Ambrose, Bishop of Milan. The See of Milan at that time and for many centuries after was wholly independent of

---

* Labb. et Coss., Tom. vii col. 1686. Paris, 1671.
† Ibid., Tom. vii. col. 1818.
‡ "Biographie Universelle," Paris, 1817, Art. Grégoire VII., p. 396.
§ Sacro. Concil., Tom. viii. cols. 93, 94; Mansi (Edit. Florent., 1762); and Binius, Concil., Tom. ii. par. i. p. 487, Colon., 1618.

the jurisdiction of the Bishop of Rome. The jurisdiction of the Bishop of Rome extended only over those churches lying "within one hundred miles round Rome, being equal in extent with that of the Roman Provost," or Prefectorate. Such was the view taken by Dr. Cave, Stillingfleet, and Beveridge.* Dupin, the French ecclesiastical historian, while maintaining the independence of the See of Milan, gives the names of seven distinct provinces as being subject to the bishop of that See.†

Milan formed no part of such outlying provinces subject to the Bishop of Rome. Proofs of the independence are incontestible. Pope Pelagius I., writing in the year 555, distinctly confesses that it was then an ancient custom that the Bishops of Milan did not come to Rome for ordination, but that they and the Bishops of Aquileia were accustomed to ordain one another.‡ Pelagius, however, like other Popes, was anxious to reduce the Bishops of Milan to dependence upon himself, and shortly after (as appears from another Epistle) he actually invoked the secular power of the Emperor's lieutenant to endeavour to effect his object.§ So far, however, was this object from being attained that Platina, the historian of the Popes (who was librarian of the Vatican under Pope Sixtus IV.), in his life of Pope Stephen IX., distinctly admits that Milan entirely withdrew itself from communion with the Church of Rome for two hundred years together.‖ That See was ultimately, but with difficulty, reduced to submission by the all-powerful Hildebrand (afterwards Gregory VII.) about the year 1059. Peter Damiani, in that year, was sent by Pope Nicholas II to interfere on his behalf in a period of great disturbance. Cardinal Baronius tells us that the interference of Damiani, instead of being at once submitted to, was met by a popular clamour, *led by the clergy*, " that the Ambrosian Church ought not to be subject to the laws of Rome; that the Pope had no power of judging or ordaining matters in that See, and that it would be a great indignity if that Church which *under their ancestors had been always free*, should now, to their extreme reproach (which God forbid), become subject to another Church." Baronius goes on to tell us that " the clamour increased; the people grew into a higher ferment; the bells were rung; the Episcopal Palace beset, the legate threatened with death."¶ This is pretty clear evidence that the See of Rome was not acknowledged to be, in its Metropolitan or Patriarchal character, the Mother or Mistress of the Church of Milan, nor had the Roman Bishop any

---

* See Bull's " Corruptions of the Church of Rome," Edition of S.P.C.K., Sect. ii.
† De Antiq. Eccl. Disciplina, diss. i. sec. 14, p. 92. Paris, 1686.
‡ Labb. et Coss., Concl., Tom. v. col. 805. Paris, 1671.
§ Ibid., col. 807, Epist. Valeriano Patricio.
‖ Plat. de Vit. Pont., p. 132. Colon., 1529.
¶ Baron. Annal., Tom. xi. p. 262, A.D. 1059, n. 43.

power or supremacy over the Bishops of that See until the eleventh century.

It is not within the object of the present treatise to examine the several passages from the voluminous works of Ambrose, forced at times into this controversy, but it may safely be admitted that nowhere does he admit an ecclesiastical supremacy in the Bishop of Rome, or that the Roman See was Mother or Mistress of the See of Milan. He admitted Rome to be an apostolically-founded See; and he had a reverence for Peter, in whom he seemed to acknowledge a precedence of honour among the Apostles; but it is equally clear that Ambrose did not place any importance on any alleged *personal* succession from Peter, nor does he anywhere say that Peter was personally Bishop of Rome.

The views of Ambrose with reference to the position of Peter in the Church may be summed up in the following extracts from his works:—" Faith," he said, " is the foundation of the Church, for it was not said of the *body* of Peter, but of the *faith* of Peter, that the gates of death should not prevail against the Church. It is the confession that conquers hell."*

Again, he said, "They do not possess the inheritance of Peter who have not the *faith* of Peter."—" Non habent Petri hæreditatem qui Petri fidem non habent." The passage thus stands in all the old Editions,† even in the Paris Edition of 1661.‡ But the text has been skilfully manipulated, by changing *fidem* into *sedem*; so they would make Ambrose say, "They have not the inheritance of Peter who have not the *chair* of Peter"! And on the gift of the keys—" To you he [our Lord] says, I will give the keys of the kingdom of heaven. . . . What is said to Peter is said to the Apostles."§ With reference to the commission to feed the flock, Ambrose gave a very different interpretation to the text from that now assigned to the thrice-repeated injunction of our Lord, " Feed my sheep." " Peter, by feeding well the flock of Christ with the food of faith, *blotted out the fault* of his former lapse; and therefore a third time he is admonished that he should feed them; a third time he is asked whether he loves the Lord, so that he should a third time confess Him whom three times he had denied before his crucifixion."‖ Again:—" And the Holy Apostle Peter, since in our Lord's passion he fell by the infirmity of human nature, because he thrice denied Him, afterwards, that he might blot out and be absolved from his fall, when he was thrice asked by Christ if he loved Him, says, ' O Lord, thou knowest that I love thee.' He said it a third time, that

---

* De Incar. Dom. Sacram., Lib. i. c. v. Tom. ii. p. 711. Benedict. Edit. Paris, 1690.
† Tom. i. p. 156. Basil. 1527.
‡ Tom. iv. col. 391, H.
§ In Psalm xxxviii. Ernarr., p. 858, Tom. i. Paris, 1690.
‖ Prologus in Lib. v., de Fide. sec. 2 Tom. ii. p. 551. Paris, 1690.

he should be a third time absolved."* And with regard to Peter's alleged primacy, the same Ambrose said:—"But what do you tell me? Immediately, not unmindful of his place, he enacted the primacy, a primacy of confession, not of honour, a primacy of faith, and not of order."†

Again:—"Nor was Paul inferior to Peter, although he was the foundation of the Church, and the former was the wise architect, knowing how to establish the footsteps of the people. Paul was not, I say, unworthy of the college of the Apostles, but might be compared with the first, and was *second to none*. For he who does not acknowledge himself to be unequal, makes himself equal."‡

The remaining point now to be ascertained as to Ambrose is, whether he submitted to the authority of the Bishop of Rome, as Supreme Pastor and Vicar of Christ. On this he clearly expressed his views in the first chapter of the third book on the Sacraments, when he said,§ "I desire to follow the Roman Church in all things; but, nevertheless, we are men who have some common sense, therefore, whatever is better preserved elsewhere, we will also properly guard. We follow the Apostle Peter himself; we adhere to his devotion. What answer can the Roman Church make to this?"

We should be glad to receive a satisfactory reply to this pertinent question!

Whatever else, therefore, Augustine, in the way of doctrine, took with him to his native country, as the teaching of Bishop Ambrose, it certainly was not that he considered it necessary to his salvation that he should be subject to the Bishop to Rome.

On his return to Africa, Augustine found a Church in direct antagonism to the Bishop of Rome. Cyprian was Bishop of Carthage A.D. 248 to 258, when he suffered martyrdom. He died not only in what would be now called schism, but in actual heresy. He maintained that the lapsed, in order to be reintroduced into the Church, or those who had been baptized at the hands of a heretic, should be rebaptized. Stephen, Bishop of Rome, held the contrary opinion, and took upon himself to call Cyprian "false Christ, and false Apostle, and deceitful worker."‖ For this piece of impertinence on the part of Stephen, Firmilian, Bishop of Cæsarea, in Cappadocia, in the Epistle last quoted, protested against the Bishop of Rome's unauthorized and impudent interference and assumed authority. He declared Stephen to be "a second Judas," and called him "an arrogant, presumptuous, manifest and notorious

---

* Lib. ii. de Sacramentis, c. 7, Tom. ii. p. 360. Paris, 1690. (Treatise attributed by Romanists to Ambrose, but of doubtful authority.)
† De Incar. Sac. [the Mystery of the Lord's Supper], Lib. i. c. iv. Edit. 1690.
‡ De Spiritu Sanct., Lib. ii.
§ See pp. 1244-5. Paris Edit. 1549.
‖ See Firmilian's Epis., lxxv.; Opp. Cyprian, Vol. ii. pp. 218, 224, 225, 227, 228. Edit. Oxon, 1682.

idiot"! Cyprian, in the Epistle No. lxxiv., addressed to Pompeius, a Bishop in Tripoli, retorted on Stephen, by declaring his theory "an error;" and he speaks of his "obstinate pride" and "hardy presumption," his "blindness of heart and corruption of manners." At a Council of eighty-seven Bishops held at Carthage, over which Cyprian presided, the insolent pretensions of Stephen were rejected. Cyprian, in his prefatory address to the assembled Bishops, pointed out that such an assumption by the Bishop of Rome was contrary to ecclesiastical custom and discipline:—"For (said he) no one of us has set himself up as the Bishop of Bishops, or has driven, by tyrannical fear, his colleagues to the necessity of obeying him, since every Bishop has his own will for the exercise of his liberty and power, and can be no more judged by another than he can judge another."*

Mosheim, in his "Ecclesiastical History," has rightly estimated the relative positions in the Church of Cyprian, as representing the African Church, and Stephen Bishop of Rome:—"With respect particularly to the Bishop of Rome, he is supposed by Cyprian to have had at this time a certain pre-eminence in the Church; nor does he stand alone in this opinion. But it is to be carefully observed that even those who, with Cyprian, attributed this pre-eminence to the Roman prelate, insisted at the same time with the utmost warmth upon the *equality*, in point of *dignity* and *authority*, that subsisted among all the members of the episcopal order. In consequence of this opinion of an *equality* among all Christian bishops, they rejected with contempt the judgment of the Bishop of Rome, when they thought it ill-founded or unjust, and followed their own sense of things with a perfect independence."

Mosheim then goes on to say:—"Whoever compares these things together, will clearly perceive that the pre-eminence of the Bishop of Rome was a pre-eminence of *order* and *association*, and not of *power* or *authority*."†

With reference to the position of Peter among the Apostles, Milman, in his "History of Latin Christianity," observed that "Cyprian, in whom the unity of the Church had taken its severest form, though practically he refused to submit the independence of the African churches to the dictation of Rome, did far more to advance the power of the primacy which he assigned to St. Peter, than he impaired it by his steady and disdainful repudiation of his authority whenever it was brought to the test of submission."

That may be to a certain extent true, but that is no reason why Romanists should exaggerate the position of Peter by a deliberate and impudent forgery, making Cyprian say in his book on "the Unity

---

* Sent. 87 Episcop. Synod. Carthag. Labb. et Coss., Tom. i. col. 786. Paris, 1671; and Cyp. Oper., Tom. i. pp. 229, 230. Oxon. 1682.
† Vol. i. pp. 214, 215, Cent. III. p. ii. sec. ii. London, 1768.

of the Church," "Upon him [Peter] He builds His Church, and to Him He commits His sheep to be fed; . . . and the primacy is given to Peter, that it might be shown that the Church is one, and the Chair one. . . . He who opposes and resists the Church, who forsakes the Chair of Peter, upon which the Church is built, can he trust that he is in the Church?" These words are not found in the Edition of Gryphius of 1537; Morellus, 1564; nor in that published at Oxford 1682, which latter Dupin describes as the most correct of all editions; and although the passages are admitted by Rigaltius into the text (Paris, 1666), he confesses their spuriousness in his notes. They were, in fact, excluded from every printed edition till the one published in 1563. But Pamelius and Manutius, two Roman Editors of Cyprian's works, retain the passages as genuine, without being equally candid. The passages are still constantly quoted as genuine. Dr. James* has given sufficient proof of this "notorious corruption in Cyprian's *De Unitate Ecclesiæ*." The following is what Cyprian did say with regard to Peter's position in the Church:—

"Peter, whom our Lord chose first, did not insolently and proudly claim or assume to himself anything, as to say he held the primacy over other bishops or apostles."†

"After his (Christ's) resurrection the like power was given to all the apostles."

"The rest of the apostles were even the same that Peter was, being imbued with the like fellowship of honour and power."‡

Milman had probably before him one of the corrupted editions of Cyprian's Epistles when he made the observation above quoted.

The independence of the African Church was maintained inviolate to the days of Augustine. A notable circumstance then occurred which reflects little credit on the Roman Church. The facts are stated by Dupin in his Ecclesiastical History,§ and in all the transactions Augustine took a prominent part.

Apiarius, a Presbyter of the African Church, being degraded and excommunicated by his Bishop, Urbanus, was unable to get a reversal of the sentence from his own Church. Apiarius sought the protection of Zosimus, Bishop of Rome. Contrary to ecclesiastical usage in such cases, Zosimus admitted this man into communion, and took upon himself to send Bishop Faustinus and two Legates to Africa to cause the restoration of Apiarius, maintaining the right of every Priest to appeal to Rome. The Bishops assembled at the Council of Milevis, A.D. 418, passed the following decree:—"If

---

* "Treatise of Corruptions of Scripture Councils and Fathers," Part II.; "Corrections of the True Fathers," pp. 74 *et seqq*. London, 1843.
† Epis. at Quintum Fratrem, Ep. lxxvi. Oper. vol. 2, p. 194. Oxon, 1682.
‡ De Unitate Eccles., p. 107, Oxon., 1682, and p. 172, cap. 2¶ Paris, 1836.
§ Vol. i. pp. 415, 417 and 637. Dublin Edit., 1723.

they think it necessary to appeal, they should not appeal unless to African Councils, or to the Primates of their provinces. But if any one appealed beyond the seas, he should *not be received into communion* by any in Africa."* Augustine's signature stands fourth in the list of Bishops who signed the decrees of this council. The deputation was asked to produce their credentials, authorizing their interference. They produced a *forged* canon as of the Council of Nice (A.D. 325). The genuineness of this document was challenged. On the 23rd of May, 419 (Zosimus was then dead; but Boniface I., his successor, continued to persist in the same course), a general synod of African Bishops, 217 in number, was assembled at Carthage, at which Augustine was also present. In the presence of Faustinus and the other Legates the African copy of the canon was read, and shown to be at variance from that produced by them. It was thereupon proposed to adjourn the sitting, until the return of deputies to be sent to Constantinople, Alexandria, and Antioch, who should examine the copies of the Nicene canons deposited with those apostolic sees. In November of the same year Cyril, Bishop of Alexandria, and Atticus, Bishop of Constantinople, forwarded to Carthage authenticated copies of the Nicene canon; and the Roman copy was thus proved to be a gross forgery.

Boniface had been scarcely dead when Celestine, his successor, made another attempt to encroach upon the Church of Africa by receiving the same Apiarius into communion, and sending Faustinus again to Africa to procure his restoration, asserting a right in Rome to hear appeals; but the African Bishops again resisted,—" seeing (as Dupin,† the Roman Catholic historian, says) of what importance it was to take care that for the future the African Councils should not be thus oppressed." They wrote to Celestine a letter of protest, which concluded as follows:—

"As for your sending Legates, we find no such ordinance in any council, nor in the writings of the Fathers. As for what you have sent us by your colleague Faustinus as a canon of the Council of Nice, we must let you know *that no such canon is to be found in the genuine and uncorrupt copies of that council* which have been transcribed and sent us by our fellow-Bishop Cyril, of Alexandria, and the Reverend Atticus, of Constantinople. These copies we sent to Boniface, your predecessor, of worthy memory. We, therefore, earnestly beg you will send no more Legates nor Ecclesiastics to execute your judgment here, lest you should seem to introduce worldly pride and arrogance into the Church of Christ."‡

The fraud was not confined to the production of this spurious canon, for the canon passed at the Council of Milevis above quoted,

---

* Lab. et Coss., Tom. iii. Conc. Milev. cap. xxii. col. 385. Venet., 1728.
† Ecc. Hist., Vol. i. p. 639. Dublin, 1723.
‡ Lab., Tom. iii. Epist. Conc. African., ad Papam Cœlest. col. 1675. Venet., 1728.

being so decisive against the Roman claim, that Romanists have even ventured to falsify that canon also, by adding,—"except it be to the Apostolic See." Even Bellarmine was obliged to admit that that addition was not warranted by the original text:—"This exception (he said) does not seem to square with the Council."*

It is important to note that throughout this disgraceful transaction, the claim of Supremacy was not founded on the pretence of a "Divine right" or privilege derived through Peter, but on a forged document in no way alluding to one or the other!

With reference to the controversy which took place between Stephen, Bishop of Rome, and Cyprian on the question of heretical Baptism, Augustine referring to that dispute, maintained that Stephen's views or decision did not bind the Church, and that Cyprian and the other African Bishops were justified in rejecting his interference,† though Augustine seems to have held the same views on re-baptism as Stephen.

With reference to Augustine's interpretation of the text Matt. xvi. 18, it is very evident that he did not place any great importance on our Lord's words as affecting Peter personally. In his 149th Sermon on the words of the sixteenth of Matthew, with reference "to the keys," he thus expressed himself‡ :—"It appears in many passages of Scripture that Peter represented the Church, and particularly in that place where it is said, I give to you the keys of the kingdom of heaven. . . . For did Peter receive those keys, and did John and James and the other apostles not receive them? . . . What was given to him was given the Church. Therefore Peter represented the Church, and the Church was the body of Christ."

And in his (so-called)§ "Retractations" he wrote, with reference to the meaning of the word "rock":—" I have said in a certain passage respecting the Apostle Peter, that the Church is founded upon him as upon a rock. . . . But I know that I have frequently afterwards so expressed myself, that the phrase 'Upon this rock,' *should be understood to be the rock which Peter confessed.* For it was not said to him, Thou art *Petra*, but, Thou art *Petrus*, for the rock was Christ. Let the reader select which of these two opinions he deems the most probable."

And in his 270th Sermon‖ :—"He says to them, 'But whom do ye say that I am?' and Peter, one for the rest, one for all, says, 'Thou art the Christ, the Son of the living God.' This he said most rightly and truly: and he deservedly merited to receive such an answer,

---

* Hæc exceptio non videtur quadrare, &c. Bell. de Pont., Lib. ii. c. 24, p. 374, Tom. i. Prag., 1721.
† De Bapt. contr. Donat., Tom. ix. pp. 98-111. Benedict. Edition.
‡ Tom. v. p. 706. Benedict. Edit.
§ Tom. i. p. 32.
‖ In die Pentecostes, Tom. v. p. 1097.

'Blessed art thou, Simon Barjona, for flesh and blood hath not revealed it to you, but my Father which is in heaven.'—'And I say unto thee,' because thou hast said this to me, listen; thou hast given me a confession, receive a blessing: therefore, 'And I say unto thee, thou art Peter:' because I am *petra*, a rock, thou art *Petrus*, Peter; for *petra*, the rock, is not from *Petrus*, Peter, but *Petrus*, Peter, is from *petra*, the rock: for Christ is not so called from the Christian, but the Christian from Christ. 'And upon this rock I will build my Church:' not upon Peter, who thou art, but upon the rock whom thou hast confessed. 'I will build my Church;' that is to say, 'I will build thee, who, in this answer, art a figure of the Church.'"

And once again in his 13th Sermon:—" Christ was the rock, Peter figuratively the Christian people. . . . Therefore, He said, 'Thou art Peter,' &c.; that is, I will build my Church on Myself, the Son of the living God. I will build thee on Myself, not Myself on thee. For men willing to build upon men, said, 'I am of Paul, and I of Apollos, and I of *Cephas*, that is *Peter*.' But others who were unwilling to be built on Peter, but would be built upon the rock, said, '*But I am of Christ*.' But the Apostle Paul, when he knew that he was chosen, and Christ contemned, said, 'Is Christ divided? was Paul crucified for you, or were ye baptized in the name of Paul?' Wherefore, as not in the name of Paul, so not in that of Peter, but in the name of Christ, that Peter may be built upon the rock, not the rock on Peter."*

And as to the commission to feed the sheep:—"When it was said to him, 'Lovest thou me? Feed my sheep,' it was said to all."†

Again, our Lord asked Peter three times, "Lovest thou me?" when he replied, He told him as many times to "feed His sheep." Augustine, far from attributing this to any appointment of governorship over the Church, applies it to Peter's fall‡:—" The threefold confession relates to the threefold denial, that the tongue might not be less submissive to love than to fear. If it was the mark of fear to deny the pastor, let it be the duty of love to feed the Lord's flock."

It is very clear, therefore, that Augustine did not conceive that the Bishops of Rome derived any pre-eminence from their assumed succession from Peter, or that the Roman branch of the Christian Church was built on Peter as on a rock. There is a remarkable passage in his exposition of the 36th Psalm, giving his view of the Church of Christ:—"Christ is our head, and we are the body of that head. But are we only the body, and not those also who lived before us? All who ever have been just from the beginning

---

* De Verbis Domini, c. i. sect. i., Tom. v. p. 415.
† De Agone Christi, c. xxx. p. 260, Tom. v. Paris, 1685.
‡ Tract. 123, in Evang. Johan., Tom. iii. pt. 2, p. 817. Paris, 1680.

of time have Christ as their head. For they believed that He was about to come, whom we now believe to have come; and they were healed by his faith, by whose faith we are healed, so that He should be head of the entire city of Jerusalem; all the faithful being collected from the beginning to the end of time, legions and hosts of Angels also being united to them, so that there should be one city under one king, and as it were one province under one emperor, happy in perpetual peace and safety, endlessly praising God and endlessly blessed."*

Again, as to those who constitute the Church:—" For He only is our head who was born of Mary, and suffered, and was buried, and rose again and ascended into heaven, and now sits at the right hand of the Father, and intercedes for us. If He is the head, we are the members; the whole of His Church which is everywhere diffused is His body, of which body He is the head. But not only those believers who now exist, but those also who existed before us, and those who are about to exist until the end of time, all belong to His body, of which body He is the head, who ascended into Heaven."†

In commenting on such passages as these the Rev. Mr. Allies, in his work, "The Church of England cleared from the Charge of Schism,"‡ says:—

"St. Augustine everywhere appeals to the Church spread throughout the whole world, as being, by virtue of that fact, the one communion in which alone there was salvation; and this, upon the testimony of the Holy Scriptures only. 'To salvation itself,' quoting Augustine's words,§ 'and eternal life no one arrives, save he who has Christ for his head, but no one can have Christ for his head except he be in His body, which is the Church, which, like the Head itself, we ought to recognize in the *holy canonical Scriptures*, nor to seek after it in the various reports, opinions and doings, sayings, and arguments of men.' But in the whole book [on the unity of the Church] there is not one word about the Roman See, or the necessity of communion with it, save as it forms part of the Universal Church. It is not named by itself any more than Alexandria and Antioch."

And in page 169 he says:—" I have as clear a conviction as one can well have, that St. Augustine *did not* hold the Papal theory of Supremacy."

If ever an opportunity presented itself to Augustine to agree with the modern Roman theory it was when he wrote the work mentioned, on the "Unity of the Church." He counted upwards of eighty-eight heresies; and surely in combating these the more ready course would have been to appeal to the "Centre of Unity,"

---

* Serm. iii. Tom. iv. p. 284. Edit. as above.
† Enarratio. in Psl. lxii., Tom. iv. p. 607.
‡ London, 1846, p. 66.
§ De Unit. Eccl., Tom. ix. p. 372, F.

if such a centre existed. But, as has been remarked, not once does he refer to Rome as of any authority. Further than this, Augustine delivered five sermons on the festivals of Peter and Paul, and these do not contain one word about any special commission or privilege descended by inheritance to the Bishop of Rome.

The following observations are made in the "Pope and the Council," by "Janus" *:—"St. Augustine has written more on the Church, its unity and authority, than all the other Fathers put together. Yet, from his numerous works, filling ten folios, only one sentence, in one letter, can be quoted where he says that the principality of the Apostolic Chair has always been in Rome—which could, of course, be said with equal truth of Antioch, Jerusalem, and Alexandria. Any reader of his Pastoral Letter to the separated Donatists on the unity of the Church, must find it inexplicable, on the Jesuit theory, that in these seventy-five chapters there is not a single word on the necessity of communion with Rome as the centre of unity. He urges all sorts of arguments to show that the Donatists are bound to return to the Church, but of the Papal Chair, as one of them, he knows nothing. Even Pope Pelagius praises St. Augustine for 'being mindful of the divine doctrine which places the foundation of the Church in the Apostolic *Sees*, and teaching that they are schismatics who separate themselves from the communion of the Apostolic *Sees*' (Mansi. Concil. ix. 716). This Pope (555-560), then, knew nothing of any exclusive teaching privilege of Rome, but only of the necessity of adhering in disputed questions of faith to the Apostolical *Churches*—Alexandria, Antioch, and Jerusalem, as well as Rome."

These citations from the writings of the Rev. Mr. Allies and "Janus" are so far important from the fact that Mr. Allies subsequently joined the Roman Church, as the result of the controversy on baptismal regeneration, and wrote a book on the "See of St. Peter," in which he nowhere refers to or attempts to displace his own evidence with regard to St. Augustine; and as to "Janus," as being written by Roman Catholics, and the reply, "Anti-Janus," by Dr. Hergenröther, a professor of great celebrity in the Roman Church, nowhere refers to the above facts, though he appears otherwise to reply very minutely to other statements made by "Janus"!

A passage from Augustine's forty-third Epistle is not unfrequently quoted as an evidence of his acknowledgment of some Supremacy in the Church of Rome. "In the Church of Rome the principality of an Apostolic Chair has always flourished." In "Romanâ ecclesiâ semper apostolicæ cathedræ viguit principatus." The words *princeps* and *principatus* were terms not unfrequently given to Bishops generally, as well by the Greek as by the Latin Fathers of the fourth and

* 2nd Edit. Rivingtons, 1869, pp. 88-9.

fifth centuries, referring to their spiritual powers, but exercised within the limits of their several jurisdictions;* and it was in that sense that the word *principatus* was used by Augustine. It was an expression properly used as applied to a Church of Apostolic origin, like that of Rome, whose Bishop exercised a supervision over the suburbicarian churches. "The Catholic Church," wrote Augustine, "was propagated and diffused over all the world by the *Apostolical Sees* and the succession of Bishops in them."†

De Maistre, in his book on "The Pope," as far as I can trace, refers only once to Augustine, where he is made to say that to Peter was by our Lord entrusted the keeping of His sheep, but we have seen that Augustine considered that the commission to feed the flock was equally entrusted to all.

Whenever Augustine speaks of the Church, Roman controversialists at once conclude that he refers to the local Roman Church. For instance, when he said "I should not have believed the Gospel except the authority of the Church had moved me thereunto,"‡ they would have us believe that he looked to the Roman Church as that authority. What possible reference can these words have to the Roman Church more than to his own Church in Africa, to the Greek Church, or any other Church? Augustine was arguing with a Manichee, who sought to enforce a gospel of his own without dispute. Augustine opposed that gospel as not acknowledged by the Universal Church. The Romish Bishop Canus has himself given the explanation. In this case he says Augustine puts the question: "What if you find one who doth not believe the Gospel? What motive would you use to such a one to bring him to your belief? I, for my part (he adds), should not have been brought to embrace the Gospel if the Church's authority had not swayed me to it."§ We have it sufficiently clear what Augustine meant by the Church from the extracts I have already given, and on that head he adds the further testimony:—"By the mouth of God, which is the truth, I know the Church of God, which is partaker of the Truth."‖ Let the Roman Church bring herself to that test!

So also in his arguments against the Donatists, a sect of Christians in Africa who, in Augustine's time, maintained for themselves exactly the position assumed by the Romish Church of the present day. They claimed to be exclusively *the Catholic Church*. In fact, the Donatists of the third and fourth centuries were in theory the same as the Romanists of the nineteenth century. Augustine denied the

---

* See Laud's Conference with Fisher, sect. xxv. p. 187. Oxford, 1849.

† Videtis certe multos præcisos a radice Christianæ societatis, quæ per sedes apostolorum et successiones episcoporum certa per orbem propagatione diffunditur. Aug. ad Madaurenses, Ep. 232, alias 42, col. 843, E., Tom. ii. Paris, 1679.

‡ Cont. Ep. Fund., c. v. Tom. viii. p. 154. Edit. as above.

§ Canus, Loc. Theol., Lib. 2, c. 8, p. 52. Colon. 1605.

‖ In Pslm. lvii., p. 545, Tom. iv. Paris, 1681.

Donatists that exclusive title, but he nowhere says that the Roman Church could assume it. Donatist Bishops set themselves up in opposition to the legitimate Bishops of the Roman See. Augustine naturally claimed for the Bishop of Rome, in opposition to this usurpation of the Donatist Bishops, to be the rightful successor in that See as an apostolically-founded Church, but in doing so he nowhere claims for the Roman Bishops a supremacy over other Bishops, though he admitted and advocated their claim as the legitimate successors in an apostolically-founded See. He rightly maintained that the Donatist was an intruder on the established successors of Bishops of that See from the time of Peter.* His answer to the claims of the Donatists is summed up in the following :—

"Let the Donatists," he said, "if they can, show their Church, not in the rumours and speeches of the men of Africa, not in the councils of their Bishops, not in the discourses of any writers whatever, not in signs and miracles that may be forged, for we are forewarned by God's word, and therefore forearmed, against those things; but in the *prescript* of the law, in the predictions of the Prophets, in the verses of the Psalms, in the voice of the Shepherd himself, in the preachings and writings of the Evangelists, that are in all the canonical authorities of the sacred Scriptures."†

Here was an opportunity for Augustine to assert the authority of the Roman Church. But no! He said that the authority of the Church is to be found in the *canonical Scriptures*. It is a true Church so long as it keeps within the bounds of the Word of God. The Holy Scripture is alone the charter of Christ's Church on earth; and so Augustine taught.

When we argue with members of the Roman Church, who, like the Donatists of old, claim to be *the* Church exclusively, we cannot do better than use Augustine's own words as applied to the Donatists. He said :—

"The question is where the Church should be. What then shall we do? Shall we seek it in our words, or in the words of our Lord Jesus? In my judgment we ought rather to seek the Church in His own words, for that He is the Truth, and knoweth His own body."‡

Again, in writing to the Donatist Bishop Petilianus, Augustine retorted on him as we now retort on members of the Roman Church :—

"Whether it be a question of Christ, or whether it be a question

---

* In the passage referred to Augustine *apparently* points to Peter as *first* Bishop of Rome. I shall presently refer again to this fact. It is evident that the text has been tampered with.
† De Unit. Eccl., c. 18, Tom. ix. p. 371. Paris, 1688.
‡ De Unit. Eccl., c. 1, sect. 2, and in Tom. ix. p. 236, Antv. Edit. 1700.

of His Church, or anything relating to our faith, or life, I will not merely say we, but I will go much farther, and add, that if even an angel from heaven were to pronounce to you anything besides what you have received in the Scriptures, in the Law and Gospel, let him be accursed."*

The head of the Church is Christ, for he says:—"His whole Church, which is spread everywhere, is His body, of which He is the head. But not only do the faithful of the present day, but those who were before us, and those who shall exist after us to the end of time, belong to His body, of which body He is the head who ascended into heaven."†

Such passages might be multiplied. The above extracts are amply sufficient to show that Augustine had no idea of localizing the Church in those over whom the Bishop of Rome presided.

I have referred to the often-quoted saying, "Rome has spoken, the cause is finished," as attributed to Augustine, and which is repeatedly and triumphantly advanced as an acknowledgment that Augustine recognized a final appeal in the Bishop of Rome. "Roma locuta; causa finita est." Augustine never made any such acknowledgment, and the words are a misquotation. The question in dispute related to Pelagianism. The passage stands thus:—"The results of two Councils [Carthage and Milevis] on the matter have been sent to the Apostolic See, and replies have come thence. The cause is ended. Would that the error may end some time or other."‡ The *question* in dispute had been decided against the Pelagians by two African Councils and a Council held in Rome, but, as a fact, it did not end the controversy, for Zosimus, the Pope in succession, immediately afterwards sided for a time with the Pelagians, and the controversy was not terminated till the Council of Ephesus.§

If, then, it be asserted, with Bellarmine, that the dogma of the Supremacy of the Bishop of Rome is the sum and substance of Christianity, and, with Pope Boniface, that it is necessary to salvation to be subject to the Bishop of that See, then Augustine lived and died a heretic!

* Cont. Lit. Petil. Don., Tom. ix. p. 302. Paris, 1688.
† Enar. in Psal. lxii., Tom. iv. p. 607. Paris, 1691.
‡ "Jam enim de hac causa duo concilia missa sunt ad sedem apostolicam unde etiam rescripta venerunt. Causa finita est: utinam aliquando finiatur error. Serm. cxxxi. col. 645, D, Tom. vii. Bassano, 1802, and col. 930, Tom. v. Pars. I. Paris 1837.
§ See Fleury's Eccl. Hist., Tom. xxiii. 44, cited by Dr. Littledale; and see "The Pope and the Council," Janus, 1869, p. 70.

CHAPTER V.

SCRIPTURE AND TRADITION.

THE Roman Church, by the first decree passed at the Fourth Session of the Council of Trent, declared that:—"Having constantly in view the removal of error and the preservation of the purity of the Gospel in the Church, which Gospel, promised by the Prophets in the sacred Scriptures, was first orally published by our Lord Jesus Christ, the Son of God, who afterwards commanded it to be preached by His Apostles to every creature, as the source of all saving truth and moral discipline; and perceiving that this truth and discipline are contained *both in written books and in unwritten traditions*, which have come down to us, either received by the Apostles from the lips of Christ Himself, or transmitted by the hands, as it were, of the same Apostles, under the dictation of the Holy Spirit; following the example of the orthodox Fathers, doth receive and reverence, *with equal piety and veneration*, all the books of the Old as of the New Testament, the same God being the author of both; and also the aforesaid traditions, pertaining both to faith and manners, whether received from the mouth of Christ Himself, or dictated by the Holy Spirit, and preserved in the Catholic Church by continual succession."

The creed of Pope Pius IV., the present binding creed on every member of the Roman Church, by its Article I. (additional) requires the following acknowledgment:—"I admit and embrace the apostolical *and ecclesiastical* traditions, and the other observances and constitutions of the Church."

Here, it will be observed, that as an addition to "Apostolical Tradition," all "Ecclesiastical Traditions and observances of the Church" are equally binding on the members of the Roman Church.

With reference to the "Canon of Scripture," the Council of Trent, by the same decree, adds that "lest any doubt should arise respecting the sacred books which are received by the Council, it had been judged proper to insert a list of them in the present decree."

A list is then given of the "Sacred Scripture" alleged to have been dictated by Divine inspiration and handed down and preserved by a continuous succession in the Church. In the list of the Old Testament are boldly inserted, for the first time, in April, 1546, the several books passing by the general title of the "Apocrypha," which are—Tobit, Judith, Wisdom, Ecclesiasticus, Baruch, two Books of Maccabees, and the rest of the Books of Esther and

Daniel—that is, from after the third verse of the tenth chapter of Esther to the end of the sixteenth chapter; and from and including the thirteenth and fourteenth of Daniel (so called), comprising the Story of Susannah, Bel and the Dragon, and the Song of the Three Children, as they at present stand in the Douay Version.

The Canon of the New Testament is the same as acknowledged by all orthodox Christians.

It is a matter of fact that the Roman Church has not authoritatively defined what questions, as relating to "faith and manners," are enforced for acceptance on the authority of "Scripture," or what on that of "Tradition." This omission is very significant, and is somewhat embarrassing when we come to discuss with them the Divine authority of any of their peculiar dogmas. I have never yet met with any precise declaration on this subject. Whenever they are hard pressed, however, in controversy on any peculiar dogma of their Church, they fall back on "Tradition," as their Bishop Canus ingenuously observed: "Because Tradition is not only of greater force against heretics than the Scriptures, but almost all disputation with heretics is to be referred to Traditions."* The importance of "Tradition" to the Roman Church is thus boldly summed up in the following startling passage from the pen of a popular Jesuit writer, Costerius, and it has not the honourable distinction of appearing either in the Prohibitory or Expurgatory Indices of Rome:—"The excellency of the unwritten word doth far surpass the Scripture, which the apostles left us in parchments; the one is written by the finger of God, the other by the pen of the apostles. The Scripture is a dead letter, written on paper or parchment, which may be razed or wrested at pleasure; but Tradition is written in men's hearts, which cannot be altered. The Scripture is like a scabbard which will receive any sword, either leaden, or wooden, or brazen, and suffereth itself to be drawn by any interpretation. Tradition retains the true sword in the scabbard; that is, the true sense of the Scripture in the sheath of the letter. The Scriptures do not contain clearly all the mysteries of religion, for they were not given to that end to prescribe an absolute form of faith; but Tradition contains in it all truth, it comprehends all the mysteries of faith, and all the estate of the Christian religion, and resolves all doubts which may arise concerning faith; and from hence it will follow that Tradition is the interpreter of all Scriptures, the judge of all controversies, the remover of all errors, and from whose judgment we ought not to appeal to any other judge; yea, rather, all judges are bound to regard and follow this judgment."†

---

* Canus. Loc. Theol. Lib. iii. cap. 3, p. 156. Colon., 1605.

† Coster. Eucharist. cap. i. p. 44. Colon., 1606. Quoted by Sir H. Lynde, *Via Devia*, sec. vii. p. 300. Lond., 1819.

The two questions, then, which we have to consider are:—

1. Whether Augustine anywhere in his writings accepted the modern Roman doctrine of Tradition as being of the same authority on matters of faith as the Holy Scriptures?

2. Whether he admitted the Apocrypha as a part of the sacred Canon of Scripture?

First, as to the Scriptures. If there is one subject insisted upon more than any other by the early Christian writers, it is the absolute sufficiency of Holy Scriptures for our rule and guidance in all questions of faith. Further, when they applied the word *Tradition* to points of doctrine, they expressly referred to the traditions handed down by the Apostles in their writings. In arguing with the heretics of his day (A.D. 140), Irenæus applied this word tradition to those doctrines which Romanists themselves admit to be clearly taught by the Scriptures. He declared that "the Scriptures are perfect, as having been dictated by the Word of God and His Holy Spirit."*

And he says:—"For we have become acquainted with the dispensation of our salvation through no other men than those through whom the gospel has come to us; which indeed they then preached, but afterwards, by the will of God, delivered to us in the Scriptures to be the foundation and pillar of our faith."†

And, in fact, this same father accused the heretics of his day of using, on this very subject, the argument invariably advanced by Protestants against Romanists of the present day:—"When they (the heretics) are confuted out of the Scriptures they turn round and accuse the Scriptures themselves, as if they were not accurate, nor of authority, and because they are ambiguous, and because the truth cannot be discovered by those who are ignorant of the tradition, for that the truth was not delivered in writing, but orally."‡

And while Tertullian (A.D. 194), in matters of discipline, set a great value on usage, custom, and tradition, which he admitted not to be authorized by Scripture, on questions of doctrine he looked to the Scriptures alone as of authority. In arguing with the heretics, he demanded from them proofs from Scripture—"If it is not written, let them fear the curse allotted to such as add or diminish." Suicer, the eminent professor of Greek, whose works are almost indispensable to the study of the Fathers, furnishes examples of the

---

* Iren. cont. Hæres., Lib. ii. c. 47, p. 173. London, 1522; and Edit. Grabe, 1853; and c. 25, p. 117. Edit. Basil., 1526.

† Iren. Advers. Hæres., Lib. iii. c. 1, p. 198. Oxon., 1702; and p. 117. Basil., 1526.

‡ Iren. cont. Hæres., Lib. iii. c. 2, in init., same edition; and p. 140. Edit. Basil., 1526.

fact that the word παράδοσις, *traditio*—tradition—was used as "identical with the written word."

The passages from the early Christian Fathers, which insist on the Scriptures as alone of authority on matters of doctrine, are so numerous and so well known, that it is at the present day almost labour and time lost to repeat them; they are to be found in almost every Protestant controversial work. I shall, nevertheless, transcribe two or three of these, merely as illustrations. What could be more striking than the words delivered at the first General Council of Nice (A.D. 325) by Eusebius, Bishop of Cæsarea, in the name of the 318 Bishops there assembled? "Believe the things that are written: the things that are not written, neither think upon nor inquire into."* And Gregory, Bishop of Nyssa (A.D. 379), said, "Let a man be persuaded of the truth of that alone which has the seal of the written testimony."† And Cyril, Bishop of Jerusalem (A.D. 386), places the matter very clearly before us. He said:—"Not even the least of the Divine and holy mysteries of the faith ought to be handed down without the Divine Scriptures. Do not simply give faith to me while I am speaking these things to you, unless you have the proof of what I say from the Holy Word. For the security and preservation of our faith are not supported by ingenuity of speech, but by the proofs of the Sacred Scriptures."‡

Such passages might be multiplied largely. They all tend to prove that the modern practice of placing Tradition on a level with Scripture, to establish a point of faith, would have been then considered most heretical. Indeed one Father, Theophilus, Bishop of Alexandria (A.D. 412), emphatically said:—"It is the part of a devilish spirit to follow the sophisms of human falsehoods, and to think anything to be divine that is not authorized by the Holy Scriptures.§"

But we have only to deal with Augustine. It may safely be asserted that there is no Latin Father whose works contain so many decisive passages on the value and importance of the Scriptures as in Augustine's. The same honourable distinction may be awarded to Chrysostom, of the Greek Church; the two most powerful champions of Christianity, in the Eastern and Western world, being of one mind in approaching the inspired Scriptures alone as the supreme and final arbiter in every question of faith and doctrine. The difficulty consists not in bringing forward evidence of this, but in

---

* Euseb. ad. Philosp. in Gelas. Cyzic. Comment. art. Nic. P. 2, c. xix. p. 185. Edit. Balf.
† Greg. Nyss. Dialog. de Anima et Resurrect., Tom. i. p. 639. Edit. Græcolat.
‡ Cyril Hieros. Catech., iv. sec. 17 p. 108. Monac., 1848.
§ Op. Epist. Paschal., i. sec. 6, in Bib. Vet. Patrum, Tom. vii. p. 617. Edit. Galland.

selecting the most appropriate.* Thus in his treatise on the "Unity of the Church," against the Donatists, he brings us at once to the source from whence the decisions on all questions controverted between Christians must be decided:—

"Let not these words be heard between us, 'I say,' or 'You say,' but rather let us hear, 'Thus saith the Lord;' for there are certain books of our Lord on whose authority both sides acquiesce; there let us seek our Church, there let us judge our cause. Take away, therefore, all those things which each alleges against the other, and which are derived from other sources than the canonical books of the Holy Scriptures. But, perhaps, some will ask, Why take away such authorities? Because I would have the Holy Church proved, not by human documents, but by the Word of God." †

"Renounce, therefore" (he further observes), "all such things, and show your Church, if you can, not in the sayings of Africa, not in the Councils of your Bishops, not in signs and lying wonders ‡ but in the writings of the Law, the predictions of the Prophets, in the Psalms, in the words of the Shepherd Himself, in the preaching and labours of the Apostles—that is, by the authority of all books of the Canonical Scriptures. For we do not say that we ought to be believed because we are in the Church of Christ, or because that Church to which we belong, was commended to us by Optatus, Ambrose, or other innumerable Bishops of our communion; or because miracles are everywhere wrought in it. These things are indeed to be approved, because they are done in the Catholic Church, but it is not thence proved to be the Catholic Church, because such things are done in it. Our Lord Jesus Christ Himself, when He rose from the dead, and offered His body to be touched as well as seen by His disciples, lest there should be any fallacy in it, thought it proper to convince them, rather by the testimony of the Law, the Prophets, and the Psalms, showing how all things were fulfilled which had been foretold; and so He commanded His Church, saying, that repentance and remission of sins should be preached in His Name, among all nations, beginning at Jerusalem. This He testified was written in the Law, the Prophets, and the Psalms; this we hold, as commended from His mouth. *These are the documents, these the foundations, these the strong grounds of our cause.* We read in the Acts of the Apostles, of some believers, that they daily searched the Scriptures if these things were so. What Scriptures? but the canonical books of the Law and the Prophets; to which are added the Gospels, the Apostolical Epistles, the Acts of

---

* In making this selection I have followed Keary's "Common Place Book of the Fathers." Lond., 1828. He quotes the Edition "Lugduni, 1562," which references I shall retain.

† De Unit. Eccl., c. 4, Tom. vii. p. 625.

‡ Is this not exactly applicable to modern Romanists ?

the Apostles, and the Revelation of St. John. Search, then, all these, and bring forth something manifest, by which you may prove the Church to have remained only in Africa, or come out of Africa."*

In another part of the same treatise he observes:—"The question between us and the Donatists is, Where is the Church to be found? What then shall we do? Shall we seek it in our words, or in the words of its head, our Lord Jesus Christ? I conceive that we ought to seek it in His words, who is the truth, and best knows His own body."† And again, excluding human authority, he adds:—"Neither must we agree with Catholic Bishops, if they err, or decide anything against God's canonical Scriptures."‡ "Faith (he remarks, in treating on Christian doctrine) will waver, if the authority of the sacred Scriptures be weakened."§ "For in those things which are clearly set forth in Scripture, are found all those things which contain matters of faith and practice."‖ In another treatise against the Donatists, on Baptism, he asks:—"Who is ignorant that the sacred canonical books, both of the Old and New Testaments, are contained within certain bounds, and ought to be so far preferred before the later writings of Bishops, that of them alone we are not to question or doubt anything written in them, whether it be right or wrong. But all other writings, since the confirmation of the canon of Scripture, may be questioned, and even the decisions of one council corrected by another."¶

"Whether it be a question of Christ" (he remarks in writing against Petilianus, the Donatist Bishop), "or whether it be a question of His Church, or anything relating to our faith, or life, I will not merely say we, but I will go much farther, and add, that if even an angel from heaven were to propound to you anything besides what you have received in the Scriptures, in the Law and Gospel, let him be accursed."** And in defence of the above work against the grammarian Cresconius:—"According to these books of Scriptures, we freely judge all other writings, whether they be faithful or unfaithful."†† In the beginning of his forty-ninth Tract on St. John's Gospel, he says:—"Our Lord Jesus Christ did many things which were not written, but that which is written is precious, the belief in which must be considered as sufficient for salvation."‡‡

The nineteenth Epistle, addressed to Jerome, contains the follow-

* De Unit. Eccl., pp. 664-6. Edit. Lugduni, 1562.
† Ibid., cap. ii. p. 622.
‡ Ibid., p. 644.
§ De Doct. Christ., Lib. i. cap. 37, Tom. iii. p. 21.
‖ Ibid., Lib ii. cap. 9, p. 39.
¶ De Bapt. Cont. Donat., Lib. ii. cap. 3, Tom. vii. p. 472.
** Cont. Lit. Petil. Don., Lib. iii. cap. 6, Tom. vii. p. 200.
†† Cont. Crescon. Gramm., Lib. ii. cap. 31, Tom. vii. p. 205.
‡‡ In Joan. Tract. 49, Tom. ix. p. 436.

ing very decisive opinion as to the light in which we should view human authority when placed in competition with the Scriptures:—
"This reverence and honour I have learned to give only to those books of Scripture which are called canonical, that I firmly believe that none of their authors could err in anything which they have written. But others I so read, that however they may excel in holiness or learning, I do not consider anything to be true, merely because they thought so; but because they were able to persuade me, either by these canonical authors, or by some probable reason, agreeable to truth. Neither do I conceive, brother, that you think otherwise, nor do I believe that you expect that I should read your books as I do those of the Prophets and Apostles, of the truth of whose writings, as being exempt from all error, we must not doubt."*
The same thoughts we find in his Epistle to Fortunatus:—"However catholic or praiseworthy any man may be, we do not appreciate his writings in the same way that we do the canonical Scriptures; but that, saving the reverence due to them, we may disapprove or reject anything in their writings if we should happen to find that they have decided contrary to truth. Thus do I judge of the writings of others, and thus do I desire to be judged myself."†

We also find in the writings of this Father many very striking descriptions of the general adaptation of the Scriptures to the wants of mankind; as well as exhortations to their universal perusal; thus, in his third Epistle to Volusian, "The mode of expression used in the Scripture, although penetrable by few, is accessible to all. Those plain things which it contains, it speaks to the heart of the unlearned and learned, like a familiar friend, without disguise. While those things which are mysterious it does not conceal under high-flown language, which unlearned men and slow of apprehension, would not dare to approach,—as the poor man fears to approach the rich,—but invites all by the homeliness of its style, not only to feed on those plain things which it contains, but to seek those which are hidden. By it the depraved are corrected, the humble nourished, and the highest intellects delighted. That mind which is inimical to its doctrine is either erroneously ignorant of its salubrity, or loathes the medicine from disease."‡

He thus exhorts his hearers in one of his sermons: "Know, my dear brethren, for a certainty, that as our flesh is, which for many days is destitute of food, so are our souls, when they do not feed upon the word of God. For as hunger and want of nourishment make our bodies lean and infirm, so the soul which does not feed upon the word of God becomes unfruitful and useless, and unfit for any good work. Continue then to hear, as you are accustomed, the Scriptures

---

* Ep. xix., Tom ii. p. 76. Edit. as above. † Ep. cxi., Tom. ii. p. 602.
‡ Ep. iii., Tom. ii. pp. 13, 14.

read in the Church, and read them again in your own houses. If any man is so occupied that he cannot read the holy Scriptures before meals, let him not neglect to read something of them at them, that thus, while his body is nourished with material food, his soul may be nourished by the word of God. For if we feed the body only, and the soul is not nourished by the word of God, we pamper the slave while we starve the mistress, and how unjust this is you cannot be ignorant."*

In his tract against the Manichean Faustus, alluding to the writings of uninspired men, he observes: "As for this kind of books we read them, not as necessarily bound to believe them, but with the liberty of judging what we read. We make a distinction between the books of later writers, and the excellency of the canonical authority of the Old and New Testaments; which, having been confirmed in the times of the Apostles, have since, by the Bishops who succeeded them, and the churches which were founded, been placed as it were upon a high throne, to be reverenced by every pious and faithful mind. And if we find anything there apparently inconsistent, we must not say that the author of the book was ignorant of the truth, but that either our copy is corrupt, the interpreter mistaken, or we ourselves are ignorant. But as for the writings of those authors who have come after them, we are at liberty, in reading or hearing them, to admit what we approve, and to reject what we dislike; so that he who rejects those passages which are not proved from Scripture, or which, at least, do not appear agreeable to the truth, is not to be reprehended."†

It has been repeatedly urged in controversy, and more particularly by Dr. Milner in his "End of Religious Controversy," as an argument against the alleged sufficiency of the Scriptures as the sole rule of faith, that Christ Himself never wrote anything. They overlook the fact that their Trent Council declared that the "sacred Scriptures were first orally published by our Lord Jesus Christ, and transmitted by the Apostles under the dictation of the Holy Spirit;" but if Augustine is to be admitted as an authority on this head, he said:—

"For as many of His actions and sayings as Christ wished us to read, *these He commanded* to be written in a book, as if it were by His own hands. For this common bond of unity, and harmonious ministry of the members, in different offices, under one head, each should understand and should receive the narrative of Christ's disciples in the Gospel no otherwise than if he saw the very hand of Christ writing it, which was attached to His own body."‡

---

* De Temp., Serm. lvi. Tom. x. p. 179—and see p. 180. Edit. as above.
† Cont. Faust. Manich., Lib. xi. cap. 5, Tom. vi. p. 309.
‡ De Consensu Evangelist., Lib. i. cap. 35, Tom. iii. pt. 2, p. 26. Paris, 1680.

We have in the above sufficient evidence that Augustine did not subscribe to Rome's modern theory of Tradition.

And Secondly.—Our next subject for investigation is whether Augustine, in appealing to the Scriptures, included the Apocrypha in the "Sacred Canon," to which he repeatedly refers.

A few preliminary observations may not be out of place here. Rome's appeal to the Fathers of the Church on the subject of the sacred canon of Scripture as testifying in her behalf, is one of their bold assertions which will not for one moment bear even the most superficial investigation.

The fatal decree above quoted, declaring the Apocrypha part of the sacred canon, was passed at the 4th Session of the Trent Council, when there were no more than forty-nine members present. There was much diversity of opinion even among these, when the subject was under discussion. The Bishops behaved so clamorously, that it was necessary to direct them to give their votes one by one, and to number them as they were received. So great was the diversity of opinion on this subject, even so late as April, 1546! It is a popular error to suppose that the Trent Council merely *declared* what was previously of faith : so far from this, some of the venerable Fathers came even to blows, and tugged at each other's beards to enforce their own private opinions. It is true they passed their decrees, and *asserted* the authority of Fathers and Apostolic Tradition in their favour ; but the assertion was not true. It was and is unsupported by evidence.

St. Paul tells us that "unto the Jews were committed the oracles of God," and this he wrote to the Romans themselves (iii. 2), as if in prophetic warning : the Jews rejected the Apocrypha, and the early Christians professed to receive the code or canon of the Old Testament from the Jews.

Neither Christ, nor any of the inspired writers of the New Testament, ever quoted the Apocrypha as of any authority.

We have several successive Christian writers who have left us lists of the sacred canon of Scripture, as accepted in their respective periods. I now name some of the leading Fathers of the early Christian Church, and other divines (all claimed as members of the Church of Rome), in each successive century, who rejected the Apocrypha, and who, therefore, bear evidence to the belief of the Church in their respective ages. The references given in a note are easily accessible. (See pp. 54 55.)

The Apocryphal books were rejected from the sacred canon, expressly by word, or indirectly by giving a list excluding them, by*—

---

* Some few of the writers here referred to admit in their list "Baruch," but these exceptions will be noticed in the note of editions, *infra.* pp. 54–55.

In the Second Century—Melito, Bishop of Sardis.
In the Third—Origen.
In the Fourth—Eusebius, Bishop of Cæsarea, and *Saints* Athanasius, Hilary, Cyril of Jerusalem, Cyprian, Gregory Nazianzen, Amphilochius, and the Bishops assembled at the Council of Laodicea,* confirmed by a decree of the General Council of Chalcedon, and by the sixth General Council in Trullo, can. 2, and therefore binding on the Church of Rome.†
In the Fifth—*Saints* Jerome, Epiphanius, and Augustine.
In the Sixth—Junilius (an African Bishop), and some add Saint Isidore, Bishop of Seville.
In the Seventh, we have no less authority than Pope Gregory the Great himself. Even the Vatican edition‡ of Gregory's Works testifies that he rejected the Apocrypha from the sacred canon.
In the Eighth—Saint John Damascene, the founder of School Divinity among the Greeks, and Alcuinus, Abbot of St. Martin's, Tours, France.
In the Ninth—Nicephorus, Patriarch of Constantinople, and the "Ordinary Gloss" begun by Alcuin or by Strabus, and enlarged by divers writers.
In the Tenth—The Monk "of Flaix" (Flaviacensis) and Ælfric Abbot of Malmesbury.
In the Eleventh—Peter, Abbot of Clugni, styled "The Venerable."
In the Twelfth—Hugo de Sancto Victore, Ricardus de Sancto Victore, Rupert, Abbot of Deutz, the author of the "Gloss upon Gratian," and the English translation of the Bible of this date in the University Library, Oxford.
In the Thirteenth—Hugo Cardinalis and Saint Bonaventure.
In the Fourteenth—Richard Fitz Ralph, Archbishop of Armagh and Primate of Ireland; Nicholas de Lyra, and Wycliffe.
In the Fifteenth—Alphonsus Tostatus, Thomas Waldensis, and Dionysius Carthusianus.
In the Sixteenth, we have the famous Cardinal Cajetan. This

---

* It may be useful here to remark that, with regard to the Council of Laodicea, the Book of Baruch and Epistles of Jeremiah, are inserted in some copies. (Labb. et Coss., Tom. i. p. 1507-8. Paris, 1671.) They are found in the version of Gentian Hervet; but in the Latin copies of previous date they have no place. (See Merlin and Crab. apud Cosin, Scholast. Hist. of the Canon, sec. lxi., note.) Neither Aristenus nor Carranza have them in their transcript. (See Beveridge's Synodicon., Tom. i. p. 481); and Carranza, Summa Conciliorum (Paris, 1677, p. 140), published with permission and approbation. And as to the 6th Gen. Council, see Binius, Concil. Laod., p. 305, Tom. i. Paris, 1636.

† The third Council of Carthage, A.D. 397, Can. 47. This Council admits some of the books, but omits Baruch and the two books of Maccabees; that is to say, no Greek copies admit them, though Dionysius Exiguus has added them to his collection. Labb. et Coss. Concil., Tom. ii. col. 1177. Paris, 1671. See the learned Bishop Beveridge's note on this canon.

‡ Rome, 1608. Ex Typogr. Vatican., Tom. ii. p. 899.

illustrious Prelate of the Roman Church wrote a Commentary on the Historical Books of the Old Testament, which he dedicated to Pope Clement VII. This book appeared only twelve years before the meeting of the Trent Council. In the dedicatory epistle,* the Cardinal adopts Jerome's rule relative to the broad distinction made by him between the Canonical Books, properly so called, and the Apocryphal. His words are:—

"Most blessed Father,—The *universal Latin Church* is most deeply indebted to St. Jerome, not only on account of his annotations on the Scripture, but also because he distinguished the Canonical Books from the non-canonical, inasmuch as he thereby freed us from the reproach of the Hebrews, who otherwise might say that we were forging for ourselves books, or parts of books belonging to the ancient canon, which they never received."*

Jerome (A.D. 418) distinctly adhered to the books constituting the Jewish canon, and expressly rejected the several Apocryphal books by name,† and this is admitted by Cardinal Bellarmine himself.‡

But what does Cardinal Bellarmine, one of the greatest controversial writers the Church of Rome has produced, say to these authorities? The facts are too notorious to be denied; so he admits them, as already stated, but blunderingly "confesses and avoids" (as lawyers say) the difficulty. "It was no sin (he said), no heresy in them [Augustine, Jerome, Gregory, &c.] to reject these books, because no General Council in their days had decreed anything touching them."§ This may be the best reason that can be advanced; but it does not support the Trent theory.

Thus, then, we have taken some leading names of men from each successive century, all (except Wycliffe) claimed by the Church of Rome as members of her communion, who rejected the Apocrypha. We come, then, to the following conclusions—that, down to April, 1546, the Apocryphal books formed no part of the canon of Scripture enjoined by the Church; that they became a part of the canon only since that date; that the Council of Trent then invented this new code, and that Romanists, in maintaining that the Apocrypha forms a part of the sacred canon of Scripture, represent a new system and teach a novel doctrine.‖

---

* Cajetan. Epis. dedic. ad P. Clem. VII. ante Comm. in Lib. Hist. V. T. Parisiis, 1546.
† Hier. Ep. ad Paulinum. Oper. Ben. Edit. 1693, Tom. iv. [col. 571-4; and Praefat. in Libros Solom., Tom. i. pp. 938, 939.
‡ De Verbo Dei, Lib. i. c. x. sec. xx. Tom. i. p. 20. Edit. Prag., 1721.
§ Ibid. sec. vii. p. 18.
‖ References to editions of the "Fathers" mentioned:—
Melito, A.D. 177 [he rejects all]. In Epist. ad Onesimum, apud Euseb. Eccles. Hist. iv. c. 26, p. 121. Cantab., 1700; Bell. de verbo Dei, Lib. i. c. xx. p. 38, sect. 15. Prag., 1721.
Origen, A.D. 200 [he rejects all]. In Expositione primi Psalmi, apud Eusebium. Hist.

The only authorities alleged in favour of the list as now proclaimed by the Roman Church of anterior date to the period covered by Augustine's writings are:—

1. The Council of Sardica, A.D. 341–347.
2. The Council of Carthage, A.D. 397.

Eccles., Lib. vi. c. 25, pp. 289, 290. Edit. Reading, Cantab., 1720. [But see Dupin, vol. i. p. 28, London, 1692, as to Esther and Ruth.]

Cyprian, A.D. 250 [or Ruffinus], excludes them all. See Bell. de Verb. Dei, Lib. i. c. 20, p. 38, Tom. i. Prag., 1721; Ibid., Can., Lib. ii. c. 11, p. 67. Colon., 1605.

Athanasius. A.D. 340 [rejects all but Baruch]. Epist. Alex. Aristoni in Epp. quæ dicuntur Canonicæ, Synopsi., Beveridge's Pandect., ii. Oxford, 1672; Athan. Oper. Synops., Tom. ii. p. 39. Paris, 1627.

Hilary, A.D. 350 [rejects all]. Prolog. in Lib. Psalm., sect. 15, p. 145. Edit. Wirceburg, 1785; Bell. de Verbo Dei, Lib. ii. c. 1, sect. 15, Tom. i. p. 38. Prag., 1721.

Cyril of Jerusalem, A.D. 370. Numbers 22 books and rejects the Apocrypha, but in these he is supposed to number "Baruch and the Epistle of Jeremiah." Catech., iv. sect. 20. Oxon., 1703.

Gregory Nazianzen, A.D. 370 [he rejects them all]. Ex Metricis ejus Poematibus, p. 194, Tom. ii. Paris, 1630; and see Beveridge's Pandect., Tom. ii. p. 178, Oxford, 1672.

Eusebius, A.D. 315, see above. Eccl. Hist., Lib. iv. c. 26; Lib. vi. c. 25, pp. 289, 290. Cantab., 1700. Chron., Lib. ii. ex Hier. versione, c. 10, p. 59. Colon., 1605.

Loadicea, Council of, A.D. 367. Can. lx.; Labbe. et Coss., Tom. i col. 1507. Paris, 1671 [rejects all], but see note above, and Bin. Concil. Laod., p. 305, Tom. i. Paris, 1636.

Amphilochius, A.D. 370 [who rejects them all]. Ex Iambis ad Seleucum., Beveridge's Pandect., ii. p. 179. Oxford, 1672.

Epiphanius, A.D. 390 [excludes them all]. De Mens. et Ponder. Tom. ii. p. 161. Colon., 1682. Hær. i. c. vi. pp. 18-19. Colon.

Jerome, A.D. 392 [rejects them all]. (Symbolum Ruffini), Tom. iv. p. 143; Præfatio in Proverbia Salomonis, Tom. iii. 8, i. k.; Præfatio in Hieremiam; Ibid., 9, c.; Præfatio in Danielem; Ibid., 9, g; Præf. in librum Regum; Ibid., p. 5, m, 6, a, b, c, Edit. Basil., 1525. Bell. de Verb. Dei, Lib. i. c. 10, sect. xx. p. 20, Tom. i. Prag., 1721.

Chalcedon, Council of, A.D. 451, which confirmed the canons of the Council of Laodicea, art. 15, can. i.; Lab. Conc., iv. col. 755. Paris, 1671.

Augustine, A.D. 420 [excludes them all from the sacred 'canon]. De Mirab. Sacræ Script. Lib. ii. c. 34, p. 26, Tom. iii. pt. i. Paris, 1686. De Civ. Dei, l. 18, c. 36, p. 519, Tom. vii. Paris, 1685. Aug. contra. Secundam Ep. Gaud., Lib. i. c. 31, p. 821. Edit. Basil., 1797.

Junilius, A.D. 545 [he excludes Judith, Wisdom, and Maccabees]. De part. divinæ legis., Lib. i. cap. 3, p. 80, Tom. xii. Bibl. Patrum. Venet., 1765.

Gregory I., A.D. 601, followed the list of Jerome. Greg. Mor., Lib. 19, on 39th chap. of Job, c. xxii. col. 13; Bened. Edit., 1705, and Romæ, 1608, Tom. ii. p. 899; see Occam. Dial., pt. 3; Tract. i. Lib. 3, c. 16. Lugd., 1495.

Damascene, A.D. 787 [rejected them all]. Orth. fid., Lib. iv. c. 18, p. 153. Basil., 1539. See Canus. Loc. Theol., Lib. 2, c. x. p. 59. Colon., 1605.

Alcuinus, A.D. 790 [rejected them all]. Advers. Elipant., Lib. i. col. 941. Paris, 1617.

Nicephorus, A.D. 800 [rejected them all]. Nicep. Patr. C. P. Canon. Script. in Operibus Pithœi, cited by H. Lynde, Via Devia, sec. 5, p. 159. Edit. 1850, London.

N.B.—For the remaining references, which, being of so late date, are only valuable as showing a succession of testimony, the reader is referred to H. Lynde's Via Devia, sect. 5. London, reprint 1850, and Birckbeck's Prot. Evidence. London, 1849, vol. 2.

I. *The Council of Sardis.* Father Calmet (A.D. 1730) was the first, I believe, who advanced this council as an authority. Independently of the fact that the genuineness of the decrees of this alleged council is challenged, we assert that these decrees, such as they are, give no list of canonical books whatever. Dupin, the famous French ecclesiastical historian, who has ransacked all the Councils, and advanced all the authorities *he* could find, does not refer to this council as an authority.

II. *The Council of Carthage.* This council is supposed, by the 47th Canon, to have included the Apocrypha in the canon or list of Scripture, alleged to have been subscribed by Augustine. The objections to this authority are the following : —

Taking for granted, for the moment, that the decree is genuine— this council was not a General, but only a Provincial Council, and cannot, therefore, be cited to establish a doctrine, or bind the Church universal. It can only be cited to establish a local custom. Cardinal Bellarmine objected to the citation of this council on another subject. He said : "This Provincial Council cannot bind the Bishop of Rome, nor the bishops of other provinces,"* because the 26th Canon of this same council declared that the Bishop of Rome was not to be called Chief Priest, and the council otherwise opposed the Roman Supremacy. Surely this was a heretical council.

But we may be reminded of Calmet's argument, that the canons of this council were confirmed by the Council of Constantinople, in Trullo, A.D. 692. Be it so ! But, alas ! for the over-zeal of Calmet, who relies on this proof. Was he not aware that this latter council was wholly condemned by Popes, as we are informed by the Jesuit Fathers, Labbe and Cossart ?† A rather awkward mistake this. But, alas ! again, for consistency—this same council in Trullo *also* confirmed the canons of the Council of Laodicea !‡ which expressly rejected the Apocrypha. Did the 211 Bishops in Trullo confirm two conflicting lists ? It is more reasonable to suppose that they confirmed those of the earlier council, whose decrees had never been questioned, but, on the contrary, had already been confirmed by the General Council of Chalcedon. And besides, the Greek copy omits the Books of Maccabees, while the Latin translators have shuffled these into the list, which bespeaks at least some suspicion !

But it may be also objected, that the Council of Laodicea was equally a Provincial Council. We admit it ; but the 60th Canon of this council, which recites the Canonical Books,§ was confirmed by the General Council of Chalcedon, A.D. 451,‖ and is therefore

---

* Bell. de Pont. Rom., Lib. ii. c xxxi. sec. viii. p. 387, Tom. i. Prag., 1721.
† Lab. et Coss. Conc. Genl., Tom. vi. col. 1316. Paris, 1671.
‡ Lab. et Coss, Conc. Genl., Tom. vi. col. 1140, can. ii. Paris, 1671.
§ Binius, Conc., Conc. Laod., can. lx. Tom. i. p. 304. Paris, 1636.
‖ See Cosin's "Scholast. Hist. of the Canon.," sec. lxxxv. London, 1672.

binding on every member of the Romish Church. And while some Romanists prefer the authority of Carthage over Laodicea, because Leo IV. (A.D. 847) is stated to have confirmed the decrees of the former, they overlook the fact that Leo IV., in the same place, confirmed the decrees of the Council of Laodicea also, and thus make a Pope confirm two contrary lists. An additional reason is thus afforded for supposing that the canon of the later council, that of Carthage, was forged, and not known to Leo IV., and the recognition falsely attributed to him.

The second difficulty Romanists have to contend with is, that the list now professed by their Church does not agree with the list supposed to be given in the 47th Canon of the Council of Carthage, the canon relied on.* For instance, the Books of Maccabees are not found in any of the Greek printed or manuscript copies of this council, but only in Latin translations, which argues a forgery somewhere. Then, again, by a strange blunder, the council has enumerated *five* books of Solomon—that is, besides Proverbs, Ecclesiastes, and the Song of Songs, which are in the Hebrew Canon, and, what is called in the Septuagint, the Wisdom of Solomon, attributed to him, —but also "the Book of Jesus the Son of Sirach," written 800 years after the death of Solomon.

Siricius was at this date (A.D. 397) Bishop of Rome, Cæsarius and Atticus being Consuls, as the council itself relates; and yet the canon which is alleged to contain the list of Canonical Books refers to Pope Boniface, who was not Bishop until 418, twenty years after,† a very cogent reason for supposing that the man who forged the canon lived so long after the council was held, that he forgot who was Bishop of Rome at the time.

Romanists are not at all agreed among themselves as to the genuineness of *this particular canon*. Cardinal Baronius, the famous annalist, was obliged to admit that—"Not all the canons of this council are established; but they are allowed in *divers other* Councils of Carthage, as, namely, that canon wherein the number of Sacred Books is defined;"‡ and Binius, the publisher of the "Councils," said "Fifty canons which were attributed to that council were not all confirmed by it, but by other Councils of Carthage, as, namely, the 47th Canon."§ So that it is a mistake after all to refer us to the Council of A.D. 397! Take for granted it was another council—say that of A.D. 419, to which the decree is sometimes shifted over—then we have another difficulty. Dupin informs us that this council merely *proposed* the list, and that other

---

* Lab. et Coss., Tom. ii. col. 117. Paris, 1671.
† See the List of the Popes. Ibid., Tom. xvi. col. 130.
‡ Baron. Annal., Ann. 397, n. 56, p. 249. Edit. Lucæ., 1740.
§ Bin. Concl. Carth. III., p. 722, Tom. i. Lutet. Paris, 1636.

churches were to be consulted for its confirmation.* But it is quite a mistake to suppose that even this council published a list; and the question is scarcely worth while arguing until Romanists are themselves agreed upon the precise council which did pass the alleged canon or list, and at what date.

So much, then, for this authority.

Augustine is supposed to have subscribed the 47th Canon of the Council of Carthage, above referred to. But I have shown that there was no such canon. Are we to suppose that he professed a different Rule of Faith from that of Jerome? If so, where is the unity of teaching? Augustine was a Bishop in *Africa ;* Jerome a Presbyter at *Rome.* But it is certain that Augustine expressly excluded these various Apocryphal books by name from the canon of Sacred Scripture ;† and he distinguished what he means by the *Divine Canon* from the ordinary canon.‡ Here Bellarmine comes again to the rescue. He says "that St. Augustine was most certain that all Canonical Books were of infallible truth; but was not alike certain that all the Books of Scripture were canonical: for, if he did think so, yet *he knew the point was not as yet defined by a General Council;* and therefore, without any stain of heresy, some books might be received by some persons for Apocryphal."§ In other words, this is an apology for Augustine for not holding, in A.D. 307, the same belief as the Council of Trent in A.D. 1546! We are quite aware that, in his "Christian Doctrine," Augustine is supposed to give a list of the canon of Scripture, in which the Apocryphal books are included. But this is easily answered; and we prefer to do so in the words of the eminent Romish divine, Cardinal Cajetan, who wrote on this subject as follows:—" Here we end our commentaries on the Historical Books of the Old Testament; for the remainder—viz., Judith, Tobit, and the Books of Maccabees, *are not included by St. Jerome among the Canonical Books*, but are placed along with Wisdom and Ecclesiasticus, among the Apocryphal. Do not be uneasy, tyro, if you should anywhere find those [Apocryphal] books enumerated among the canonical, either by holy councils, or by holy doctors; for the words both of councils and of doctors must be reduced to the judgment of Jerome; and, according to his decision, *these books* [the Apocryphal books enumerated], and if there are any others like them in the canon of the Bible, *are not canonical—*that is to say, do not contain rules for *confirming Articles of Faith ; they may, however, be called canonical, as containing rules for the edification* of the faithful, inasmuch as they have been ad-

---

* Dupin, Vol. i. pp. 8, 9, fol. edit. London, 1699.
† Aug. de Civit. Dei, Lib. xvii. c. 20, p. 508, and p. 483; Lib. xviii. c. 26, Tom. vii. Paris, 1685.
‡ De Mirab. Sacræ Scrip., Lib. ii. cap. 34, p. 26, Tom. iii. Paris, 1680.
§ Bell. de Verbo. Dei, Lib. i. cap. x. sec. vii. p. 18, Tom. i. Prag., 1721.

mitted into this canon of the Bible, and authorized for this very purpose. With *this distinction*, you will be able to discern the meaning of *the words of Augustine* (de Doctr. Christ., lib. ii.), as also the decrees of the Council of Florence, under Eugenius IV., and of the Provincial Councils of Carthage and Laodicea, and of Popes Innocent and Gelasius."*

It may be mentioned, by the way, that Cajetan was most highly esteemed by his contemporaries: he was called the "incomparable theologian"—"to whom, as to a common oracle, men were wont to resort in all difficult questions of theology."

Now, what do we learn from this illustrious Doctor and Cardinal of the *ante*-Trent Roman Church? *First*, that the Church of Rome, in his day (A.D. 1533), did not admit the Apocrypha into the *sacred* canon of Scripture as of any authority on *questions of faith*, but allowed them to be read for the *edification of the faithful*, assigning to them exactly the same value as that accorded by the Church of England, in her Sixth Article, at the present day. On the other hand, the Council of Trent (which now rules the teaching of the Church of Rome), twelve years after Cajetan wrote the above, placed the two classes of books exactly on the same level, as being of equal authority in establishing questions of faith, and for which purpose they are now quoted. The same council, too, cursed to all eternity all who presumed to oppose this, her modern innovation! And, *secondly*, we learn from Cajetan in what light we are to regard the word "canonical" when used by Augustine and the other authorities relied on, who make a marked distinction between the *sacred* canon, as authority in questions of faith, and the ordinary phrase "Canon of the Bible" (*in canone Bibliorum* are his words). Since Cajetan wrote, the alleged lists of Carthage, Innocent, and Gelasius have been proved to be spurious.

Augustine (on the sixth Psalm, sec. 9) said, "The *Jews carry the volume* on which the Christian faith is built; they have been constituted our librarians." And his contemporary, Jerome, said—"The Church knows nothing of the Apocrypha; recourse *must be had to the Hebrew books*, from which the Lord speaks, and out of which the disciples take their example."†

We may here mention that Cardinal Bellarmine, in his extreme anxiety to press Augustine into the service of Rome,‡ quotes a passage from a work entitled "Ad Orosium," to prove "Ecclesiasticus" canonical Scripture; but, when the same tract is quoted against the Church of Rome on another of her dogmas, with the short memory peculiar to this Jesuit writer, he says—"It is not St.

---

* Cajetan in omnes authenticos Vet. Test. Hist. Lib. Comment., p. 482. Parisiis, 1546.
† Hieron., Præf. in Paralipom.
‡ Lib. i., De Verbo Dei, cap. 14.

Augustine's work, as learned men confess."* We should not have thought this worth mentioning, were not Bellarmine Rome's great controversial authority.

Augustine, therefore, when he treated of doctrine, as we have seen, refers to the "Sacred Canon of Scriptures," and there cannot be the slightest doubt but that he excluded the Apocrypha when he so referred to the Scriptures. Nor am I aware that he anywhere refers to the Apocrypha when he is treating of doctrine. And here I may note that, with reference to the "Canon of Scripture," Dr. Wordsworth, in his "Letters to M. Gondon," Letter III., Third Edition, 1848, p. 102, quotes the following passage from Augustine's work on "Christian Doctrine" (ii. 13, Benedictine Edition):—
"In Canonical Scriptures you must follow the judgment of the majority of the Churches. You will prefer those which are received by *all* Catholic Churches, to those which are not received by some," &c.

The Doctor detects an artful perversion of Augustine's meaning. Augustine's words are " quæ *apostolicas* (plural) sedes habere et epistolas accipere meruerunt." Whereas, in their "Jus. Canon. Decret., i. Dist. xix. c. 6," they have artfully made Augustine say: " Quas *apostolica* (singular) sedes habere et *ab eâ* alii meruerunt habere epistolas," evidently pointing to *Rome*, whose judgment we are to follow!

It requires the experience of a literary detective to enable us to discover the arts and wiles of controversy!

CHAPTER VI.

TRANSUBSTANTIATION.

THE doctrine and teaching of the Roman Church is clearly defined on "Transubstantiation." On the consecration of the elements of bread and wine, they tell us that the whole *substance* of the bread is changed into the body, and the whole *substance* of the wine is changed into the blood of Christ; the same Christ that was born of Mary that walked on this earth, that was crucified and ascended into heaven—the same "body, blood, bones and nerves, soul and divinity, of our Lord"; and that in the so-called Sacrifice of the Mass, the same Christ is offered up as a propitiatory sacrifice for the sins of the living and the dead, as was offered on the cross; and

---

* Bell. de Miss., Lib ii. c. 12, p. 913, Tom. iv. Edit. Colon., 1617.

that the consecrated elements are to be adored with the same Supreme worship as that which is offered to the Divinity itself.

That some of the early Christian writers used very extravagant expressions when referring to the Eucharist, and more especially the Eastern Bishops, we freely admit. For instance, Chrysostom said that the mouth became red with gore on partaking of the Sacrament; but not one of them refers to the consecrated elements as having been *changed in substance*. Indeed their writings prove to the contrary. To name a few, Gelasius, Bishop of Rome (A.D. 492), wrote:—"Certainly the sacraments of the body and blood of the Lord, which we receive, are a Divine thing; because by them we are made partakers of the Divine nature. Nevertheless, the *substance or nature of the bread and wine ceases not to exist;* and assuredly the *image* and *similitude* of the body and blood of Christ are celebrated in the action of the mysteries."*

Cardinal Baronius, and some other zealous Romanists, have endeavoured to deny the authenticity of this passage by attributing the work to Gelasius of Cyzicus (of the fifth century, nevertheless), and Rome, ashamed of its teacher, has placed the passage in question in the Roman Expurgatory Index.† There are, however, honest men in that Church, such as Dupin and others, who admit its authority as the genuine production of the Bishop of Rome of that name.

To go still higher, Theodoret,‡ Bishop of Cyrus (A.D. 430), wrote that—"The mystical signs do not depart from their nature, but remain in their former substance, figure, and form." This passage has also been tampered with.§

Again, we have Chrysostom (A.D. 406), who, in his Epistle to Cæsarius, said:—"Before the bread is consecrated, we call it bread; but when the grace of God, by the priest, has consecrated it, it is no longer called bread, but is esteemed worthy to be called the Lord's body, *although the nature of bread still remains in it.*"‖

Cardinals Perron and Bellarmine, feeling the force of this formidable passage, accused Peter Martyr (A.D. 1548) of having forged the treatise in question, and actually asserted that the epistle never existed; though they do not undertake to explain how it is that this same epistle was quoted as the genuine production of Chrysostom by John Damascene (A.D. 740), Anastasius (A.D. 600), and the Greek Father Nicephorus (A.D. 800), as shown by Wake. To

---

* Gelas. de Duabus in Christo Naturis, contra Eutychen et Nest. in Bibl. Patr., Tom. iv. par. i. col. 422. Paris, 1589; and p. iii. Tom. v. p. 671. Colon., 1618.
† See Mendham's Literary Policy of the Church of Rome, p. 121. London, 1830.
‡ Theodor. Oper. Dialog., Lib. ii. c. 24, p. 924. Paris, 1608.
§ See Faber's Difficulties of Romanism, B. ii. c. iv. p. 274. London, 1853.
‖ Chrysost. ad. Cæsarium Monachum, Tom. iii. p. 744. Bened., Paris, 1721.

this we may add the words of the French ecclesiastical historian, Dupin, "It appears to me that one ought not to reject it as a piece unworthy of Chrysostom."*

Again, we have Ephrem of Antioch (A.D. 336), who testified as to the belief in his day:—"The body of Christ, which is taken by the faithful, *neither departs from its sensible substance*, nor remains separated from intellectual grace on the other hand."†

This passage has also been perverted in the Latin version of the Jesuit editor with native adroitness.‡

The signal failure of the attempts to prove these passages to be spurious, tampering with them, putting them in the Roman Index as prohibited, establishes our case triumphantly.

Further than this, while the Trent decree excludes the possibility of a *figurative* interpretation, or a *spiritual* presence in the consecrated elements, the early Christian writers, Irenæus, Origen, Cyril of Jerusalem, Macarius, Gregory of Nazianzus, Clement of Alexandria, Tertullian, Eusebius of Cæsarea, Ambrose, Jerome, Augustine, Theodoret, and others, clearly understood our Lord's phraseology not *literally*, but *figuratively*. In their writings all these authors refer to the consecrated elements as *types, antitypes, figures, symbols, images*, or *representations* of the body and blood of Christ; expressions wholly irreconcilable with the present Romish theory.§

We have, however, to deal with Augustine. No person who peruses the following extracts can assert that Augustine held the modern Romish theory.

But first let me transcribe one of the many passages from a work on "The Sacraments," attributed to Ambrose of Milan, remembering that Augustine derived his first impressions on Christian doctrine from that illustrious Bishop:—"In eating and drinking, we *signify* the body and blood that was offered for us; *you receive the sacrament of a similitude:* it is a *figure* of the body and blood of our Lord; you drink the *likeness* of His precious blood."‖

It is in the writings of the great Augustine that we find the clearest evidence against this, as, indeed, against every other error with which Romanism has darkened the light of truth. Thus, how appropriate to our present subject are the following excellent rules for the interpretation of Christian doctrine:—"We must beware

---

* Dupin, Nouv. Bib. des Auteurs Eccl., Tom. iii. p 37. Paris, 1698.
† Ephraem. Theopolitan. apud Phot. Bibl., cod. ccxxix. p. 794. Edit. Rothomag., 1653.
‡ See Rivet. Critici Sacri, Lib. iv. cap. xxvi. p. 1148. Roterodami, 1652.
§ These passages are so frequently quoted, that it would be superfluous to repeat them here. The reader will find a very admirable selection in Faber's "Difficulties of Romanism," 3rd Edit., 1853, part ii. cap. iv.
‖ De Sacramentis, Lib. 4, c. iv. and v. Paris, 1539.

that we take not a figurative speech literally, for to this the Apostle's declaration applies, The letter killeth."* "In treating of signs, I say thus, that no man consider what they are, but rather of what they are signs—that is, what they signify."† "If the phrase be preceptive, either forbidding a great crime or wickedness, or commanding a beneficial thing, it is not figurative. But if it seems to command a crime or wickedness, or forbid a useful or beneficial thing, it is figurative." Having thus laid down the rule, he gives us the example:—"Unless ye eat the flesh of the Son of Man, and drink His blood, ye have no life in you. Now this seems to command a crime, or horrid thing, *therefore it is a figure*, commanding us to communicate in the passion of our Lord, and sweetly and profitably to treasure up in our memory, that His flesh was crucified and wounded for us."‡

In his Tract against the Manichean Faustus, he uses language nearly similar:—"Thus Christians celebrate the memory of that perfect sacrifice by the holy Oblation" (or Sacrament) "and the participation of the body and blood of Christ. Which sacrifice of the body and blood of Christ, before His advent, was promised by the similitude of the (Levitical) sacrifices. In the passion of Christ, it was rendered by the *very truth of the thing itself*; since His ascension it is celebrated by a *sacramental memorial.*"§

When Augustine uses the word *Sacrifice*, he cannot be construed to mean a sacrifice in the modern Roman signification of that term. In his 149th Epistle (ad. Paulin. n. 16), he speaks of a dedication of ourselves at the altar of God as a main part of that oblation or sacrifice which is there offered to Him:—"But let all things which are offered to God be devoted to Him, chiefly the Oblation of the Holy Altar, in which Sacrament that greatest of our vows is proclaimed, by which we promise that we will abide in Christ, as in the unity of the Body of Christ." This is much after the same strain of our own service, where the Eucharist is spoken of as a sacrifice—"a sacrifice of praise and thanksgiving"—in which "we offer and present ourselves, our souls and bodies," to the Lord, beseeching Him that we may be "fulfilled with His grace and heavenly benediction."

In his great work, "De Civitate Dei" (Lib. x. c. 6), after the expression of the same sentiments, St. Augustine uses the strong language that the Church was herself offered up in that very oblation which she did offer:—"Since, therefore, works of mercy are true sacrifices, which are referred to God, whether they are done to ourselves or to our neighbour, but works of mercy are done for

---

* De Doctrina Christiana, Lib. iii. cap. v. Tom. iii. p. 59. Lugd. 1532.
† Ibid., Lib. ii. cap. i. p. 23.
‡ Ibid., Lib. iii. cap. xvi. Tom. iii. p. 66.
§ Contra. Faustum Manich., Lib. xx. cap. ix.-xxi. Tom. vi. pp. 402-6.

nothing else than that we should be freed from misery, and thereby be happy . . . the result, therefore, is that the whole city of the redeemed, *i.e.*, the congregation and society of the Saints, should be offered as an universal *sacrifice* to God by the great High Priest, who also offered Himself in suffering for us, that we might be the body of so great a Head, according to the form of a servant. For this He offered, in this was offered, because, according to this, He was our Mediator, our Priest, and Saviour."

Many other passages might be adduced to illustrate the wide signification Augustine gave to the expression *Sacrifice*, and to which I shall have again to refer.

The compilers of the Expurgatory Index actually condemn Augustine for saying that the Eucharist was not a Sacrifice, but the memorial of a Sacrifice.*

In the 27th Tract on the Gospel of St. John, Augustine wrote: —" When ye shall see the Son of Man ascending where He was before, then shall ye see that He giveth not His body in the manner you suppose—then will ye understand that His grace is not consumed by morsels."† Again, in the questions on Leviticus:— " The thing which is signified is often called by the name of that which it signifies. St. Paul did not say the rock signified Christ, but the rock was Christ; which it was—not, indeed, in substance, but by signification." ‡ And in another place:—" The Law and the Prophets had sacraments, touching, a thing that was to come. But the sacraments of our times testify that the thing is come which, by these sacraments, was signified."§

How scriptural is the following definition of a worthy and unworthy participation of this rite?—" This is, therefore, to eat that meat, and drink that drink; to remain in Christ, and to have Christ remaining in him; and by. this, he that remaineth not in Christ, and in whom Christ does not abide without doubt, neither spiritually eats His flesh, nor drinks His blood; although he carnally and visibly presses with his teeth the sacrament of the body and blood of Christ, and thus rather eats and drinks the sacrament of so great a thing for judgment to himself, because that, being unclean, he presumed to come to the sacraments of Christ." ‖ " For this (he remarks, a little before, in the same Tract) is to eat the living bread, to believe on Him. He that believeth on Him, eateth; he is invisibly fed, because he is invisibly degenerated. He is inwardly a babe, inwardly renewed; where he is renewed, there he is nourished."¶

---

* See the extracts given in Chapter III.
† In Joan. Tractatus 27, Tom. ix. p. 284.
‡ Quæst. super. Levit. Quæst. 57, Tom. iv. p. 292.
§ Contra. Lit. Petil., Lib. ii. cap. xxxvii. Tom. vii. p. 138.
‖ In Joan. Tractatus 26, Tom. ix. p. 282.
¶ Ibid., p. 273.

In no mode of conveying instruction should we be more precise than in that which is intended for the young and unlearned. Such was the opinion of this Father, when, in compliance with the request of a friend, he wrote a treatise upon the best method of teaching the ignorant. Among other subjects, he speaks of the Sacrament, and thus states the doctrine, which, on that important point, should be impressed on the neophyte:—"He was to be taught that sacraments are *signs* of heavenly things, but invisible things are to be honoured in them. Nor is he to regard the species which have been blessed and sanctified, as if they were in common use. Let him be told also what the words mean which he has heard, what is hidden in it, and whose likeness that thing (the Sacrament) bears. On which occasion also, he must be admonished, that if he hear anything, even in the Scriptures, that sounds carnal, if he does not comprehend it, he must yet believe that it has a scriptural meaning."* "If we look to the things themselves, by which the sacraments are ministered (he remarks in his Tract on Baptism, against the Donatists) who knows not that they are corruptible? but if we consider what is wrought by them, who does not see that it cannot be corrupted?"† Again, in the 23rd Epistle, we find the following:—"If sacraments did not in some way resemble the things of which they are sacraments, they could not be sacraments at all; and on account of this resemblance, they often bear the name of the things themselves. *As therefore the sacrament of the body of Christ is, after a certain manner, the body of Christ,* and the sacrament of Christ's blood is (similarly) the blood of Christ, so likewise the sacrament of faith is faith."‡ "I may interpret that commandment ['This is my body,' he observes] to consist in a sign, for our Lord doubted not to say, This is My body, when He gave a sign of His body."§ And in his discourse on the 98th Psalm, he introduces our Saviour as thus speaking on the subject:—"Understand spiritually what I say; you shall not eat this body which you see, nor drink that blood which they shall shed that will crucify Me. I have commended a certain sacrament unto you, that, being spiritually understood, will quicken you Although it is needful that this be visibly celebrated, yet it must be spiritually understood."‖

From the preceding extracts, as Mr. Keary justly observes, there can, we conceive, be little doubt of the opinion entertained by Augustine on the question before us. His views were far too scriptural to admit of his believing in a dogma so opposed to spiritual

---

* De Catechizandis, &c., cap. xxvi. Tom. iv. p. 356. Edit. as above.
† De Baptist. Cont. Donat., Lib. iii. cap. x. Tom. vii. p. 491.
‡ Ep. 23, ad Bonifac, Tom. ii. p. 102.
§ Cont. Adimantum, Tom. vi. p. 231.
‖ In Psal. 98 and Tom. viii. col. 1105. Basil., 1556.

Christianity. And while he rested with implicit confidence on the Saviour's promised presence with His Church, even to the end of the world, he thought not of any visible appearance, but of that superintending care with which He watches and protects His believing people; or, as he expresses it, and which may properly conclude the evidence of antiquity against Transubstantiation—"According to the presence of His majesty, we have Christ always with us; but according to the presence of His flesh, Christ truly said to His disciples, Me you have not always with you."*

CHAPTER VII.

INVOCATION OF SAINTS.

THE question between the Roman and the Reformed Churches is not whether Angels and departed Spirits in heaven are occupied in praying for us on earth (even of this we know nothing), but whether they can hear our prayers, either " mental or verbal," as explained by their Trent Council, and that they may be lawfully prayed *to* as mediators, and whether we can plead their supposed superabundant merits (called " Treasure of the Church ") on our behalf.

The present Roman Creed does not leave this practice of Invocation of Saints an optional duty. It is imperative. " Likewise, that the Saints reigning with Christ *are to be honoured and invocated* with Christ."

The doctrine presupposes that the Saint invocated is actually in heaven, or in a beatific state. The state of the departed was a subject of speculation, even in the Roman Church, for many centuries. In proof of this we may refer at once to Augustine. In his time it was a question, and not easily to be determined, " Whether at all, or how far, or after what manner, the Spirits of the dead did know the things that concerned us here."† In another place he says, that " the Spirits of the dead are removed beyond the power of seeing what is done by men, or what befalls them in this life."‡

In the old Liturgies we find that the Patriarchs, Prophets, Apostles, and even the Virgin Mary, are prayed *for*, and not prayed *to*. It was not until many years after the days of Augustine that these prayers were altered by praying *to* them. Indeed Véron, an acknowledged

---

* In Joan. Tract 50, Tom. ix. p. 456. Lugduni, 1562.
† August. in Psal. cviii. Tom. iv. part 2, p. 1221. Paris, 1681.
‡ De Cura Gerend. pro Mort., c. xiii. sec. 16, Tom. vi. col. 526. Paris, 1685.

authority, in his "Rule of Catholic Faith,"* candidly admits that it was not decided by the Roman Church until the beginning of the fifteenth century, at the Council of Florence, A.D. 1439, "whether the souls of the blessed are received into heaven and enjoy the clear vision of God, before the resurrection and the last day of final judgment."

The late Rev. J. Endell Tyler, in two exhaustive treatises, entitled "The Primitive Christian Worship," and "The Worship of the Virgin Mary,"† has clearly established the fact that the practice was wholly unknown to the early Christians for a period at least of four hundred years after Christ.

No one who has had the advantage of perusing the writings of Augustine can doubt for one moment of his sentiments and teaching on the subject of Invocation of Saints. The passages here again are so numerous that the difficulty is to make an appropriate selection, without wearying the reader.

We may feel assured that the enlightened mind of Augustine would have rejected so antiscriptural a tenet; for, to one so deeply impressed with his need of the Saviour's all-prevailing merits, dependence on any other would appear in its true light as subversive of the fundamental principles of Christianity. He expresses this very strikingly in the following passage:—" Whom should I find that might reconcile me unto Thee? *Should I have gone to the Angels? with what prayer? with what sacraments?* Many seeking to return unto Thee, and not being able to do so by themselves, as I hear, have tried these things, and have fallen into the desire of curious visions, and were accounted worthy of illusions. Thus have these over-proud people fallen into the hands of the devil, who is transformed into an angel of light. We must therefore (he concludes) seek as our Mediator Him who combines the divine and human nature, namely, Jesus Christ."‡ In his Sermon on the 64th Psalm, we find the same train of thought :—" He is the Priest, who having now entered within the vail, there *alone*, of those who have been partakers of the flesh, making intercession for us. As a type of which thing, among that first people, and in that first temple, the priest only did enter into the holy of holies, while all the people stood without."§

In the first tract on the First Epistle of St. John, on that text, "If any man sin, we have an advocate with the Father, Jesus Christ the righteous," "St. John (he says), though so great a man, did not say *ye* have, nor *ye* have me, nor *ye* have Christ Himself, but put in Christ, not himself, and also said, *we* have, not *ye* have. Because

---

* Waterworth's Translation. Birmingham, 1833, p. 82.
† Society for Promoting Christian Knowledge.
‡ Augustin. Confess., Lib. x. cap. xlii. Tom. i. p. 264. Lugd. 1562.
§ In Psal. 64, Tom. viii. p. 791.

he would rather include himself in the number of sinners, that he might have Christ for his advocate, *than put himself for an advocate, instead of Christ, and so be found among the proud, that shall be damned.*"* And in his treatise against Parmenian, the Donatist, —"If he (St. John) had expressed himself thus—I have written this unto you, that you sin not, and if any man sin, ye have me a mediator with the Father, I make intercession for your sins" (as Parmenian, in one place, makes the Bishop a mediator between the people and God), *"what good and faithful Christian would endure him; who would look upon him as the apostle of Christ, and not rather as Antichrist."*† He makes a similar observation respecting St. Paul:—" Paul did not make himself a mediator between God and the people, but required that they should pray one for another, being all members of the body of Christ."‡

Not only does he give his own opinion on the question, but states that of the Catholic or Universal Church, as decidedly opposed to such vain superstitions:—" In the Catholic Church, it is divinely and singularly delivered, *that no creature is to be worshipped by the soul, but He only who is the Creator of all things.*"§ And, in his book of the true religion, he asserts:—" *The worship of dead men shall form no part of our religion,* for if they lived piously, they are not to be considered such as would seek that kind of honour, but would have Him to be worshipped by us, through whose enlightenment they rejoice that we are made partakers of their merits. *They are to be honoured therefore for imitation, not to be religiously adored.*"‖ With respect to angels, he comes to a similar conclusion:—" *We honour them with love, not with service;* neither do we build temples to them, for they do not wish to be so honoured by us, because they know that we ourselves, if good, are temples of the Most High God. And therefore it is rightly written, that a man was forbidden by an angel to worship him, but God alone, under whom he was his fellow-servant."¶ "If we should build a temple of wood and stone (he observes) to any Angel, however excellent, should we not be anathematized, and separated from the truth of Christ and the Church of God? because we should be rendering to the creature a service due only to the Creator."**

He argues also against the worship of Saints from their ignorance of what is passing upon earth; and in proof of this he quotes that passage from Isaiah (lxiii. 16), "Doubtless thou art our Father,

---

* Tract. 1, in 1 Ep. Joan., cap. ii. Tom. ix. p. 716.
† Cont. Ep. Parmen., cap. viii. Tom. vii. p. 36.
‡ Ibid.
§ De Quantitate animæ, Tom. i. p. 823.
‖ De Vera Religione, cap. lv. Tom. i. p. 1046.
¶ Ibid.
** Cont. Maxim., Lib. i. Tom. vi. p. 859.

though Abraham be ignorant of us, and Israel acknowledge us not." On which he observes:—" If such great patriarchs as these were ignorant of what was done to the people who descended from them, unto whom, believing in God, these very people were promised to come from their stock, how do the dead interpose themselves in knowing and furthering the acts and deeds of the living? The Spirits of the dead are there, where they neither see, nor hear, those things that happen unto men in this life."* " If the souls of the dead could interest themselves in the affairs of the living, surely my good mother would no night forsake me, who, while she lived, followed me day and night, both by land and sea. But certainly that which the Psalmist tells us is true, my father and mother have forsaken me, but the Lord took me up."† " We must never sacrifice (he says in his 49th Epistle) to a spiritual intelligence, however holy it may be, because in proportion to that holiness, and consequent submission to God, it knows that it is not worthy of this honour, which pertains to God only."‡

I conclude the evidence of Augustine against the Invocation of Saints with some decisive passages from his great work, the "City of God." In the eighth book we find the following:—" We do not erect temples, raise altars, or offer sacrifices to the martyrs, because not they, but their God, is our God. We honour their memory indeed, as holy men of God, who contended unto death for the truth, that the true religion might be propagated, and the false abolished. But which of the faithful ever heard the Priest, standing at the altar, erected to the honour and worship of God, over the bodies of the martyrs, say in the prayers,—I offer sacrifice to thee, O Peter, or Paul, or Cyprian, when at their memorial churches it is offered to God, who made them both men and martyrs, and associated them to the angels in heavenly glory; that by this solemnity we may give thanks to the true God for their victories, and that we, by renewing in ourselves the remembrance of them, may be excited, by imitating them, to strive for such crowns and palms as they have obtained. Therefore the religious ceremonies performed at the martyrs' tombs are ornaments to their memories, not sacrifices unto the dead as gods. Those, consequently, who bring their banquets there,—which the better sort of Christians are not accustomed to do,—having set them down and prayed over them, take them away to eat, or distribute in charity, merely desiring that they might be sanctified by the martyrs, in the name of the God of martyrs. But he who knows the only sacrifice which Christians offer to God, knows also, that these are no sacrifice to the martyrs: for we do not worship our martyrs with God's honour, nor men's crimes, as they worship their gods,

---

* Du Cura pro Mortuis, cap. xii. Tom. iv. p. 314.
† Ibid.
‡ Ep. 49, ad Deo gratias, Tom. ii. p. 224.

neither do we offer sacrifice to them, nor change their disgrace into their religion."*

"We believe (he says, in the 15th chapter of the 9th book,) that we need not many, but one Mediator, and that such a one by whose participation we are made happy; that is, the Word of God, not made, but by whom all things were made. And he has shown us that, in order to attain this blessedness, we must not seek many mediators, by whom we are to make our degrees of approach to God, because God Himself, by partaking of our nature, hath shown the shortest way for our partaking of His divine nature. Neither, when delivering us from mortality and misery, does He lead us to immortal and blessed angels, that by participating with them we should become immortal, but to that Trinity by whose participation the angels themselves are blessed."†

The whole of the 9th book is taken up in discussing the question, whether spiritual intelligences could be mediators, or intercessors, between the Creator and His creatures, and he concludes in the following striking manner:—"What need we say more? No man of common understanding will maintain that these Spirits are to be worshipped in order to attain eternal life hereafter! But perhaps it will be said, the gods are good, but of these Spirits, some are good, and some bad, and therefore the former should be worshipped, in order, by their aid, to attain eternal life: how far this opinion holds good, the next book will show."‡ He then demonstrates the absurdity of the proposition, as applicable to the plurality of heathen deities, while he denies, on behalf of the Christians, that any worship whatever is due to Angels, or the departed Spirits of the just; summing up his argument in these words:—"*Immortal and blessed Spirits, however they are called, which are made and created, are no mediators to bring miserable mortals to blessedness and immortality.*"§

It is true that we meet in Romish works quotations alleged to be from the pen of Augustine, of prayers to Saints and the Virgin Mary, and more especially in Liguori's "Glories of Mary," but the works purporting to be quoted have been so repeatedly exposed as admittedly spurious works, that we are only left to wonder at the boldness of any one at the present day making use of such materials. I have placed at the foot of this chapter some of these quotations attributed to Augustine, from the "Glories of Mary."

The adoration of the Virgin Mary, and faith in her merits and intercession, are leading features in the present Roman system. The

---

* De Civit. Dei., Lib. viii. cap. xxvii. Tom. v. p. 513.
† Ibid., Lib. ix. cap. xv.
‡ Lib. viii. cap. xxvii. Tom. v. p. 514.
§ Lib. ix. cap. xxiii. Tom. v. p 551.

Rev. J. Endell Tyler,* after a careful investigation, testifies that from the first to the last page of Augustine's voluminous works there is not a single expression which would lead us to suppose that he ever invoked her himself, or was aware of her invocation forming any part of the worship of his fellow-Christians, either in their public assemblies or their private devotions; nor is there a single expression which would induce us to believe that Augustine looked to her for any aid, spiritual or temporal, or placed any confidence in her mediation or intercession. On the contrary (he adds), there is accumulated and convincing proof that he knew nothing of her worship, let it be called *dulia* or *hyperdulia*; that he knew nothing of her Immaculate Conception, of her Assumption into heaven, or of festivals instituted to her honour; in a word, that, though he maintains strong opinions on some points left open by our Church, his belief and sentiments correspond in all essential points with the belief and sentiments of the Church of England, and were utterly inconsistent with the present belief and practice of the Church of Rome.

Mr. Tyler then proceeds by precise references to prove that, although Augustine speaks of Mary dying, he does not allude to her Assumption; that he speaks of the conception of her by her father and mother; but he expressly says she was herself conceived and born in sin, though she herself conceived without spot or stain of sin, and gave birth to a sinless Saviour.

To support these statements Mr. Tyler quotes numerous passages from the genuine writings of Augustine, so that no doubt whatever is left in our minds as to the doctrine and teaching of Augustine on this most popular branch of Romish devotion. With reference to the "Assumption of the Virgin Mary," there is a tract under that title in the Appendix to the Sixth Volume, p. 250, of the Benedictine Edition, which is frequently quoted; but the Benedictine editors themselves have excluded this treatise from their collection of the genuine works of Augustine, and they are unable to give it any certain author. The fact being that Augustine himself was utterly ignorant of what, if true, would rank among the most signal miracles of the Gospel dispensation.

Considering the importance Romanists attach to the fact that Mary gave birth to our Saviour, I cannot better conclude this branch of our subject than by presenting the reader with the two following extracts, as examples of the estimation in which Augustine held Mary as the mother of Jesus:—

"It is written in the Gospel, that when the mother and brethren of Christ, that is, His relations after the flesh, were announced to

---

* Worship of the Virgin Mary, pt. v. cap. ii. London, 1851.

Him, and waited without, not being able to approach Him by reason of the crowd, He answered, 'Who is my mother, and who are my brethren?' and, pointing to His disciples, He said, 'These are my brethren, and whosoever shall perform the will of my Father, he is my brother and mother and sister.' What else did He teach us by this, but that we should prefer our spiritual to our carnal relationship, nor that men are therefore blessed because they are carnally related to righteous and holy men, but because they adhere to them by their obedience and their imitation of them in doctrines and morals. Mary, therefore, *was more blessed in adopting the faith of Christ than in conceiving His flesh.* For when some one said to Him, Blessed is the womb that bare Thee, He answered, Yea, rather blessed are they that hear the word of God and keep it. Lastly, what did that relationship profit His brethren, that is, His relations after the flesh, who did not believe in Him? Thus also her *maternal* relationship would have profited Mary *nothing*, if she had not borne Christ more blessedly in her heart than in her flesh."*

"Wherefore, when the Lord appeared wonderful in the midst of the crowd, working signs and wonders, and showing what was hidden in the flesh, certain persons admiring, said, Blessed is the womb that bare thee. But He answered, Verily, blessed are they who hear the word of God and keep it. That is to say, My mother, whom thou hast called blessed, is thence blessed because she keeps the word of God, not because the Word was made flesh within her."†

I have referred to the use that has been made of the name of Augustine by the compiler—Liguori, a canonized saint of the Roman Church—of the "Glories of Mary" to support their extravagant praises of the Virgin Mary. The following passages (extracted from that erratic book) attributed to Augustine are, without exception, taken from treatises which their own theologians, for instance, Cardinal Bellarmine, Possevin, Erasmus, the divines of Louvain, &c., have condemned as decidedly spurious and utterly unworthy of the pen of Augustine.

I quote from the 1852 Edition, bearing the following approval of the late Cardinal Wiseman :—

"We hereby approve of this translation of the 'Glories of Mary,' and cordially recommend it to the faithful."

A similar approval of Cardinal Manning is appended to the reprint, 1868 :—

"We heartily commend this translation of the 'Glories of Mary' to all the disciples of her Divine Son.— ✠ HENRY E., Archbishop of Westminster."

---

* De Sancta Virginit. c. iii., Tom. vi. p. 342. Benedict. Edit., Paris.
† Tenth Treatise on the 2nd Chap. of John's Gospel, Tom. iii. p. 370.

With reference to the quotations themselves, the translator says in his preface (p. xix.) :—" I have carefully compared and corrected all these quotations with the originals from which they are taken. In the few instances in which I have been unable to procure the authors or to find the quotations I have put the sign †, not to doubt that they do not exist, but simply to indicate that I do not pledge myself to them."

Thus it appears every care has been taken to arrive at accuracy, and yet there is not one single intimation that the passages quoted as from Augustine's works are notoriously spurious. Nay, further, the translator encourages the reader to place implicit reliance on the accuracy and authority of the book in question by stating (p. xviii.) —" Remember that it has been strictly examined by the authority which is charged by God Himself to instruct you, and that that authority has declared that it contains NOTHING [in capitals] worthy of censure."

The following are the quoted passages:—

1. (p. 3) "St. Augustine, in common with most writers, says that Mary co-operated by her charity in the spiritual birth of all members of the Church.—*Lib. de Virginitate*, c. vi."
2. (p. 5) "That if all the tongues of men were put together, and even if each of their members was changed into a tongue, they would not suffice to praise her [the Virgin Mary] as much as she deserves.—*Int. Op. St. Aug. in App.*, Tom. v."
3. (p. 23) "St. Augustine declares, 'As she then co-operated by her love in the birth of the faithful to the life of grace, she became the spiritual mother of all who are members of the one Head, Christ Jesus.'—*De S. Virginitate*, cap. vi."
4. (p. 54) "With reason does an ancient writer call her 'the only hope of sinners,' for by her help alone can we hope for the remission of our sins.—*In. Op. St. Augustini*, Serm., cxciv., de Sanctis."*
5. (p. 90) "The only hope of sinners."—Same as last reference.
6. (p. 125) "If there is nothing else to take away our fear of exceeding in the praise of Mary, St. Augustine should suffice; for he declares that whatever we may say in praise of Mary is little in comparison with that she deserves, on account of her dignity of Mother of God."—No reference.
7. (p. 256) "The author of the book already quoted from the works of St. Augustine says 'that we must certainly believe that Jesus Christ preserved the body of Mary from corruption after death; for if He had not done so He would not have obeyed

---

* N.B.—This is the same as the sermon on the Annunciation of the V.M., as next quoted.

the Law,' which 'at the same time that it commands us to honour our mother it forbids us to show her disrespect.'—*Lib. de Assump.*"

Had the compiler, or the translator, or the two Cardinals who have issued, authorized, and endorsed this translation had the slightest intention to deal fairly, they would have boldly stated that this work was none of Augustine's, and had been utterly condemned as spurious.

8. (p. 303) "'Answer then, O Sacred Virgin,' says St. Augustine, or some other ancient author, 'why delayest thou giving life to the world?'—Serm. ii. *de Annunciat.*"
9. (p. 307) "Mary's humility became a heavenly ladder, by which God came into the world."—Same reference.
10. (p. 308) "St. Augustine asks: 'Whence have they made Thee flee, unless it be from the bosom of Thy Father into the womb of Thy Mother?'" †
11. (p. 326) "St. Augustine, addressing the Blessed Virgin, says: 'Through thee do the miserable obtain mercy, the ungenerous grace, sinners pardon, the weak strength, the worldly heavenly things, mortals life, and pilgrims their country.'—*Serm. de Assump.*"
12. (p. 417) "St. Augustine assures us that 'the cross and nails of the Son were also those of His Mother.'" †
13. (p. 451) "St. Augustine says that 'when Mary consented to the incarnation of the Eternal Word, by means of her faith she opened heaven to men.'" †

These are all the references to Augustine. Not one of them is genuine, and yet we have an author, a canonized saint, in whose works, after a most rigid examination, "not one word had been found worthy of censure,"* whose translator has vouched for the accuracy of the citations, and two English Cardinals cordially recommending the book to "the faithful," without the slightest intimation from either of them that their readers are being shamefully and wickedly imposed upon, and all to enhance the glory of their supreme Goddess; for we read in the same volume, p. 146:—

"AT THE COMMAND OF MARY ALL OBEY, EVEN GOD."

The following passages are decisive on the opinion of Augustine as referring to the modern dogma of the Immaculate Conception of Mary. If we turn to his work, "De Peccatorum Meritis et Remissione,"† we read:—"He (Christ) alone, being made man, but remaining God, never had any sin; nor did He take on Him a flesh of sin, though from the flesh of sin of His mother ('Quamvis de maternâ carne peccati'). For what of flesh He thence took, He

---

* Dublin Calendar, 1845, p. 167.
† The Benedict. Edit., Paris, 1690, Tom. x. p. 61 B, lib. ii. c. 24, sec. 38.

either when taken immediately purified, or purified in the act of taking it."

Again:—"Mary, the Mother of Christ, from whom He took flesh, was born of the carnal concupiscence of her parents (de carnali concupiscentia parentum nata est); not so, however, did she conceive Christ, who was begotten not by man, but by the Holy Ghost."*

Augustine himself informs us that the assertion that the Virgin Mary was sinless is due to a heretic, Pelagius.† Indeed we can trace almost all Rome's innovations to some exploded heresy.

I cannot more appropriately close this chapter than by bringing home to the Church of Rome, on the testimony of Augustine—to whom she virtually appeals on the question of Masses celebrated in honour of Saints—the clear distinction between the custom as practised in the days of Augustine and the teaching of the Roman Church of the present day, as established in the sixteenth century at the Council of Trent.

The third chapter of the Twenty-second Session, on "Masses in honour of Saints," is as follows:—

"Although the Church is accustomed to celebrate sometimes Masses in honour and memory of the Saints, nevertheless it teaches that sacrifice is not offered to them, but to God only, who has crowned them with glory; hence the priest does not say, '*I offer sacrifice to thee, Peter, or Paul*,' but giving thanks to God for their victories, *he implores their patronage, that they whom we commemorate on earth may vouchsafe* to intercede for us in heaven."

The following is the prayer in the "Ordinary of the Mass," which will further explain the meaning of the Council:—

"Receive, O Holy Trinity, this oblation which we make to Thee in memory of the passion, and resurrection, and ascension of our Lord Jesus Christ, and in honour of the Blessed Virgin Mary, ever a virgin, of blessed John the Baptist, the holy Apostles Peter and Paul, and of all the Saints; that it may be available to their honour and our salvation; *and may they vouchsafe to intercede for us in heaven,* whose memory we celebrate on earth. Through the same Christ our Lord. Amen."

Now, the early Christian custom of celebration in memory of Martyrs and Saints (holy men), as testified by Augustine—and the appeal in the above extract of the Council, no doubt to the testimony of Augustine—is very different from the modern innovation,

---

* Idem. Op. Imperf. contra Julian. Lib. vi. 22, Tom. x. p. 1344 A. We find further corroboration of Augustine's views in this same work (cont. Julian. Pelagian.), Lib. v. xv. Tom. x. p. 654 E; and De Genesi, ad Literam, Lib. x. c. xviii. Tom. iii. pp. 268-9.

† De Naturâ et Gratiâ, c. xxxvi.

for there is not in the former the most distant intimation of any *patronage*, or *intercession*, or invocation for their assistance.

The passage from Augustine, found in the last chapter of the eighth book, "On the City of God," is as follows, and is worth repeating :—

"We honour the memories of the Martyrs as of holy men of God who have contended even unto the death of their bodies for the truth, and that the true religion should be proved and the false ones convicted. But who ever of the faithful has heard a priest, standing over the holy body of a Martyr at an altar built for the honour and worship of God, say in his prayers, 'I offer thee the sacrifice, Peter, or Paul, or Cyprian?' whereas the offering is made to God at their memories, who made them both men and Martyrs, and associated them with His Holy Angels; *in order that by that celebration we may both render thanks to God for their victories, and encourage ourselves to the emulation of their crowns and palms, He being called to our assistance by the renewal of their memories.*"

We need not further comment on this clear distinction between the ancient and modern practice. But we must express our astonishment at the boldness of Roman controversialists when they appeal to Augustine to support their modern Trentisms.

CHAPTER VIII.

PURGATORY.

THE Roman Church teaches that, besides Heaven and Hell, there is yet a third place, where the souls, or bodies—Romanists do not seem to be agreed which—those who have "departed this life in Christ" and are justified, but who have not fully expiated the consequences of sin, and are not "fully purified and purged in this world, are there purified and rendered fit to enter Heaven." There remains, they tell us, for these, an obligation to the payment of temporal punishment in Purgatory.* This Purgatory is represented as a place of torment, a "*fire* where pious souls for a definite time are tortured."† Indeed, it was Cardinal Bellarmine who said that it was the general teaching of almost all divines, that the fire of Hell and fire of Purgatory are the same elements,‡ and that the sufferings of the damned and those in Purgatory are the same.

---

* Concil. Trid., sess. vi. can. xxx. ; sess. xxii. cap. ii.
† "Est Purgatorius *ignis*, quo piorum animæ ad definitum tempus *cruciatæ* expiantur." Catech. Concil. Trid., Pars i. sec. v. ; Purg. Ignis., p. 61. Paris, 1848.
‡ Bell. de Purg., Lib. ii. c. vi. Tom. i. col. 633. Paris, 1608.

Purgatory is a source of great profit to the priest, by sale of Indulgences, which are said to extend (by way of suffrage) to souls in Purgatory, and by traffic in Masses for the dead. Purgatorial Societies have been formed, for the purpose of releasing persons out of Purgatory on payment of certain subscriptions for Masses to be said by the Directors of the Society. A notable Society was established in Paris, under the direct sanction of the late Pope Pius IX. Their Report, a copy of which is deposited in the Library of Lincoln's Inn, London, lays down the scale of subscriptions and the rules by which provision is made for saying Masses, one of the prominent advantages being that the life subscriber will be relieved of all personal trouble, and without incurring any responsibility.

In a popular little book bearing the authority of the Romish Bishop, Dr. Murray, and sold in penny numbers, we read :*—" Holy Indulgences diminish the pains which you must suffer in Purgatory. I will here mention some of many Indulgences which you can obtain. First, he who hears Mass gains an indulgence of 3,800 years. They who say five *paters* and *aves* in honour of the passion of Jesus Christ, and of the dolors of the Virgin Mary, gain an Indulgence of *ten thousand years.*"

The theory depends on the antecedent process of the so-called Sacrament of Penance—that is, the penitent armed with imperfect repentance,† called *attrition,* on confession to a priest obtains absolution, and with it the forgiveness of the sin itself, " however great or however often repeated," and with it the *eternal* punishment, leaving *temporal* punishments to be expiated here or in Purgatory; which temporal punishments are wiped away either by Indulgences or by the Mass, a process alleged to have the same propitatory character as the Sacrifice on the Cross; or they may be satisfied by deputy, and this is in a pre-eminent sense a property of this part of the Sacrament of Penance; with this nice distinction, however, that the work performed by the deputy is not a part of the sacrament; but the act of the penitent himself attending to it that it should be performed for him is a part of the sacrament.‡

---

* Liguori on the Commandments. London and Dublin, 1862, pp. 292-3.

† " The sorrow of *attrition* is a sorrow for having offended God, which the soul conceives from a less perfect motive, such as from the consideration of the deformity of sin, of having deserved hell, or of having lost heaven, in punishment of her sin. Thus, *contrition* is a sorrow for sin on account of the injury offered to God; *attrition* is a sorrow for an offence offered to God on account of the injury it does us. By contrition the soul immediately obtains the grace of God, before the penitent receives sacramental absolution from a confessor, provided he has at least the implied intention of going to confession and receiving the Sacrament of Penance. This we learn from the Council of Trent. But by *attrition* the penitent obtains sanctifying grace only when he actually receives absolution, as we learn from the same Council."—Pp. 255-6, " Liguori on the Commandments," as above.

‡ Satisfacere potest unus pro alio. In eo vero summa Dei bonitas et clementia maximis laudibus et gratiarum actionibus prædicanda est, qui humanæ imbecillitati hoc

I need hardly say that we in vain search through the pages of Augustine for even the most distant allusion to such a system of theology.

It is a favourite device, however, to assert that the early Christians prayed *for* the dead, and we are constantly reminded that Augustine himself records in his "Confessions" a fervent prayer for his deceased mother, Monnica. We are asked to what end did the early Christians pray for the dead if they did not pray for the release of souls from Purgatory? It is admitted by Romanists that the Patriarchs, Prophets, Apostles, and the Virgin Mary, and the Martyrs, did not go to Purgatory, and yet we find in the early Liturgies all these included in the prayers for the departed. Dr. Wiseman attempted to meet this difficulty by the lame explanation: —"There is no doubt" (he says) "that in the ancient Liturgies the Saints are mentioned in the same prayer as the other departed faithful, for the simple circumstance that they were so united before the public suffrages of the Church proclaimed them to belong to a happier order."*

That is, we presume, by the process of Canonization. But as the first recorded act of Canonization is placed at the latter end of the tenth century, in a Council at Rome,† these "Saints" must have been a long time in torture! As a fact, however, it was not until the Council of Florence (A.D. 1439) that the Church of Rome came to the decision that the Saints did "belong to a happier order."‡

In fact, the state of the departed was a subject of constant debate and doubt. We have a remarkable admission by the Benedictine Editors of the works of Bishop Ambrose in their "Admonition to the Reader":—"It is not, indeed, wonderful that Ambrose should have written in this manner about the state of souls; but it may seem almost incredible how uncertain and how little consistent the holy Fathers have been on that question from the very times of the Apostles to the Pontificate of Gregory XI. *and the Council of Florence, that is, in the space of nearly fourteen hundred years.* For not only do they differ one from another, as in matters not

---

condonavit, ut unus posset pro altero satisfacere; quod quidem hujus partis poenitentiæ maxime proprium est. . . . Ita qui divina gratia præditi sunt, alterius nomine possunt quod Deo debetur persolvere; quare fit ut quodam pacto (Gal. vi. 2) alter alterius onera portare videatur.—Nec vero de hoc cuiquam fidelium dubitandi locus relictus est, &c.—"Catech. Concil. Trid.," pars. ii. De Pœnitentiæ Sacramento, No. cix. et cx. p. 312. Edit. Paris, 1848. And Donovan's Translation, p. 292. Dublin, 1829. Utiliter interim imponitur pro pœnitentia sacramentali, ut pœnitens curet pro se fieri opera satisfactoria per alios: verum illa per alios facta non sunt pars Sacramenti; sed actus ipsius pœnitentis curantis ea fieri pro se est pars Sacramenti—Dens, Theologia De satisfactione pro peccatis in Generali, No. 172. Tomus v. p. 242. Dublinii, 1832.

* The Moorfields Lectures, Lect. xi. vol. ii. p. 67. London, 1851.
† Labb. et Coss., Concil., Tom. ix. col. 741. Paris, 1671.
‡ Véron's "Rule of Catholic Faith." See p. 67 *ante*.

[yet] defined by the Church as likely to happen, but they are not even sufficiently consistent with themselves."*

We have yet to be informed what new revelation was given to the Church of Rome which induced the divines assembled at the Florentine Council to pass a dogmatic decision on the vexed question, and on which we have no revelation.

It is, however, true that we do read in Augustine's "Confessions" that he offered up a prayer for his mother,—"Although she" (he writes) "having been made alive in Christ, even while not yet released from the flesh, so lived that Thy name should be praised in her life and conversation, yet I dare not say that, from the time that Thou didst regenerate her by baptism, no word came out of her mouth contrary to Thy commandments," and therefore he prayed for her forgiveness. But mark the sequel. He adds: "*I believe Thou hast already done what I ask*, but accept, O Lord, the freewill offering of my mouth."

Now, when Augustine uttered this prayer, so often quoted, he believed what he asked—the forgiveness of his mother—had already been granted; it is impossible, therefore, to conclude that he was praying her soul out of the torments of Purgatory. Her dying request was that her son "would remember her at the Lord's altar, wherever he might be"—as if referring to the propitiatory character of the Mass. But we are not left in doubt as to Augustine's teaching on the subject of a Purgatory.

It was Origen, of the third century, who first broached the idea of a limited punishment in Hell; and he considered that all, good and bad, must go through that ordeal, and eventually come out free. That theory is said to have been condemned by a General Council (A.D. 553),† and certainly by Augustine himself.‡

Augustine thus states the faith of the Catholic Church on the subject in question; and how his sentiments are opposed to the doctrine of the Church of Rome it is needless to point out. In his 10th Homily on the 1st Epistle of St. John, he recognized only a state of bliss or a state of misery:—"For as to the man who lived and is dead, his soul is hurried off to other places, his body is laid in the earth . . . [as to his soul] either in Abraham's bosom he rejoices, or in eternal fire he longs for a drop of water; while his corpse is senseless in the sepulchre." Again, in his 19th Homily on St. John:—"They that have done well will go to live with the Angels of God; they that have done ill, to be tormented with the Devil and his angels." Again, "The first place on which the Catholic faith, by Divine authority, believes in is the Kingdom

---

* S. Amb. Oper., Tom. i. p. 385, Admonitio ad Lectorem. Benedict. Edit. Paris 1686.
† Bals. apud Beveridge, Synod., Tom. i. p. 150. Oxon., 1672.
‡ Lib. de Hæres., Tom. viii. p. 10. Paris, 1685.

of Heaven, from which the unbaptized are excluded. The second is Hell, where all apostates, and those who are alienated from the faith of Christ, shall suffer everlasting punishment. *Of any third place we are entirely ignorant, neither shall we find that there is any such place in the Holy Scriptures.*"* In his 80th Epistle, "ad Hesychium," he observes:—"In whatever state his last day shall find each person, in the same state the last day of the world shall find him: for such as every man in this day shall die, such in that day shall he be judged."† He describes, in the "City of God," the different states of blessedness and misery, as eternal and unchangeable:—"We have our own peculiar peace with God, here by faith, and we shall have it in eternity by sight. And this peace all shall have unto all eternity, and shall be sure to have it, and hence the blessedness of this peace, or the peace of this blessedness, shall be the height and perfection of goodness. But those who do not belong to the city of God shall suffer that eternal misery which is called the second death, because neither can the soul be said to live there, where it is separated from the life of God, nor the body, which is subjected to eternal torments. For which cause, this second death shall be so much the more terrible, as it will never have an end. But what can be conceived more dreadful and bitter than that, where the will is opposed to the passion, and passion to the will, so that this deadly hatred shall never cease by victory declaring on the side of either. In our earthly conflicts, either pain overcomes, and death deprives us of feeling, or nature conquers, and health relieves the pain; but there, pain afflicts, and nature suffers eternally, both enduring the continuance of inflicted punishment."‡

We must not omit to note an expression in Augustine's "Confessions" on the funeral of his mother:—"So, when the body was carried to burial, we went and returned without tears. For neither in those prayers which we poured forth unto Thee, when the *sacrifice of our ransom* was offered up unto Thee for her," &c. What meaning did Augustine here attach to the word "Sacrifice"? In addition to my former observations, I may add the following passages:—"By the daily sacrifice spoken of in the Prophet Malachi is meant (Augustine tells us) the prayers and praises of Saints."§ The views are more clearly expressed in the 10th book and 6th chapter of his great work, the "City of God," where we read:—

"A true sacrifice is any work which is done to keep up our league of amity with God, having reference to Him as our sovereign good, in whom we may enjoy real happiness. Hence, compassion

* August. Pelag. Hypognost., Tom. vii. p. 884. Lugduni, 1562. (The authority of this work has been doubted.)
† Tom. ii. p. 399.
‡ De Civit. Dei, Lib. xix. cap. xxvii. and xxviii., Tom. v. pp. 530, 531.
§ Lib. ii. Cont. Lit., cap. lxxxvi. p. 272, Tom. ix. Paris, 1688.

by which a fellow-man is succoured, if it is not shown for the sake of God, is not a sacrifice. For sacrifice, though it be done or offered by man, is still a divine thing; and therefore the ancient Latins called it by the name of sacrifice. Hence, man himself, consecrated by the name of God, and dedicated to God, so far as he dies to the world that he may live to God, is a sacrifice. For this belongs to the mercy which a man shows upon himself. . . . Seeing then that true sacrifices are works of mercy, whether to ourselves or to our neighbours, which have reference to God, and that the end of such works is to free us from misery and make us happy; which is attainable only by that good whereof it is said, It is good for me to hold me fast by God; it follows that the whole of the redeemed city itself, that is, the congregation and society of the Saints, must be offered as an universal sacrifice to God by our Great Priest, Who also in His Passion offered Himself for us (that we might be the Body of so great a Head), in His form of a servant. For this form He offered, in this was He offered; because through this He is our Mediator, in this He is our Priest and our Sacrifice. Since then the Apostle has exhorted us to present our bodies a living sacrifice, holy, pleasing to God—our reasonable service—and not to be conformed to this world, but to be transformed in the renewing of our minds, that we may prove what is the will of God, what is good, acceptable, and perfect; all which sacrifice we are: for, says he, 'as we have many members in one body, so we, being many, are one body in Christ'—this is the Christian's sacrifice: we, who are many, are one body in Christ. This the Church celebrates in the Sacrament of the Altar, so well known to the faithful, wherein is shown to her that, in the oblation which she makes, she herself is offered."

The intention therefore of the celebration referred to was not that the soul of Monnica should be released from Purgatorial pains, by the offering up of the sacrifice of the Mass—Augustine nowhere utters such a thought—but in conformity with the early Liturgies of the Church, it was a rendering of thanks for her departure, and to pray for the completion of her happiness in the world to come, a prayer, as we have already seen, he considered had already been answered.

There is a passage often quoted wherein Augustine is represented as saying, "The souls of the dead are relieved (*relevari*) by the piety of the living, when the Sacrifice of our Mediator is offered for them, *or alms are distributed in the Church*."* Presuming even such passages to be genuine, we have another parallel passage in his 172nd Sermon†: "It is not to be doubted that the dead are helped

---

*Enchirid. ad Laurent., c. cx. Tom. vi. p. 238. Paris, 1685.
† De Verb. Apost., Tom. v. p. 827.

(*adjuvari*) by the prayers of the Holy Church, by the salutary sacrifice, *and by alms.*" It is admitted that the early Liturgies did include prayers for the dead, but these prayers were offered, as I have already noted, *for* those whom the Roman Church will not admit went to Purgatory, namely, Prophets, Apostles, the Virgin Mary, and Martyrs. In those services there is no pretence for saying that there was offered up a propitiatory sacrifice. That phase of the process was not introduced until the thirteenth century under Innocent III., and after the dogma of Transubstantiation had been by conciliar decree—namely, by the fourth Lateran Council, A.D. 1215—for the first time declared to be an article of faith. The service was then altered by the introduction of five prayers, while the elements of bread and wine are being offered up for the sins of the living and the dead. These five prayers commence respectively:— "Suscipe, sancte Pater," "Offerimus tibi," "In spiritu humilitatis," "Veni sanctificator," and "Suscipe, sancta Trinitas." In no other part of the service is there any offering of the bread and wine as a propitiatory sacrifice. Thus for the first time the theory was started of assimilating the offering of the consecrated elements (supposed to be changed into the very same body and divinity of Christ) to the offering of Christ Himself on the Cross.

That these five prayers are modern interpolations, we have the testimony of various authors, confirmed by no less an authority than that of Cardinal Bellarmine. His words are:—

"These five prayers [naming them as above] are neither very ancient, nor were they read in the Roman Church five hundred years ago, and hence it is that neither Walafridus, nor Rupert, nor Amalarius, nor Alcuin, nor Innocent III., nor other old expositors, have made any mention of these prayers."* Previous therefore to this addition to the service the Mass was not a *Sacrifice*, and had no propitiatory character; and by a strange oversight the compilers of these five prayers made the awkward and unaccountable blunder of inserting them *before the act of consecration*, therefore simple bread and wine are now offered up as a propitiatory sacrifice! Hence it is quite clear that Augustine meant no more than what the old Liturgies sanctioned, namely, a prayer for the consummation or perfection of happiness of the defunct—they had then no fixed idea of any middle state,† and therefore there is not the slightest necessity for connecting the words of Augustine with the sulphurous torments of Vatican imposition.

Much reliance is placed on the statement we find in Peter's First Epistle (iii. 18), with reference to Christ's preaching to the spirits in prison, and that prison it is pretended was *Purgatory*. But

---

* Bellar. de Missa., Lib. 2, c. xvii. ed. 1601, and col. 850, Tom. iii. Paris, 1613.

† In one place Augustine observes, that during the time between death and resurrection they were kept in hidden receptacles. (Enchirid. ad Laurent. cap. xxix. Tom. vi. col. 237. Paris, 1685.)

Augustine, who wrote at very considerable length on this verse, nowhere hints at a Purgatory. "It may be (he says) that what the Apostle Peter says concerning the spirits shut up in prison who did not believe in the days of Noah, may not after all have any reference to the realms beneath, but rather to those times whose resemblance he transferred to the present time. . . . For before Christ came once in the flesh to die for us, He came often in the Spirit to those whom He would, giving them by visions such spiritual intimations as He wished; by which Spirit He was also quickened, when, during His passion, He was man in the flesh."*

We are repeatedly reminded that in the Book of Maccabees prayers for the dead are encouraged as a "wholesome thought" (ii. xii. 46), and it is alleged that the sin-offering was made for the dead. This is not so. The sin-offering was for the living, according to the Levitical Law (iv. 13–35). The sentiment as to the praying for the dead was the private opinion of the author who wrote the Book of Maccabees. The slain died in mortal sin, idols being found on their persons. According to the modern Roman theory, such would not go to Purgatory but to hell. Augustine, however, expressly rejected the Books of Maccabees as uncanonical scripture.† When, however, the authority of these books was quoted, it was objected against him that Razis killed himself, and therefore it was lawful according to the Scriptures for a man to commit suicide. Augustine, however, returns this answer:—"The Jews do not esteem this Scripture called the Maccabees, in such sort as the Law, the Prophets, and the Psalms, to which Christ gave testimony of him, saying, 'It behoveth that all these things should be fulfilled that are written of Me in the Law, the Prophets, and the Psalms;' but it is received of the Church not unprofitably, so that it be read and heard with sobriety, especially because of these Maccabees, which endured grievous persecutions for the law of God."‡

There is a Sermon, number one hundred and four, and published in the Appendix of the fifth volume of the Benedictine Edition of Augustine's works (col. 185), which treats of the fire referred to by Paul: "He himself shall be saved, yet so as by fire," which savours very much of the Papal Purgatory, but the editors attribute this treatise to Cæsarius of Arles. And again, the 103rd Psalm is quoted, but here he refers to a supposed transitory fire at the general consummation. Indeed, all these sermons are either of doubtful authority or evidently tampered with.

We may then safely aver that the Papal doctrine of Purgatory is inconsistent with the opinions held in the Primitive Church, on the state of the souls both of the righteous and the wicked, after their

---
* Ep. 164, ad Evodium, c. vi. sec. xviii. Tom. ii. col. 578 G, 580 C. Bened. Paris Edit.
† De Mirab. Sacr. Scrip., p. 26, Tom. iii. part 1, Paris, 1636; and p. 519, Tom. vii.
‡ Aug. Cont. secundam Ep. Gaud., Lib. i. c. 31, p 821. Basil., 1797.

departure from this world. We find but two regions spoken of, the one of happiness, the other of woe; and although they seem to have held various opinions as to the degree of blessedness on the one hand, and the intensity of suffering on the other, in which they should pass the intervening time between death and the day of judgment, yet this was a mere speculative idea, not bearing on the question of a third state, in which satisfaction was to be made for sins committed here. Nothing, indeed, can be more opposed to the truth of Christianity than the assertion that anything which we can do or suffer, either in time or eternity, can avail for the pardon of our sins, and peace with God. The one Oblation on the Cross is the only effectual means of reconciliation with Him, and every departure from a simple dependence on its all-prevalent efficacy will tend, either to foster self-righteous pride, or strengthen that propensity to sensual indulgence so deeply engrafted in our fallen nature.

CHAPTER IX.

IMAGES.

No charge against a Christian communion could be more serious than that of idolatry, or idol worship. The characteristic of all heathen nations is the use of images in their religious exercises. The introduction of images into Christian worship has been designated as baptized heathenism. "Beyond all doubt," said Lactantius, the Christian Cicero, "wherever an image is there is no religion."[*] And if there is one fact more clearly established than another, it is that the early Church knew nothing of the introduction of images in their worship, and that they strenuously opposed any religious use of them. Erasmus, who was ordained Priest A.D. 1492, said:—"Down to Saint Jerome's time (that is, contemporary with Augustine), those of the true religion would suffer no image, neither painted nor graven, in the Church; no, not the picture of Christ." And he adds:—"No man can be free from show of superstition that is prostrate before an image, and looks on it intentionally, and speaks to it, and kisses it; nay, although he does but pray before an image."[†]

Cornelius Agrippa, a divine of great and varied attainments, who

---

[*] Divin. Inst., Lib. ii. c. xix. Edit. Lugd. Batav., 1660.
[†] Erasm. Symbol. Catech., Tom. v. p. 1187. Edit. L. Bat., 1703.

died 1535, said:—"The corrupt manners and false religion of the Gentiles have infected our religion also, and brought into the Church images and pictures, with many ceremonies of external pomp, none whereof was found amongst the first and true Christians."*

To go up to a higher date, Agobard, Archbishop of Lyons (A.D. 816), said:—"The orthodox Fathers, for avoiding of superstition, did carefully provide that no pictures should be set up in churches, lest that which is *painted on the walls* should be worshipped. There is no example in all the Scriptures or Fathers of adoration of images: they ought to be taken for an ornament to please the sight, not to instruct the people."†

Such testimony we might multiply, but to what purpose? Romanism stands self-convicted.

It is necessary to understand that in the Roman Church religious service is ranked under three grades: *Doulia*, given to Saints, *Hyperdoulia*, a higher degree, given to the Virgin Mary; and *Latria*, the highest degree, given to the Deity. They are all, nevertheless, degrees of religious worship. The three classes above enumerated are, as a fact, represented in the Romish Church by images, hence it has been a question for discussion what degree of worship is to be rendered to the respective images which purport to represent the Divinity, the Virgin, or any of their so-called Saints. Cardinal Bellarmine, in the 2nd Book and 20th Chapter on "*Sacred Images*," gives the opinions of theologians of his Church. Under the second series of opinions, he says that—"*The same honour is due to the image as the exemplar;* and thence, that the image of Christ is to be worshipped with the WORSHIP OF LATRIA [that supreme worship which Papists render to God], the image of the Blessed Virgin with the worship of *Hyperdoulia*, and the images of the other Saints with the worship of *Doulia*. Thus Alexander, part 3, quest. 30, last art.: the blessed Thomas [Aquinas], part 3, quest. 25, art. 3; and thus also Cajetan, the blessed Bonaventura, Marsilius, Almayne, Carthusian, *and others.*"

In addition to these authorities, I quote the following:—James Naclantus, the celebrated Bishop of Chioggia, wrote about four years after the sitting of the Council of Trent, of which he was one of the principal members, and was described as "shining among the doctors and bishops there, as the day-star among the lesser luminaries."

The works of Naclantus were specially dedicated to the Pope of Rome. It will not, therefore, be unreasonable to look to him as a faithful exponent of the true sentiments of the Tridentine

---

* Cornel. Agrippa, de incert. et vanit. Scient., c. lvii. p. 105, Tom. ii. Lugduni.
† Agobardi Opera, Lib. de Imag., Tom. i. p. 226. Edit. Baluzius. Paris, 1665.

Fathers, and consequently of the Romish Church in general, on the subject of image worship. His words are:—" We must not only confess that the faithful in the Church worship before an Image, as some *for caution's sake* affirm; but we must furthermore confess, without the slightest scruple of conscience, that *they adore the very image itself*: for, in sooth, they venerate it with the identical worship wherewith they venerate its prototype. Hence, *if they adore the prototype with that Divine worship which is rendered to God, and which technically bears the name of Latria, they adore also the image with the same Latria or supreme Divine worship*: and, if they adore the prototype with Doulia or Hyperdoulia, they are bound also to adore the image with the selfsame species of inferior worship."*

Gabriel Biel, Peter de Meduarus, and Aringhi, all redoubtable doctors and theologians of the Romish Church, maintain the same opinions.

" If there shall be Images of Christ, they are *adored with the same species of adoration as Christ Himself—that is, with the supreme adoration called Latria*: if of the most blessed Virgin, with the worship of Hyperdoulia."†

" We must say, that to our Lady the Mother of God, there has been granted the remarkable privilege of being physically and really present in some of her statues or images. Hence we must piously believe, that in some celebrated statues or images of herself, she is inherent and present, *personally, physically, and really;*—in order that, in them, she may receive, from faithful worshippers, *her due adoration.*"‡

" This image, translated from the city of Edessa, is at once preserved as a bulwark against mad image-breakers, and is set forth to be taken up and ADORED by the faithful "§

" Within these few years, under every Pope successively, some or other of our sacred images, especially of the more ancient, have made themselves illustrious, and have acquired a *peculiar worship and veneration*, by the exhibition of fresh miracles: as it is notorious to all who dwell in this city."‖

It is, however, alleged, and with some truth, that this is not the recognized teaching of the Roman Church; and we are invited to consult the dogmatic ruling of Councils, which alone ought to be followed. But we find that Councils of the Church were not at all agreed on this subject. The first important decree passed

---

* Jacob. Naclant. Clug. Expos. Epist. ad Roman., cap. i. Edit. Venice, A.D. 1567, p. 202.
† Gabriel. Biel. super Can. Miss., Lect. xlix. Brixen., 1574.
‡ Pet. de Meduarus. Roset. Theolog., p. 311.
§ Aring. Rom. Subt., Lib. v. chap. iv.
‖ Ibid., vol. ii. p. 464.

was by the thirty-sixth canon of the Council of Elvira, or Illiberis, in Spain (A.D. 305). That Council decreed that—"No pictures should be in churches, lest that should be worshipped which was depicted on the walls."

Augustine, in his day, complained of the practice:—"I have known," he said, "that many are adorers of sepulchres and pictures, but the Church herself condemns them, and studies to correct them as bad children."*

In successive centuries religion became corrupt, so much so, that in the year 730, a Council of Constantinople, under the Emperor Leo III. (the Isaurian), passed a decree not only against the abuse, but against the use of any images or pictures in churches. Perceiving how the Christian Church was becoming immersed in gross idolatry, and feeling that the Arabian imposture (Mohammedanism) would be promoted by such an innovation on Christianity, Leo undertook to abolish the sinful practice altogether. He issued an edict, directing that images should be removed from churches and sacred places, and be broken up or committed to the flames, with the threat of punishment for disobedience of orders. Constantine V., to whom the image worshippers, in derision, gave the name of Copronymus, followed in his father's footsteps. In the year 754, he summoned another Council at the same place, which was attended by 388 Bishops, who enjoined the absolute rejection of every image or picture from every church.

In 787, at the Seventh Session of the Second Council of Nice, images, &c., were, for the first time, authoritatively permitted. It was declared that "there should be paid to them the worship of salutation and honour, and not that true worship which is accorded by faith and belongs to God alone;" and that "*the honour so paid to them was transmitted to the originals they represent.*" In this year, the Empress Irene, the Jezebel of that day (who became regent on the death of her husband, Leo IV., and during the minority of her son, Constantine VI.), convoked a council, and was mainly instrumental in effecting the firm establishment of image worship. She was heathen by instinct, and conceived the idea that this idolatry would soon make the world forget the profligacy of her past life. But, in 794, the Council of Frankfort, by its second canon, condemned the said decree of the Second Council of Nice, and all worship of images; as did also, in 815, a Council of Constantinople, which decreed that all ornaments, paintings, &c., in churches should be defaced. In 825 the Council of Paris condemned the decree of the Second Council of Nice, declaring that it was no light error to say that even some degree of holiness could be attained through the means of images. This Council

---

* De Morib. Eccl. Cathol., Tom. i. col. 713. Edit. Bened., 1680.

of Paris was continued at Aix-la-Chapelle; the French Bishops still resisting the decree of the Second Council of Nice, though the Pope had approved it. But in 842, at the Council of Constantinople, under the Emperor Michael III. and Theodora, his mother, the decree of the Second Council of Nice was confirmed, the image-breakers anathematized, and images restored to churches.

In 870, at the Tenth Session of the Council of Constantinople, the third canon again enjoined the worship of the Cross and the images of the Saints. And at the same place, at another Council, A D. 879, in the Fifth Session, the decrees of the Second Council of Nice were approved and confirmed.

Again, in 1084, at another Council of Constantinople, the decree made in the Council of 842, in favour of the use of images, was confirmed. Thus, after a contest of 110 years, image-worship was victorious over all the East, except the Armenian Church.

The worship of images, after this time, appears to have taken such deep root, even in the West, that, in 1549, the Council of Mayence decreed that people should be taught that images were not set up to be worshipped; and priests were enjoined to remove the image of any Saint to which the people flocked, as if attributing some sort of a divinity to the image itself, or as supposing that God or the Saints would perform what they prayed for by means of that particular image, and not otherwise.*

Such was the fearful idolatry to which the introduction of images into churches led; so that the assembly of French Bishops, at the celebrated Conference at Poissy, A.D. 1561, enjoined on the priests to use their endeavours to abolish all superstitious practices; to instruct the people that images were exposed to view in the churches for no other reason than to remind persons of Jesus Christ and the Saints; and it was decreed that all images which were *in any way indecent*, or which merely illustrated fabulous tales, should be entirely removed†—a proof of the corruption of the times that

---

* The following are references to the above Councils :—

"Placuit picturas in ecclesiâ esse non debere; ne quod colitur et adoratur in parietibus depingatur." Council of Eliberis, A.D. 305, Can. xxxvi. Labb. et Coss. Conc., Tom. i. col. 974. Paris, 1671.
Council of Constant., A.D. 730. Ibid, Tom. vi. col. 1461.
Council of Constant., A.D. 754. Ibid, Tom. vi. col. 1661.
Council of Nicæa II., A.D. 787. Ibid, cols. 449, 899, Tom. vii.
Council of Frankfort, A.D. 794, Can. ii. Ibid, Tom. vii. col. 1013.
Council of Constant., A.D. 815. Ibid, Tom. vii. col. 1299.
Council of Paris, A.D. 825. Ibid, Tom. vii. col. 1512.
Council of Constant., A.D. 842. Ibid, Tom. vii col. 1782.
Council of Constant., A.D. 870, Session x. Can. iii. Ibid Tom. viii. col. 962.
Council of Constant., A.D. 879, Session v. Ibid, Tom. ix. col. 324.
Council of Mayence, A.D. 1549. Ibid, Tom. xiv. col. 667.

† See Landon's "Manual of Councils," p. 495. London, 1846.

such a decree should be needed. And the Council of Rouen (A.D. 1445), in its seventh canon, condemned the practice of addressing prayers to images under peculiar titles, as "Our Lady of Recovery," "Our Lady of Pity," of "Consolation," and the like, alleging that such practices tended to superstition, as if there was more virtue in one image than in another.*

It remained for the Council of Trent (at the Twenty-fifth Session, A.D. 1563) to confirm, and for Rome to give its authoritative sanction to the worship of images, and their use in churches, as part of the religious worship of Christians.

The decree passed at the Trent Council now binds the Roman Church, with which alone we have to deal. At the Twenty-fifth Session, A.D. 1563, "all Bishops and others sustaining the office and charge of teaching" were directed "especially to instruct the faithful that images of Christ, the Virgin, and other Saints are to be especially had and retained in churches, and that *due* honour and veneration are to be awarded to them, not because there is any divinity or virtue in them on account of which they are to be worshipped, nor because anything is to be asked of them, nor that confidence is to be placed in images as of old was done by the heathens, who placed their hopes in idols, *but because the honour which is shown to them is referred to the prototypes which they represent; so that in the images which we kiss, and before which we uncover our heads and fall down, we worship* Christ, and venerate the Saints *whose likeness they bear*."†

Now, it was exactly this system of *relative worship* of images, practised by the heathens, that was condemned by the early Christians.

Arnobius, who flourished at the beginning of the fourth century, was himself a zealous Pagan before his conversion to Christianity, and therefore practically knew what he was writing about. He thus remonstrated with the heathen idolaters of his day:—

"You say, 'We worship the gods *through* the images.' What then? If these images did not exist, would the gods not know they were worshipped, nor be aware of any honour being paid to them by you? . . . . What can be done more unjust, more disrespectful, more cruel, than to recognize one as a god, and offer your supplication to another thing; to hope for help from a divine being, and pray to an image which has no sense?"

Again he proceeds: "But ye say, 'You mistake; we do not consider materials of brass, or silver, or gold, or other things of which the statues are made, to be, of themselves, gods, or sacred

---

* Labb. et Coss. Concil., Tom. xiii. Concil. Rothomagense, Can. vii. col. 1307. Paris, 1671.
† Sess. xxx. Lab. et Coss. Concil., Tom. xiv. col. 895. Paris, 1671.

divinities; but in these materials we worship and venerate those gods, whom the holy dedication brings in, and causes to dwell in the images wrought by the craftsmen.'"*

The following passage from Origen (A.D. 230) also bears strongly on the question :—" What sensible person would not laugh at a man who . . . . looks to images, and either offers up his prayer to them, or, *beholding them, refers it to the being contemplated in his mind,* to whom he fancies that he ought to ascend, from the visible object, which is the symbol of Him (the unseen Deity)."†

St. Ambrose (A.D. 397) to Valentinian, thus speaks:—" This gold, if carefully handled, has an outward value; but inwardly it is mere ordinary metal. Examine, I pray you, and sift thoroughly the class of Gentiles. The words they utter are rich and grand; the things they defend are utterly devoid of truth; *they talk of God—they worship an image.*"‡

We now come to the testimony of Augustine. Arguing against this nice distinction made by the heathen idolaters of his day, his remarks exactly apply in condemnation of the present Romish theory :—

"But those persons seem to themselves to belong to a more purified religion who say, 'I worship neither an image nor a demon [this does not mean a *devil,* but a departed spirit], but I regard the bodily figure as the *representation of that Being whom I ought to worship.'* . . . . And when, again, with regard to these, they [the more enlightened heathens] begin to be pressed hard on the point, that they worship bodies, ... they are bold enough to answer that they do not worship the images themselves, *but the divinities which preside over and rule them.*"§

And, again, he says :—

"But some disputant comes forward, and, very wise in his own conceit, says, 'I do not worship that stone nor that insensible image; your prophet could not say they have eyes and see not, and I be ignorant that that image neither hath a soul, nor sees with his eyes, nor hears with his ears. *I do not worship that, but I adore what I see, and serve him whom I do not see.*' And who is he ?—a certain invisible divinity, which presides over that image."‖

And, once again, he says :—

"And lest any one should say, 'I do not worship the image, but that *which the images signify,*' it is immediately added, ' And they worshipped and served the creature more than the Creator.' Now,

---
* Leipsic Edit., 1816, Lib. vi. c. ix. and xvii.
† Cont. Cels., Lib. vii. c. xliv. Paris, 1733.
‡ Epist., chap. i. sec. xviii. Venice, 1781.
§ Aug., in Psalm xciii., Part ii. Tom. iv. p. 1261. Paris, 1679.
‖ Aug., in Psalm xcvi., Tom. iv. p. 1047.

understand well, they either worship the image or a creature; he who worships the image converts the truth of God into a lie."*

These sentences are directed to be expurgated† from the works of Augustine. Augustine, in his great work, "The City of God,"‡ refers to a remarkable admission of the heathen philosopher, Varro:—"The gods are better served without images," to which he gives his unqualified approval. What would Augustine say were he to appear again amongst us? To witness churches decorated with images, people falling prostrate before them, special veneration given to particular images, and to witness even pretended miracles wrought by their instrumentality? Would he honour them by uncovering the head, by kissings, and prostrations? We think not.

CHAPTER X.

THE SACRAMENTAL SACERDOTAL SYSTEM.

THE next, and perhaps the most important, subject in a Roman point of view is the Sacramental System, by means of which alone the salvation of sinners is assured; the instrument, be it remembered, being, in every instance, the PRIEST. The Roman Priest, by virtue of his Ordination, by means of those imaginary implements, "the Keys of the Kingdom of Heaven," alleged to be entrusted to him, claims the power not only of condemning sinners, but of forgiving sins, and of remitting the temporal and eternal punishments otherwise consequent on their sins, through the tribunal of Penance. They claim also the power of relieving the living and the dead by the process of the Mass, in which they profess to offer up the same propitiatory sacrifice as was once effected on the cross, and this by a miraculous conversion of the consecrated elements of bread and wine into Christ's very same body, blood, bones and nerves, soul and divinity—the same body which was born of the Virgin Mary, crucified, and ascended into heaven. Priests are, therefore (they tell us), "justly called not only Angels but Gods, holding, as they do, the place and power and authority of God on earth." This "power consists in consecrating"—*conficiendi* is the word, which is more than consecrating, of actually making, or creating—

---

* Aug., Serm. cxvii., Tom. v. p. 905. Edit. Paris, 1679.
† See Index Expurg., Madrid, 1667, p. 59, col. 2; and see *ante*, Chap. III. No. 30.
‡ Lib. iv. c. xxxi. Tom. vii. p. 112. Paris, 1685.

"and offering the body and blood of our Lord, and of remitting sins;" a power, they further tell us, "which cannot be comprehended by the human mind" [305].*

In common with other Christians, and as a first principle, the Church of Rome holds that we are all born in, and subject to, sin [525], entailed on us by the original sin of Adam [28], and that our destiny is ultimate eternal happiness or immediate eternal misery in a future state. But beyond these general principles, the Roman Church holds exclusive and peculiar theories founded on her *Sacramental System*. Sins, they tell us, are of two natures, *mortal* and *venial* [301-2], and punishment for sin is either *eternal* or *temporal* [59]; the former in Hell, the latter to be expiated either in this world or in Purgatory, previous to the soul entering Heaven. On the truth or falsehood of this distinction hang, in fact, the whole aim and alleged efficacy of their Sacramental System. We need scarcely be called upon to prove the negative that Augustine knew of no such system; we do not find any such system throughout his writings.

The Church of Rome teaches that the Sacraments "are a necessary means of salvation" [135], and that they all, more or less, but that each of them conveys a sanctifying grace [152] by the action of the Priest (technically, *ex opere operato*). If we deny this power in Sacerdotal Sacramentalism, they tell us that we are surely damned.†

The Council of Florence (A D. 1439)—to quote the expression of the Jesuit writer Suarez—first insinuated the precise number of *seven* Sacraments, which the Council of Trent afterwards decreed as a matter of faith. The first canon of the Seventh Session of the Council of Trent declared:—"If any shall say that all the seven Sacraments of the new law were not instituted by Christ, or that there are more or less than seven, viz., Baptism, Confirmation, the Eucharist, Penance, Extreme Unction, Orders, and Matrimony, or that any of these is not truly and properly a Sacrament, let him be accursed."

Augustine nowhere endorses such a system. He mentions only two Sacraments, properly so called, *Baptism* and the *Lord's Supper*. He continually refers to them as the twin Sacraments of the Church, allegorically represented by the blood and water which came out of the side of Christ when He was pierced on the cross.‡ He further tells us that—"Our Lord and His Apostles have delivered unto us a few Sacraments instead of many, and the same

---

* These figures in [ ], to avoid repetitions, refer to the pages of Donovan's Translation of the Trent Catechism, Dublin Edit., 1829, the authorized Maynooth Edition. The original was published by command of Pius V.

† Concil. Trident., Sess. vii. can. viii., Decretum de Sacramentis.

‡ In Joh. Tract. 15, p. 409, Tom. iii. pars. 2. Paris, 1680.

for performance easy, for signification most excellent, for observation most revered, as is the Sacrament of Baptism and the celebration of the body and blood of our Lord."* And again, in another place, he declares these to be the two or twin Sacraments of the Church.† In a general sense, he includes many other things as Sacraments. "Signs, when they are applied to godly things, are (he says) Sacraments,"‡ which are not admitted by the Roman Church. For example, he mentions as a Sacrament "the sign of the cross." But in its proper signification, as ordained by Christ, Augustine only admitted two Sacraments of the Church.

We may here enumerate, as we proceed, the great value attached by the Roman Church to each Sacrament, through which we are said to be saved from sin and all its consequences.

First, as to *Baptism*. "The law of Baptism (they tell us) extends to all, insomuch that unless they are regenerated through the grace of Baptism, be their parents Christians or infidels, they are born to eternal misery and everlasting destruction!" [Catechism as before, pp. 171-2]. The effect is stated to be "to remit original sin and actual guilt, however enormous" [177]—" not only is sin forgiven, but with it all the punishment due to sin" [180]. It "also remits all the punishments due to original sin in the next life" [181], and "it opens to us the portals of Heaven, which sin had closed against our admission" [186].

Though Augustine did not express himself so strongly as the above, he still had very high notions of the efficacy of Baptism. In fact, he held what may be classed as "High-Church" notions of "Baptismal regeneration."

The next is *Confirmation*, which is said "to perfect the grace of Baptism," and "it also remits sin" [202-3]. I am not aware that Augustine even mentions Confirmation; we, nevertheless, have it admitted by an eminent Roman theologian, called the "Irrefragable Doctor," Alexander of Hales, "that the Sacrament of Confirmation, as it is a Sacrament, was not ordained either by Christ or by the Apostles, but afterwards was ordained by the Council of Melda."§ This was only a provincial Council of no note, held A.D. 845. Certainly we do not find Confirmation anywhere mentioned by Augustine as a Sacrament.

We then have *Penance*. This so-called sacrament is a complicated piece of ecclesiastical machinery. The parts are stated to be contrition—or rather *attrition*—confession to a priest, his absolution, and the performance of satisfaction by the penitent. These are

---

* De Doct. Christ., Lib. iii. c. ix. Part 1, col. 49, Tom. iii. Paris, 1679.
† De Symbol. ad Catechum., col. 562, Tom. vi.
‡ P. 412 Tom. ii. Paris, 1679.
§ Fol. 193, Col. Agrip., 1622.

alleged to be the necessary component parts to give the entire efficacy to the Sacrament. It was Peter Lombard, in the year 1140, who first determined these three parts of Penance;* and it was Bishop Canus, in 1551, who first broached the doctrine that *attrition*—that is, imperfect repentance, joined with confession and satisfaction—would be sufficient to obtain forgiveness of sins in the Sacrament of Penance.† Augustine nowhere refers to any such combination of parts.

Compulsory Sacramental Confession to a Priest was first imposed as a law of the Roman Church by a decree of the fourth Lateran Council (A.D. 1215), under pain of Mortal Sin.‡

Augustine certainly did not practise nor recommend confession to a Priest. Such a process was evidently repugnant to his feelings. He exclaimed:—"To what purpose do I confess my sins to men who cannot heal my wounds?—to a set of men inquisitive in inquiring into the lives of others, but indolent in amending their own. And how shall they, who know nothing of my heart but by my confessions, know whether I say true or not? For no one knows what is in man, but the spirit of man that is in him."§

Absolution is the next process,—save, perhaps, the awful pretension of the Roman Priest of first making or creating his God out of a piece of bread,‖ then worshipping it with supreme worship due to the Divinity, and then eating it,—the assumed power of *judicially* forgiving sins—anticipating the judgment of the Almighty—is the most dangerous and fearful delusion to which a Romanist is subjected. More especially when we are told that the efficacy, in reality in both cases, depends on the private *intention* of the officiating Priest to do what his Church prescribes! Nay, further, their Council teaches that even those Priests who are living in *mortal* or *deadly* sin exercise the function of forgiving sins as the Ministers of Christ,¶ and this because (as their Trent Catechism informs us) they "represent the character and discharge the functions of Jesus Christ—as Ministers of God they really absolve us from sin" [256-260.] Can we conceive a murderer or adulterer—a Priest in mortal sin—representing JESUS CHRIST, "who knew no sin"?

---

* See Neander's Church History, vol. vii. p. 483. London, 1852.

† Melchior Canus de Loc. Theol., Dist. xiii., de Pœnit, Art. vii. Nos. 5, 6. Louvain, 1569. See *ante*, p. 77, note †.

‡ Labb. et Coss. Concil., Tom. xi. Decret. xxi. cols. 171-3. Paris, 1671. And see Fleury, Eccl. Hist., Tom. xvi. p. 375. Paris, 1739.

§ Confess., Lib. x. c. iii. Tom. i. p. 171. Paris, 1672.

‖ Pope Urban II., while presiding over a Council, gravely and deliberately asserted, in solemn assembly, that "the hands of the Priest are raised to an eminence granted to none of the Angels, of *creating God, the Creator of all things*, and of offering Him up for the salvation of the world." To this the whole assembly, with the utmost unanimity, responded a solemn "Amen"! (Lab. et Coss. Concil., Tom. x. col. 617. Edit. Paris, 1671.)

¶ Session xiv. cap. vi. can. x.

It is in these two characters, of creating their God, and of Priests forgiving sins, that, as I have said, they proclaim themselves to be "not only Angels but Gods," by assuming " the power and authority of God on earth "! [304-5].

"The power with which the Priests of the new law are invested is not *simply to declare* that sins are forgiven, but as Ministers of God, *really to absolve* from sin " [259]. "It is not to be considered as merely a ministry *to publish the Gospel*, or *to declare* the remission of sins, but as *of the nature of a judicial* act, by which sentence is pronounced by him as a judge."* And if we refuse to accept this assertion, the same Council consigns us to eternal damnation.

Augustine knew of no such judicial power in the Priesthood. More than once he disclaimed it. In his 99th Sermon on the words of the seventh chapter of St. Luke's Gospel, on the remission of sins, written against the Donatists, who in this, as in many of their other assumptions, anticipated modern Romanism, and maintained that their priests were invested with the same *judicial* powers to forgive sins as now assumed by the Roman Priesthood, Augustine said :†—

"What did the Jews say? Who is this who forgives sins also? Does man dare to usurp to himself this power? What, on the other hand, does the *heretic* say? I forgive, I cleanse, I sanctify. Let Christ, and not myself, answer him : O man, when I was thought by the Jews to be simply a man, I gave the forgiveness of sin to faith. It is not I, it is Christ who answers you. O heretic, you are but man, and you say, Approach, O woman, I will save thee ; but I, when I was thought to be a man, said, 'Depart, O woman, thy faith has saved thee.' They answer, as the Apostle says, ignorant of the things of which they talk and which they affirm ; they answer and say, If men do not forgive sins, then what Christ says is false ; Whatsoever ye shall loose in earth shall be loosed in heaven ; ye are ignorant wherefore this was said, and how it was said. The Lord was about to give the Holy Spirit to men, and He wished it to be understood that sins were remitted to His believers by the Holy Spirit Himself, and not by the merits of men. For what are you, O man, but a sick person about to be healed ? Do you wish to be a physician to me ? Come with me and seek the physician. For the Lord, in order that He might show this more evidently, namely, that sins were remitted by the Holy Spirit which He gave to His believers, and not by the merits of men, thus says in a certain passage when He had risen from the dead, Receive the Holy Ghost, and when He had said receive the Holy Ghost, He

---

* Sess. xiv. c. vi., De Pœnitentia.
† Tom. v. p. 525. Paris Benedictine Edition.

immediately added, Whosoever sins ye remit are remitted, that is to say, it is the Spirit who remits and not you. But the Spirit is God; God therefore remits and not you. But what connection have you with the Holy Spirit? Are ye ignorant that ye are the temple of God, and that the Spirit of God dwells in you? And again, are you ignorant that your bodies are the temple of the Holy Ghost which is in you, whom ye have from God; God, therefore, dwells in His holy temple, that is to say, in His holy believers in His Church; through them He remits sins because they are living temples."

And to the same effect he wrote against the letter of Parmenianus.* Commenting on the text John xx. 22, 23, he continues thus:— "But since the words are introduced, 'When He had said this He breathed upon them and said, Receive the Holy Ghost,' and then was conferred upon them either the remission or the retention of sins, it is sufficiently evident that *they themselves* did not do this, but the *Holy Spirit* by their agency, as he says in another place, It is not you that speak but the Holy Spirit who is within you." It is thus made clear that Augustine considered this power of absolution a *ministerial* act, as in our Church, which proclaims to the repentant sinner that "He (God) pardoneth and absolveth all them that *truly repent* and unfeignedly believe His holy gospel," and that this remission in no way depends on the will, caprice, or hidden *intention* of a Priest.

The absolution having been pronounced, the *mortal* sin and *eternal* punishment are supposed to be remitted, leaving *temporal* punishments, called "Satisfaction," to be undergone in this life or in Purgatory; the absolved sinner being considered "justified" and in a "state of grace." This "Satisfaction" is stated in their Trent Catechism to be "a compensation made by man to God, by *doing something* in atonement for the sin which has been committed but forgiven." "The nature of the sin regulates the satisfaction .... which is imposed at the will and discretion of the Priest" [294–296]. "This punishment which the sinner endures," they tell us, "disarms the vengeance of God, and prevents the punishment decreed [by the Priest] against the penitent" [285, 290]. "It is the full payment of a debt; for when satisfaction is made nothing remains to be supplied" [285].

These Sacramental Satisfactions are:—"Punishments, which usually consist in some *painful good works*, which the sinner does himself or *accepts from others*, such as fastings, *prayers*, almsdeeds, mortifications, humiliations, and the afflictions and tribulations *in this life*, when they are accepted and borne patiently."† If

---

* Lib. ii. Tom. ix. p. 42, same Edition.

† "Catechetical Conferences on Penance," by the Right Rev. Dr. James Lanigan, [Romish] Bishop of Ossory, p. 89. Dublin, 1833.

these penitential works are not accomplished in this life, they are to be substituted by the tortures of Purgatory, until some kind relative or friend relieves the unfortunate by the purchase of Masses or Indulgences, which are "applicable to souls in Purgatory."

It need scarcely be pointed out to the reader that this process of "justification" by merit and *good works* was unknown to Augustine. We are, therefore, happily spared the trouble of again going over the ground so often traversed by the contending factions in the Roman Church.

The importance to the Priest of this so-called Sacrament of Penance is evident when we are told "that it is a powerful engine of salvation in his hands." "It is as necessary as is Baptism for those who have not been already baptized;" "it washes away all sins of thought or deed committed after Baptism" [257]. "There is no sin however grievous, no crime however enormous, *or however frequently repeated*, which Penance does not remit" [260]; "*it may be repeated and becomes necessary as often as we may have sinned after Baptism*" [251], which "Penance" the reader must not mistake for *penitence* or *repentance*. "To it belongs, in so special a manner the efficiency of remitting *actual guilt*, that without its intervention we cannot obtain or even hope for mercy" [861]. Augustine nowhere advocates such a process.

As to Extreme Unction. The practice was derived from the Valentinian heretics, who assumed the gift of the Apostles, and anointed their sick with oil on the approach of death. They, like modern Roman Priests—for, be it understood, almost all modern Roman innovations are derived from condemned heresies—the Valentinians pretended that this anointing, with prayers, would conduce to the salvation of the soul, not to the healing of the body. This superstition found no supporters, except among heretical impostors, until long after Augustine's times. Innocent I., at the beginning of the fifth century, in his letter to Decentius, Bishop of Eugubium, refers to the custom of anointing the sick with oil, which was to be exercised not merely by the priesthood but by all the faithful, and was, therefore, evidently not considered then as a Sacrament. The custom subsequently gained ground, and early in the sixth century Felix IV., Bishop of Rome, engrafted it on other Christian ceremonies, and first instituted the rite of Extreme Unction, by declaring that such as were *in extremis* should be anointed.* It was not authoritatively reckoned as a Sacrament until 1439, at the Council of Florence. And we need scarcely add that Augustine nowhere alludes to this process as a Sacrament, or for the healing of the body or soul.

The alleged benefits supposed to attend this ceremony are also

---

* Polydore Vergil, B. v. c. iii. p. 102. London, 1551. De Invent. Rerum.

important. We are told by their Catechism that it " was instituted to afford us, when departing this mortal life, an easier access to Heaven " [301-2]. This " Sacrament remits sins, especially lighter offences, or, as they are commonly called, venial sins. Its primary object is not to remit mortal sins; for this the Sacrament of Penance was instituted, as was that of Baptism for the remission of original sin. Another advantage arising from Extreme Unction is, that it removes the languor and infirmity entailed by sin, with all its other inconveniences." " Another, and the most important advantage is, that it fortifies us against the violent assaults of Satan " [301-2]. On all this Augustine is silent.

Marriage. As this was deemed a civil contract—and did not require the intervention of a Priest—until very shortly previous to the meeting of the Trent Council, it is difficult to discover how they make it out to be a Sacrament instituted by Christ. Augustine, in all his voluminous writings, nowhere assists them. A characteristic of a Sacrament is alleged to be that the act of receiving it confers a grace. We fail to perceive what grace is conferred, say in an ill-assorted marriage of " convenance," as the French have it. Indeed their own Canon Law declares that Marriage is not one of those Sacraments which confers the consolation of Divine grace,* and several of their divines, such as Durandus, Peter Lombard, and others, held the same opinion.†

We may safely dismiss this so-called Sacrament from Augustine's list.

We have now only left priestly " *Orders.*" Here again members of the Roman Church are themselves at variance. Cardinal Bellarmine admits that the very learned doctor of his Church, Dominicus Soto, declared :—" That Episcopal ordination is not, truly and properly (*vere et proprie*), a Sacrament."‡ There can be no doubt that Augustine held the office in high veneration, but that is very different from the assertion that " Orders " were instituted by Christ, and that the act of ordination was a Sacrament of the Church. It was not, in fact, so declared until the Council of Florence, 1439, which substituted a new *form* for ordination, the giving of the cup and paten in the place of the ancient admitted form of laying on of hands. It is difficult to understand how the succession is maintained in the Roman Ministry when their Catechism declares that the slightest deviation in the use of the *form* nullifies the Sacrament [259].

I have dwelt more largely on the Roman Sacerdotal Sacramental System than, perhaps, may be considered necessary. But as at the

* Tom. i. col. 1607. Ludg., 1671.
† See Bellarmin. de Matr., Lib. i. cap. v. Tom. iii. p. 506. Colon., 1615. And see Cassander. Consult. de Num. Sacr., p. 951. Paris, 1616.
‡ Bellarm., Tom. iii. p. 718. Edit. Prag., 1721.

present day that phase which Christianity has unhappily assumed is now made the great test of a true Church, I have, therefore, not considered it out of place in the present treatise to show that Augustine could have known of no such system as the present Sacramental Sacerdotal System, as recognized in the Church in his day.

CHAPTER XI.

BELLARMINE AND AUGUSTINE.

IN examining the writings of Augustine, we cannot but admire the fervent zeal and Christian piety which are apparent in almost every page. At the same time, we must not allow our admiration to warp our judgment in receiving, as gospel all that we find placed before us, even though what is presented to us may have the appearance of being the genuine production of his pen. We have seen the difficulty of separating the genuine from the spurious. Even as to his genuine writings, Augustine himself leaves us at liberty to weigh and consider his opinions, and to accept them so far only as they may accord with Scriptural truth.* Indeed the members of the Roman Church have largely availed themselves of this privilege, which, as I have shown, they have not scrupled to exercise, even to the disparagement of Augustine himself. Surely we have a right to exercise the same privilege. We know that many spurious works are attributed to Augustine, and it is from these principally that we find quotations made in support of modern theological theories which are attempted to be vindicated as *doctrines* supplied by the authority of antiquity.†

Again, even in his genuine works, we are by no means certain that passages have not been interpolated to give colour to such innovations.‡ When we find a writer takes most decided views on a

---

* "That Augustine should have written the large series of volumes still preserved to us, without being betrayed by his zeal into a single rash statement, is hardly to be imagined. But he endeavoured to correct these at the end of his life by a volume of 'Retractations,' in which he strove to clear up questions which had arisen from the use of incautious language. Our rule, however, after the lapse of fifteen hundred years, is a very simple one. Augustine was right—was a safe guide so far, and only so far, as he 'followed Christ.'"—*Anonymous*, "*Record.*"

† See J. Endell Tyler's "Primitive Christian Worship," and "Worship of the Virgin Mary." Society for Promoting Christian Knowledge.

‡ Bellarmine cites a passage, purporting to be from the 24th Chapter of the 22nd Book of Augustine's great work, "The City of God," in proof of Purgatory (De Purg., p. 330, Tom. ii. Prag., 1721). Ludovicus Vives, the learned commentator on this work, says:—" In the ancient copies which are at Bruges and Cologne, these ten or twelve

particular subject, we are startled to meet sentiments quoted from the same writer repugnant to opinions which have been previously expressed by him.

It is true that we do not often meet with such passages in the admittedly genuine writings of Augustine, but when they do present themselves, they should be accepted with caution.

In addition to these difficulties, a desperate struggle is made by Romish writers—and particularly by Cardinal Bellarmine—to extract from those passages in Augustine's works, which have been condemned as heretical, proofs in support of their modern theories. An examination of these efforts may not be inappropriate as a sequel to the previous chapters.

And first on the question of the assumed right claimed by the Bishop of Rome of hearing appeals from Africa. We have seen that Zosimus, Bishop of Rome, attempted to impose on a Council of African Bishops, at which Augustine assisted, a forged canon, represented as having been passed at the first General Council of the Church, that of Nice (A.D 325), which purported to vest in the Bishop of Rome the right to receive all appeals from members of other Christian Churches. This canon turned out to be a forgery, and accordingly the Bishops assembled at the Council of Milevis passed a decree prohibiting any such appeals out of Africa. Bellarmine, in order to get out of this difficulty, and remove the shame attaching to such a disgraceful proceeding, admitted that "the Nicene Council was alleged, but that the Sardican Council was meant, and at that Council it was decided that the Africans might appeal to Rome."* The Sardican Council is supposed to have been held A.D. 347, though various dates are given, so uncertain even is the tradition of such a Council. Indeed there are very grave reasons for doubting that any such Council was ever held, and more particularly, if even held, that any such canon was passed as now relied on. The very form gives the appearance of corruption; for, limited as the powers of appeal are, they nevertheless are not in any way supported by, or in accordance with, the admittedly genuine canons passed by the first four General Councils of the Church, which clearly gave independent ecclesiastical jurisdiction to every metropolitan Bishop over his own diocese; and besides, this Council of Sardica was only a provincial Council. Again, the African Church is said to have been represented by thirty-six Bishops, who scarcely would have submitted to any such indignity,

---

printed lines are not to be found, nor in the edition at Friburg." And in his notes on the 8th Chapter of the 22nd Book, on Miracles, he tells us that "there are many additions in that chapter, without question, foisted in by such as make a practice of depraving authors of great authority" (Edit. 1610, p. 890). These are only two of the many examples that might be cited.

* De Rom. Pont., Lib. ii. c. xxv. See *ante* Chap. IV., for a history of this transaction.

seeing that, from the days of Cyprian, Bishop of Carthage, to the time of Augustine, every encroachment on the part of the Bishop of Rome was resisted.

But even supposing the canon to be genuine, it went no further than that, in certain cases, Julius, the then Bishop of Rome, might direct a cause to be reheard by a greater Synod. Bellarmine, it appears, either did not make himself sufficiently acquainted with the facts, or a candid acknowledgment was not convenient. Be this as it may, the attempt to foist this forgery as a genuine canon of the Council of Nice was a miserable failure, and the attempt to cover the shame by this subterfuge only makes the matter worse.

Augustine's opinion on *Justification and Merits* has been sufficiently considered, and we have seen the theory condemned authoritatively by the Expurgatory Index and by Romish divines. Bellarmine, nevertheless, comes again to the rescue, and asserts that Augustine's treatise "On Faith and Works," cap. 15, is fatal to the theory of "Solifidianism" or faith alone. But it is clear that Augustine is speaking in that work against those who were so confined in the faith as to neglect good works, resting secure on the profession made in Baptism. Augustine warns us against sheltering ourselves under any such a pretext. He nowhere speaks against *good works*, except when advanced as a meritorious cause of justification. And when Augustine says— which he does repeatedly—that when God crowns our merits He crowns nothing else but His own gifts, Bellarmine, in order to nullify the force of this, says that Augustine meant only "such merits as be in us from ourselves, that is to say, without the grace of God."* That is ingenious, but such is clearly not Augustine's meaning. The words of Augustine are "tanquam dona sua," not as our merits, but "as His gifts." He is speaking of the faithful, who are in a state of salvation. The authors of Rome's Expurgatory Index took a bolder course, by directing the passage to be expunged from Augustine's works as absolutely heretical.

Other subtle evasions of Augustine's palpable meaning are advanced; but Augustine is too clear to be mistaken as to what he did teach. Good works without faith in God will not avail a man; it is not the good work that saves, but good works resulting from a justifying faith, which are acceptable to God, as they are His own gifts; such was Augustine's teaching.

With regard to the practice of *Invocation of Saints*, Bellarmine and others quote—and I believe this is the only passage they advance—from Augustine's 17th Lecture, "De Verb. Apostoli," where he says, "It is an injury to pray for a martyr by whose prayers we on the other side ought to be recommended." The question between us, on this head of the controversy, is not whether Saints

---

* Lib. i. de Justif. c. xxv.

or Angels in heaven are occupied in offering up prayers on our behalf; we know nothing of their occupations, though it is to be hoped that they may be so occupied. The question is, are we justified in praying to them, "mentally or verbally," for their help, assistance, or intercession? This solitary passage gives us no such instruction or encouragement. But here again the Expurgatory Index comes largely to our assistance, and we have on this head a selection of passages from Augustine condemned.

As to *Image Worship.* When Augustine declared that no image (*imago*) ought to be worshipped, and that it was unlawful to erect any such imago (*simulacrum*) to God in a Christian Church,* Bellarmine excuses him by saying that he wrote this in his early days of conversion. He then goes into a subtle argument on the difference of the expressions "imago" and "simulacrum;" but it will be seen, in my selection of expurgated passages, that Augustine makes no such distinction in using the two expressions.

In fact, the language of Augustine, which I have given in a previous chapter, is too plain to be misunderstood. And the compilers of the Expurgatory Index, as I have shown, continually use the word "simulacrum" to condemn Augustine for his views on the subject. (*Ante*, p. 22.)

Tradition. Augustine, in his Treatise on Baptism against the Donatists, constantly reminds us that whatsoever the Universal Church holds, though not ordained by any Council, and yet always retained, is rightly believed to be an Apostolic tradition.† But Augustine, as I have stated in the last chapter, was not here treating of a matter of *faith*, but the Baptism of Infants, a matter of discipline. And, by the way, with regard to Infant Baptism, Bellarmine has the following acknowledgment :‡—"For although we do not find it expressly commanded that we should baptize infants, yet this is *sufficiently clearly gathered* from the Scriptures, as we have already shown." And in the "Table of Reference" given with the present edition in use of the Rhemish Version of the New Testament we read: "For the Baptism of Infants see St. Luke xviii. 16, compared with St. John iii. 5." So that Augustine was justified in designating Infant Baptism as a genuine Apostolic tradition. Even this passage Dr. James, in his "Corruptions of the True Fathers," detects as a corruption, and as none of Augustine's.§ The only other passage I have met with is from his 118th Epistle, to Januarius, where Augustine says: "All those things that we hold without writing, only by unwritten tradition, were commanded and ordained either by the Apostles themselves, or by General

---

* Ep. 119, ad Januar. cap. xi., and De Fide et Symbolo, cap. vii.
† De Genesi ad literam, Lib. x. c. xxiii.
‡ Boll. de Sacramento Bap., Lib. i. c. ix.
§ See p. 114, Edit. 1843.

Councils." Here, again, he was not referring to matters of faith, but of Church Constitutions, for he immediately refers to the yearly celebration of Christ's Passion, His Resurrection and Ascension.* All these passages are quoted by Bellarmine.

I have already referred to the oft quoted saying that Augustine would not believe the Gospel, but that the authority of the Church moved him. Bellarmine quotes this also. Having the concurrent authority of the entire Christian world, Augustine believed, and such concurrent authority induced him to believe, the Gospel. He was converted to Christianity. Christianity was founded on the Gospel, which the entire Church accepted. What better motive could a man have, in passing from Paganism or other heresy to Christianity? Religion is a matter of education, not a spontaneous inspiration. Bellarmine desired us to believe that Augustine pointed to the authority of the *Roman Church* as his inducement to accept the Gospel. Rome was but a small part of the whole of Christendom. Had the Roman Church never existed, Augustine would have had the same motives for belief in the Gospel.

As to the *Canon of Scripture*. I have already answered the objection that Augustine is said to have conformed to the Council of Carthage, which is alleged to have included the Apocrypha in the Sacred Canon. But we have also seen that Augustine made a marked distinction between the *Sacred* Canon of Scripture and such books as might be read for edification. We may pass over, therefore, objections on this head, though Bellarmine struggles to enlist Augustine under the banner of Rome as a believer in the Apocrypha.

Communion in one Kind. In his Commentary on Leviticus (4. Qu. 57), Augustine said: "All that would have life are exhorted to drink of the blood;" and in Qu. 49 we read: "The whole Church having received the Cup, answereth Amen." I have not met any counter explanation to these acknowledgments of the custom in Augustine's time of the universal partaking of the wine at the Sacrament by the laity, except that he is censured in the Expurgatory Index for saying that both species are to be given to children. Bellarmine is prudently silent on this subject!

As to the *Number of Sacraments*. We have seen that Augustine stated that the Sacraments delivered to us were but few; the words are: "Sacramentis numero paucissimis"—as being easy in observance, &c. ("sicuti,") as in Baptism and the Lord's Supper. Bellarmine,† as usual, quibbles. "Sicuti," he means to say, does not restrict the number of the Sacraments. But we have other places in which Augustine specially names the two as the twin-Sacraments of the Church. If it be contended that we are to receive all

---

* See "Faith of Catholics," vol. i. p. 39, Edit. 1846.
† Lib. ii. de Effect. Sacr., c. xxvii.

Augustine mentions under the general word Sacrament, then we must admit many more Sacraments than the Church of Rome acknowledges.

Transubstantiation. Augustine, in the 33rd Psalm, is represented as saying that when Christ said, "This is my body," He bore Himself in His own hands—"Ferebatur Christus in manibus suis."* This was a curious error in St. Augustine's translation of 1 Sam. xxx. 13. Referring to David, the text is: "And feigned himself mad in their hands." Augustine, however, translated the passage: "He bore himself in his own hands." This seemed to puzzle him. He said it could not be meant for David literally, and he therefore took it to allude to Christ. Bellarmine makes the most he can out of this. We have seen that Augustine did not believe in a *literal* presence. He explains himself thus: he bore himself in his own hands "*after a certain manner*"—not literally, as he expresses himself in the 23rd "Ep. ad Boniface." "Sicut secundem quendam modum sacramentum corporis, corpus Christi est; ita sacramentum fidei, fides est." As much as to say "This Sacrament, *after a sort*, is the body of Christ; not literally, but as the baptism of faith (the Sacrament of faith) is called faith, to wit, figuratively and improperly."† If he thought there was a literality in the expression, he would not have said "after a certain manner." But these are extravagances of expression we often meet with in early Christian writers.

And, lastly, we are told that Augustine taught the Romish doctrine of the adoration of the Host when in his Commentary on the 98th Psalm he said: "None doth eat the flesh of Christ (nisi prius adoraverit) before he adores it." First let me record, as an historical fact, that the elevation of the Host for adoration was first instituted by Honorius III., A.D. 1217.‡ I have no desire to enter on the subtle arguments raised between *Sacramentum* and *rem Sacramenti*. But let us look at once at the intention of Augustine. He said as plainly as one could explain himself, that he did not take Christ's words literally. In interpreting Christ's words in St. John's Gospel, chap. vi., he thus expresses himself: "You shall not eat this body which you see. I have proposed to give a sacred sign, which, being spiritually taken, will quicken you; for though this Sacrament be visibly celebrated, yet it must be spiritually conceived."§

Having thus clearly explained the interpretation he gave to eating and drinking the body and blood of Christ, we can appreciate the meaning of his words, "None doth eat the flesh of Christ before he

---

* See "Faith of Catholics," vol. i. p. 439, Edit. Lond., 1846.
† See Birckbek's "Protestant's Evidence," p. 299. London, 1849.
‡ See Fleury's "Eccl. Hist.," Tom. xv. lib. liv. p. 663. Paris, 1719.
§ See *ante*, p. 65.

adoreth it." As that eating must be spiritually conceived, so must the adoration, but not of the elements.

I thus dispose of Bellarmine's efforts to clear Augustine of heresy, if his statements were taken literally, and to enlist him into the ranks of the Papacy. The fact of these efforts being made shows clearly the importance which Romanists attach to the opinions of Augustine. But the more remarkable fact still remains to be accounted for, how is it that no notice is taken by Bellarmine of the numerous passages I have quoted from Augustine, which, if uttered by a Bishop or Priest of the Roman Church at the present day, would brand him as a heretic? His attempt to shield Augustine is in strange contradiction to those who have actually condemned the very same passages as decidedly heretical.

CHAPTER XII.

CARDINAL WISEMAN AND AUGUSTINE.

Dr. Wiseman delivered sixteen lectures "On the Principal Doctrines and Practices of the Catholic Church," which he afterwards republished when he became "Cardinal Archbishop of Westminster,"* covering 580 octavo pages. Being in his day the first Romish authority in England, with the reputation of a great scholar and divine, my task could scarcely be complete were I to omit to examine the evidence on which the Cardinal relies for the "Doctrines and Practices" of his Church as of ancient date, as being proved by the works of Augustine.

It must be borne in mind that Dr. Wiseman distinctly admitted that we must not seek for proofs of Romish doctrines in the Scriptures alone, but in Scripture and Tradition; and should any difficulty arise regarding any doctrine, the method to be pursued would be to examine most accurately the writings of the Fathers of the Church, in order to ascertain what, in different countries and ages, was by them held, and then, collecting the suffrages of all the world and of all times, not to create new Articles of Faith, but to define what has always been the Faith of the Catholic Church.† He resolves the question purely into a historical inquiry, and in that view of the question the Doctor appeals to the evidence of the early Christian writers, and, among others, to Augustine.

* London, 1851.   † See *ante*, Chap. II. p. 8.

It will now be my task to examine every single quotation as from Augustine's writings cited by Dr. Wiseman in these Lectures, and I venture to state that the reader will be satisfied that the appeal results in a lamentable failure.

I. The first passage quoted is in Lecture V., on "The Catholic Rule of Faith" (p. 140):—"Disputing with a Manichee—he says expressly, as it should be rendered from the peculiarity of the style—'I should not have believed the Gospel if the authority of the Catholic Church had not led or moved me.'"

I have already fully examined this citation, and it is only necessary to add that Augustine nowhere gives us to understand that the Catholic Church was localized in the communion over which the Bishop of Rome presided, or that he derived his knowledge of, or belief in, the Gospel from that quarter.

II. In order to lead us to believe that Augustine held the Roman doctrine that the Scriptures are not in themselves sufficient as a guide, but that Tradition is necessary, Dr. Wiseman quotes as follows:—"That the whole Church observes what was not decreed by Councils, but always retained, is justly believed to be of Apostolic origin."* To this the Doctor adds—"Such a principle surely implies a conviction that the Church can never fall into error."

Augustine was discussing the subject of Infant Baptism, which is not a doctrine or article of faith, but a practice apparently handed down from the time of the Apostles. We may safely concede to a Roman Catholic that what the whole Church observes, and *has always retained*, may be accepted as of Apostolic origin. But that is exactly the test which not one single article of Pope Pius's Creed will bear. Not one of them was accepted by the Church in the days of Augustine; we conclude, therefore, that they are not Apostolic Traditions. The passage cited, therefore, may go to prove that Augustine believed that Infant Baptism was practised by the Apostles, and that if any other practices can be proved to have the same authority, they might be accepted as Apostolic Traditions. (See *ante*, p. 102.)

III. The modern Roman Church we know has assumed to itself exclusively the term "Catholic"; and, by an unfortunate concession, that term has, in our modern times, been adopted in common parlance to mean a member of the Romanist Church. But it was not so in the days of Augustine; and for Dr. Wiseman, or any one else, to apply the two following passages to the Roman Communion is an impudent assumption for which there is not the remotest authority. The two extracts are:—"It is our duty to hold to the Christian religion, and the communion of that Church which is Catholic,

---

* De Bapt. cont. Donat., Lib. iv. c. xxiv.

and is so-called, not by us only, but by all its adversaries. For whether they be so disposed or not, in conversing with others they must use the word Catholic, or they will not be understood." Again —" Among the many considerations that bind me to the Church is the name of *Catholic,* which not without reason, in the midst of so many heresies, *this Church alone has so retained,* that although all heretics wish to acquire the name, should a stranger ask where the Catholics assemble, the heretics themselves will not dare to point out any of their places of meeting."

The reference given is "Contra Ep. Fundam. c. iv." Augustine was writing against the Donatists, who, like modern Romanists, I must be excused for repeating, claimed for themselves alone the title "Catholic." To suppose that Augustine pointed to the Roman or Latin branch of the Christian Church exclusively as the Catholic Church would be the height of absurdity. He counted eighty-eight heresies in his day. The Catholics were the orthodox believers, according to Augustine's notions of Christianity.

But here the compilers of the "Faith of Catholics" come to our aid.* They quote the following passage from Augustine's letter against Petilian, a Donatist, which shows us in what sense Augustine used the term:—" Petilian said, 'If you say that you hold fast to the Catholic Church—Catholicos ($\kappa\alpha\theta o\lambda\iota\kappa o\varsigma$) is that which, in Greek, signifies the *alone,* or the *whole.* Now you are not in the whole, seeing that you have sunk into a part.' Augustine replies— 'For my part, I have indeed attained to a very slight, scarcely any, knowledge of the Greek language, yet do I say, without presumption, that I know that ὅλον means, not *one,* but *the whole,* and καθ' ὅλον *according to the whole,* so that the Catholic Church received its name when the Lord said, '*You shall be witnesses unto me*" [not in *Rome* but] "*in Jerusalem, and in all Judæa, and in Samaria, and even to the uttermost part of the earth*' (Acts i. 8). Behold wherefore she is called Catholic." It was, as I stated, the Donatists who assumed to themselves the title, so Augustine continues—" Behold wherefore she is called Catholic. But you, with closed eyes, so stumble against that mountain which, from a small *stone,* according to the prophecy of Daniel, 'increased and filled the whole earth'—as to say to us that 'we have sunk into a part, and that we are not in the whole,' we whose communion is diffused throughout the whole world." So that when Augustine uses the word *Catholic,* it is clear that he is pointing to the orthodox Christians scattered throughout the world, and not localized under the presidency of the Bishop of Rome.

If in the present day any one in London were to inquire for the "Catholic Apostolic" Church, he would not be directed to a

* Vol. i. p. 200. Edit. 1846.

Papist chapel, but to the church of the "Irvingites" in Gordon Square [London].

IV. The next passage is to be found in Lecture XI., "On Satisfaction and Purgatory." I have already shown that Augustine neither accepted nor taught the Roman doctrine of "Satisfaction" nor of Purgatory. Dr. Wiseman quotes two passages, which he has garbled. They are correctly rendered in the 1846 Edition of the "Faith of Catholics,"* from which I now quote:—"'*A sacrifice to God is a contrite spirit; a contrite and humble heart God does not despise.*' Not only, therefore, did he offer up with devotion, but also by saying this he shows what ought to be offered. For it is not enough to reform our manners, and to withdraw from evil deeds, if we do not, for those things which have been done, satisfy God by the sorrow of penitence, by the grieving of humility, by the sacrifice of a contrite heart, alms co-operating."†

V. The other passage, as quoted in "The Faith of Catholics," is as follows:—"Implore mercy, but lose not sight of justice; it is mercy to pardon the sinner, justice to punish the sin. What then? Dost thou seek for mercy, and shall sin remain unpunished? Let David answer, let the lapsed answer, let them answer with David, that they may deserve mercy like David, and let them say, 'No, Lord, my sin shall not be unpunished; I know His justice whose mercy I seek; it shall not be unpunished, but therefore do I seek that Thou punish me not, because I punish my own sin; therefore do I ask Thee to forgive because I forget not.'"‡

How these passages apply to the Roman doctrine of Purgatory it is impossible to conceive, so we presume they are intended to refer to their teaching on "Satisfaction," that title being adopted by the compilers of the "Faith of Catholics," where these passages appear. Now, "Satisfaction" is one of the component parts of their so-called Sacrament of Penance; but we seek in vain to discover from these or any other passages from Augustine that previous private confession to a Priest is a first requirement, followed by his absolution, to remove the guilt and eternal punishment, leaving "Satisfaction" to wipe away the remaining *temporal* punishment, either in this life or in Purgatory. The passages, in fact, apply as little to "Satisfaction" as they do to Purgatory! I have shown that a "contrite heart," or "Contrition," is no part of the Sacrament of Penance, but "Attrition," or *imperfect* repentance, is.§ Indeed, it has been boldly maintained by a Jesuit writer of considerable repute, P. Valentia—and his statement has never been censured by the Roman Church—that perfect repentance is not at all necessary in order to

---

* Vol. iii. p. 127. 1846.   † Tom. v. Serm. cccli. n. 12, col. 2019.
‡ "Tom. iv. on Ps. 1, n. 7, col 661."   § See *ante*, p. 77.

obtain a remission of sins through the absolution of a Priest in the tribunal of Penance, the principal effect of the Sacrament, but, on the contrary, *such contrition is rather a hindrance than otherwise.**

The proposition is startling. What one Jesuit publishes is binding on all, and the Jesuits being now in the ascendant in the Roman Church, we must, it may fairly be presumed, accept this as the present theory of that Church.

In the same Lecture† we have again brought before us the oft-quoted passage wherein Augustine refers to prayers *for* the departed, and, also coupled with this, Augustine's commentary, only partly given, on the text 1 Cor. iii. 12, 13: "If a man build upon this foundation gold, silver, precious stones, wood, hay, and stubble; every man's work shall be made manifest: for the day shall declare it, because it shall be revealed by fire; and the fire shall try every man's work of what sort it is."‡

Dr. Wiseman pretends that Augustine considered the fire referred to by Paul to be the Popish Purgatory, and that "the prayers of the Church or of good persons are heard in favour of those Christians" whose lot is cast to pass through the torments of Purgatory; for it is Dr. Wiseman himself who vouches as a fact that the souls in Purgatory suffer "most cruel and bitter torments."§

In citing these two passages he says:—"I have no hesitation in saying that the two doctrines [prayers for the dead and a Popish Purgatory] go so completely together that if we succeed in demonstrating the one [prayers for the dead] the other [Purgatory] necessarily follows;" || and with grave simplicity he asks, if they did not pray for the relief of souls suffering in this painful state, what did they pray for? If we admit this theory we are, as I have before observed, to suppose the Patriarchs, Prophets, Apostles, Martyrs, and even the Blessed Virgin Mary, suffered the excruciating torments, according to Bellarmine, of the damned, until it pleased the Church of Rome to take upon herself to declare that all these "Saints" belonged to a happier order."¶

---

* "Voilà tout ce qui se peut dire, si ce n'est qu'on veuille ajouter une conséquence, qui se tire aisément de ces principes; qui est, que la contrition est si peu nécessaire au sacrement, qu'elle y seroit au contraire nuisible, en ce qu'effaçant les péchés par elle-même, elle ne laisseroit rien à faire au sacrement. C'est ce que dit notre P. Valentia, ce célèbre Jésuite. Tom. iv. disp. 7, q. 8, p. 4. 'La contrition n'est point du tout nécessaire pour obtenir l'effet principal du sacrement, mais au contraire, elle y est plutôt un obstacle. *Imo obstat potius quominus effectus sequatur.*'" (Pascal, Lett. Prov. x. Tom. iii. p. 94. Amsterd., 1767.)

† XI., p. 63, vol. ii.
‡ "Enar. in Psal. 37, Tom. iv. p. 275."
§ Lives of St. Alphonsus, &c., p. 202. London, 1847.
|| Lecture XI., vol. ii., p. 54.
¶ See *ante*, p. 67.

The first of the two passages quoted under this head is from the 24th chapter of the 21st book "On the City of God," as follows:—
"The prayers of the Church or of good persons are heard in favour of those Christians who departed this life not so bad as to be deemed unworthy of mercy, nor so good as to be entitled to immediate happiness. So also, at the resurrection of the dead, there will some be found to whom mercy will be imparted, having gone through those pains to which the spirits of the dead are liable. Otherwise it would not have been said of some with truth that their sins shall not be forgiven neither in this world nor in the world to come (Matt. xii. 32), unless some sins were remitted in the next world." It did not require an Augustine to tell us of the hope that God in His mercy will forgive us our sins; but the Popish Purgatory is not a place for *forgiveness* of sin. Purgatory is for the pious who have died in grace, the sins being supposed to have been forgiven in their Sacrament of Penance. And, further, we have this fact, that it is very doubtful if Augustine ever penned such a sentiment; for Ludovicus Vives, a learned Roman Catholic and commentator on this particular work, admits that in the ancient copies, printed at Bruges and Cologne, the above extract is not to be found, nor is it found in the copy printed at Friburg.* And as to the passage founded on the text 1 Cor. iii. 12, 13, which text the Doctor also quotes on page 62 as positive Scriptural evidence in support of Purgatory, on the faith of Augustine, it so happens that there is perhaps no text in the New Testament on which a greater divergence of opinion exists among the Fathers and Doctors, bearing in mind that the Roman Creed absolutely requires that the Fathers must be unanimous in their interpretation of any given text before that text can be quoted as an authority. Once for all, and at the expense of tiring the reader, let me quote in full what Bellarmine has recorded on the various interpretations of this text:†—

"The difficulties of this passage are five in number.

"1. What is understood by the builders? 2. What is understood by gold, silver, precious stones, wood, hay, and stubble? 3. What is understood by the day of the Lord? 4. What is understood by the fire, of which it is said that in the day of the Lord it shall prove every one's work? 5. What is understood by the fire, of which it is said, he shall be saved, yet so as by fire? When these things are explained the passage will be clear. The first difficulty, therefore, is, who are the architects who build upon the foundation? *Augustine*, in his book on faith and works, chapter 16th and elsewhere, thinks that all Christians are here called by the apostle architects, and that all build upon the foundation of the faith either good or bad works. *Chrysostom, Theodoret, Theophylact,* and *Œcumenius,*

* Lud. Vives on Lib. De Civ. Dei, Lib. xxi. c. xxiv. note *a*, p. 865. London, 1610.
† Bell. De Purg., Tom. ii. c. iv, Lib. i. pp. 332 *et seqq*. Prag., 1721.

appear to me to teach the same upon this passage. Many others teach that only the doctors and preachers of the Gospel are here called architects by the apostle. *Jerome* insinuates this in his second book against Jovinianus. The blessed *Anselm* and the blessed *Thomas* hold the same opinion on this passage, although they do not reject the former opinion. Many more modern think the same, as *Dionysius the Carthusian, Lyra, Cajetan,* and others.

"The other difficulty is rather more serious. For there are *six* opinions. Some by the name of foundation understand, a true but an ill-digested faith; by the names of gold, silver, and precious stones, good works. By the names of wood, hay, and stubble, mortal sins. Thus Chrysostom upon this place, who is followed by Theophylact. The second opinion is, that Christ or the preaching of the faith is understood by the name of foundation; that by the names of gold, silver, and precious stones, are understood Catholic expositions; by the name of wood, hay, and stubble, are understood heretical doctrines, as the commentary of *Ambrose* and even *Jerome* seem to teach. The third opinion by the name of foundation understands living faith, and by the name of gold, silver, and precious stones, understands works of supererogation, &c. Thus the blessed *Augustine* in his book on faith and works. The fourth opinion is that which is held by those who explain by gold, silver, &c., to be meant good works, by hay and stubble, &c., venial sins. Thus the blessed *Gregory* in the fourth book of his dialogues, chapter 39th, and others. The fifth is of those who understand by gold, silver, &c., good hearers, and by stubble bad hearers, &c. Thus *Theodoret* and *Œcumenius.* The sixth opinion, which we prefer to all, is, that by the name of foundation is to be understood Christ, as preached by the first preachers. By the name of gold, silver, &c., is to be understood the useful doctrine of the other preachers, who teach those who have now received the faith. But by the name of wood, hay, &c., is to be understood the doctrine, not heretical or bad, but the singular doctrine of those preachers who preach catholically to the catholic people, but without that fruit and profit which God requires.

"The third difficulty regards the day of the Lord. Some understand by the name of day the present life, or the time of tribulation. Thus *Augustine* in his book on faith and works, c. 16, and *Gregory* in his 4th book of dialogues, c. 39. . . . But all the ancients seem to have understood by that day, the day of the last judgment, as *Theodoret, Theophylact, Anselm,* and others. The fourth difficulty is, what is the fire which, in the day of the Lord, shall prove every one's work? Some understand the tribulations of this life, as *Augustine* and *Gregory* in the places noted, *but these we have already rejected.* Some understand eternal fire, but that cannot be, for that fire shall not try the building of gold and silver. . . .

Some understand it to be the pains of Purgatory, but that cannot be truly said. First, because the fire of Purgatory does not prove the works of those who build gold and silver. But that fire of which we speak shall prove every one's work what it is.

"Secondly, the apostle clearly makes a distinction between the works and the workmen, and says concerning that fire, that it shall burn the works but not the workers: for he says, if any one's work shall remain, and if any work shall burn: but the fire of Purgatory, which is a true and real fire, cannot burn works, which are transitory actions, and have already passed. Lastly, it would follow, that all men, even the most holy, would pass through the fire of Purgatory, and be saved by fire, for all are to pass through the fire of which we are speaking. But that all are to pass through the fire of Purgatory and to be saved by fire is clearly false: for the apostle here openly says, that only those who build wood and hay are to be saved as by fire: the Church, also, has always [?] been persuaded that holy martyrs and infants dying after baptism are presently received into heaven, without any passage through fire, as the Council of Florence teaches in its last Session. *It remains, therefore, that we should say that the apostle here speaks of the fire of the severe and just judgment of God, which is not a purging or punishing fire, but one that probes and examines.* Thus *Ambrose* explains it on Psalm 118, and also Sedulius.

"The fifth and last difficulty is, what is understood by the fire, when he says, but he shall be saved, yet so as by fire?

"Some understand the tribulations of this life, but this cannot properly be said, because then even he who built gold and silver would be saved by fire. Wherefore *Augustine* and *Gregory*, who are the authors of this opinion, when they were not satisfied with it, proposed another, of which we shall speak by-and-by. *Some understand it to be eternal fire, as Chrysostom and Theophylact.* But this we have already refuted. Others understand the fire of the conflagration of the world. It is, therefore, the common opinion of theologians, that by the name of this fire is understood some purgatorial and temporal fire, to which after death they are adjudged, who are found in their trial to have built wood, hay, or stubble."

To quote such a text to establish a doctrine to be believed under pain of eternal damnation is a theory that could be conceived only by a dogmatic and arrogant Priesthood.

We have a ready key to the interpretation of the prayers alluded to by Augustine in the following, which, by the way, Dr. Wiseman gives, but it stands in a note of two pages, where it is least likely to be found by an ordinary reader[*]:—"When, therefore, the sacrifice of the altar, or alms, are offered for the dead; in regard to those whose lives were very good, such offices may be deemed acts

[*] Lect. XI., p. 67, vol. ii.

of thanksgiving; for the imperfect, acts of propitiation; and though to the wicked they bring no aid, they may give some comfort to the living (Enchirid. cap. cx.)."

VI. There is another reference to Augustine, and that is in Lecture XII., on "Indulgences." He tells us that—"St. Augustine gives us another ground whereon mitigation of Penance was sometimes granted; that is, when intercession was made in favour of the repenting sinner by persons justly possessing influence with the Pastors of the Church. In the same manner, he tells us, as the clergy sometimes interceded for mercy with the civil magistrate in favour of a condemned criminal, and were successful, so did they, in their turn, admit the interposition of good offices from the magistrates in favour of sinners undergoing penance (Epist. ad Maced. 54)."

Now, in all popular Manuals, an "Indulgence" is defined to be a "remittance of *temporal* punishments due to sin, the guilt and eternal punishment having been previously remitted by the Sacrament of Penance;" that is, by previous attrition and confession to a Priest, and his absolution, which last act remits the *eternal* punishment otherwise consequent on sin. The definition of an Indulgence is given in a book published by "R. Grace and Son," 45, Capel Street, Dublin (the authorized or recognised publishers of Papal books), entitled "Indulgences granted by Sovereign Pontiffs to the Faithful, collected by a Member of the Sacred Congregation of Indulgences in Rome, translated into English with the permission of Superiors." As this book appears to be for all time, it bears no date, but is now on sale. In page 5, we read:—

"An indulgence is the remission of the temporal punishment which generally remains due to sins already forgiven, in the Sacrament of Penance, as to the guilt and eternal punishment. This remission is made by the application of the merits and satisfactions which are contained in the treasures of the Church. These treasures are the accumulation of the spiritual goods arising from the infinite merits and satisfaction of Jesus Christ, with the superabundant merits and satisfaction of the holy martyrs, and of the other saints, which ultimately derive their efficacy from the merits and satisfactions of Christ, who is the only Mediator of redemption. These CELESTIAL TREASURES, as they are called by the Council of Trent, are committed by the Divine bounty to the dispensation of the Church, the sacred spouse of Christ, and are the ground and matter of indulgences. They are *infinite* in reference to the merits of Christ, and *cannot, therefore, be ever exhausted.*"

Dens, in his text-book, informs us that—"This treasure is the *foundation* or *matter* of indulgences, and is that infinite treasure made up in part from the satisfactions of Christ, so as never to be exhausted; and it daily receives the superabundant satisfactions of pious men."*

I would now ask any honest-minded reader to compare this statement of the Roman teaching on Indulgences, and say whether he can trace the slightest pretence for asserting that Augustine, in the passages above referred to, taught the modern Roman practice of "Satisfaction." Whom did Dr. Wiseman expect to deceive? Surely not members of his own communion?

VII. And lastly, in proof of the Roman theory of Transubstantiation† we have, of course, quoted the passages—" When committing to us His body He said, This is My body. Christ was borne in His own hands. He bore that body in His hands."—" 'How was He borne in His hands?' he asks in the next Sermon on the same Psalm.—' Because, when *He gave His own body and blood*, He took into His hands *what the faithful know*, and He bore Himself *in a certain manner* when He said, *This is my body*."

I have elsewhere examined this passage, showing that Augustine fell into an error, not knowing the Hebrew language, but he fully explains himself when he stated that in saying " This is my body," He gave the *sign* of His body, and that He warned the Disciples not to fall into what otherwise would be an obvious error:—" You shall not eat this body which you see, nor drink that blood which they will shed that will crucify Me. I have commanded a certain Sacrament unto you, which, being spiritually understood, will quicken you."‡

I have now quoted every single reference to Augustine contained in Dr. Wiseman's sixteen Lectures, covering 580 octavo pages. And what do they amount to? That Augustine would not have believed the Gospel if the authority of the Church had not moved him; that Infant Baptism was an Apostolic Tradition; that the orthodox Christians in his day were known as Catholics; an abortive effort to make us believe that the " sacrifice of a contrite spirit, a contrite and humble heart, which God will not despise," had reference to Rome's modern theory of " Satisfaction;" and that because, in the justice of God, He will punish the sinner, therefore that punishment must be in the Roman Purgatory, and that the early custom of praying for the dead necessarily implied a belief in Purgatory, and that this Purgatory has Scriptural authority in Cor. iii. 12; and that He bore Himself in His own hand when He kept the Passover with His Disciples in offering them bread and wine; and lastly, that the alleged ancient custom of showing mercy to

---

* Dens' Theologia, Tom. vi. p. 417, No. 30, Tract. de Indulg. Dublin, 1832.
† Lecture XVI. p. 230.
‡ Enarratio in Psalmum xcviii. Tom. viii. col. 1105. Basiliæ ex off. Frob., 1556.

condemned criminals by the intercession of the clergy before magistrates, was the same as the modern theory of Indulgences!

Not one of the citations, however, carries out the intentions for which they are quoted, and the fact still remains, in the present case, that Dr. Wiseman has avoided the citation of the numerous passages found in Augustine's works which, had they been fairly quoted, would have entirely demolished his theories. This is only one other desperate effort to induce us to believe that the great Augustine, Bishop of an African See, was in fact a Romanist!

CHAPTER XIII.

DR. JOHN MILNER AND AUGUSTINE.

I NOW proceed to examine the citations from the writings of Augustine made by Dr. Milner in his Letters addressed to an imaginary community of Protestants under the equivocal title of "The *End of Religious Controversy.*" If by the *end* he meant to convey that his arguments had brought the controversy to a conclusion, he has lamentably failed, since these same Letters have brought into the field against him a host of opponents. If he meant the *object* of controversy, namely (to quote Dr. Newman's words), "not to refute error, but to establish the *truth*," it has been conclusively proved by his numerous critics that *truth* seems to be the very last object he had in view.

The estimation in which these Letters are held by contending parties is somewhat remarkable. The late Charles Butler, a lay advocate of the Roman Church, declared the Letters to be "the ablest exposition of the doctrines of the Roman Catholic Church *on the articles* contested with her by Protestants, and the ablest statement of the proofs by which they are supported, and of the historical facts with which they are connected, that has appeared in our language."* The same work has been put forward by Romanists as "the herculean shield, which not only confounds, but fritters away the ingenious subtleties of the sophist, the specious distinctions of the critic, the empty theories of the sceptic, and all the impotent attacks of misguided reason against our holy religion."† By another editor it is styled "The golden work of the Right Rev.

* Book of the Roman Catholic Church, p. 10, quoted in the Letters of the Bishop of Exeter, 1826, p. 16.
† In the Preface of the 1820 Edition, Dublin.

John Milner, &c., &c." It is recommended as a "book particularly adapted for the perusal of inquiring Protestants; the one of all others which the Catholic Priest or layman wishes to place in the hands of such persons as best able to assist their search after truth." Again, the same editor adds—" We may, in fact, safely say that no other controversial work of modern times, has had equal success in effecting conversions to our holy religion. Indeed, there are probably few converts who have arrived at it without being, partly at least, indebted to this excellent work."*

While, on the other hand, Dr. Milner's work has been designated by Protestant writers of credit as the most unscrupulous production that has been put forward under the garb of religion, and with the affectation of candour and learning. The Rev. Joseph Mendham, in his "Literary Policy of the Church of Rome," said:—" I cannot forbear adding, with respect to this plausible, because deceitful work, that the reflection which but a cursory examination of it most constantly and forcibly impresses upon the mind, is the facility with which, particularly when *aided by opportune suppression*, invention, and adjustment, Romanists may prove anything, since the authors and authorities respected by them have maintained everything." The Rev. Geo. Stanley Faber, in his "Difficulties of Romanism,"† asserts—" In point of dexterity and plausibility the work of Dr. Milner, which he has entitled 'The End of Religious Controversy,' is strongly marked by what I have noted to be the grand characteristics of productions written in favour of Popery, and in opposition to the Reformation; these are *unscrupulous misrepresentations* on the one hand, and bold allegations on the other." And Mr. Gavin, in his able refutation of part of the work in question, declares—and his statements are founded on proofs—that Dr. Milner "has displayed an impudent disregard of historical truth"; that "his 'End of Religious Controversy' bears one of the most prominent marks of the beast on its very front—there is downright lying and imposition."

In conducting an examination with reference to the citations from Augustine, we have not to complain so much of falsification as of "opportune suppression." Augustine is so far quoted only as suits the object of the astute Doctor. The deliberate suppression of the whole truth is equivalent to the suggestion of a falsehood—*Suppressio veri suggestio falsi* is an admitted axiom.

In the fifty Letters, covering 494 pages of the stereotyped 1843 edition, from which my quotations will be taken, there are twenty-five references to Augustine, including some repetitions, the usual leading fallacy being, that wherever Augustine refers to the "Church," or to "the Catholic Church," Dr. Milner would have his

---

* From Preface to the 8vo Edition, 1842.
† See Preface to 3rd Edition, p. xxxiv.

readers necessarily believe that Augustine pointed to the communion of Christians presided over by the Bishop of Rome. The result is that by far the greater number of these citations are of that character. The following are examples:—

"See (says St. Augustine) into how many morsels those are divided who have divided themselves from the unity of the Church." (Let. viii. p. 100, and Let. xv. p. 181.)

"Augustine uses this argument against the Donatists—'In the Scriptures we know Christ, in the Scriptures we know the Church. If you hold to Christ, why not hold to the Church?'" (Let. x. p. 128.)

"It would fill a large volume to transcribe all the passages which occur in the works of the great St. Augustine, in proof of the Catholic Rule, and the authority of the Church in making use of it: let therefore two or three of them speak for the rest:—'To attain to the *truth of the Scriptures*,' he says, 'we must follow the sense of them entertained by the Universal Church, to which the Scriptures themselves bear testimony. True it is, the Scriptures themselves cannot deceive us; nevertheless, to prevent our being deceived in the question we examine by them, it is necessary we should advise with that Church, which these certainly and evidently point out to us. (Let. i. Contra Crescon.) This (the unlawfulness of rebaptizing heretics) is not evidently read either by you or by me, nevertheless, if there were any wise man, to whom Christ had borne testimony, and whom He had appointed to be consulted on the question, we could not fail to do so: now Christ bears this testimony to His Church.—Whoever, therefore, refuses to follow the practice of the Church, resists Christ Himself, who by His testimony recommends this Church.' (De Util. Credend.) Treating elsewhere the same subject, he says—'The Apostles, indeed, have prescribed nothing about this; but the custom must be considered as derived from their Tradition, since there are many things observed by the Universal Church which are justly held to have been appointed by the Apostles, though they are not written.' (De Bapt. cont. Donat. lv.)" (Let. x. pp. 135-6.)

The "practices," as I have already observed, were not questions of *faith*, but ecclesiastical *observances*. But Dr. Milner omits to tell us that in regard to the question of rebaptism Augustine repudiated the right of the Bishop of Rome to interfere in the case of the controversy with Cyprian.

"He [Augustine] tells the Donatist schismatics, 'Whoever is separated from this *Catholic Church*, however innocently he may think he lives, for this crime alone, that he is separated from the unity of Christ, will not have life, but the anger of God remains upon him.' (Concil. Lab., Tom. ii. p. 1520.)" (Let. xiv. p. 179).

"Augustine says, 'All the assemblies, or rather divisions, who call themselves Churches of Christ, but which, in fact, have separated themselves from the congregation of Unity, do not belong to the true Church. They might indeed belong to her, if the Holy Ghost could be divided against Himself; but as this is impossible, they do *not* belong to her.' (De ver. Don., Serm. ii.) In like manner, addressing himself to certain sectaries of his time, he says, 'If our communion is the Church of Christ, yours is not so; for *the Church of Christ is one, whichsoever she is;* since it is said of her, '*My dove, my undefiled is one; she is the only one of her mother.*' Cantic. vi. 9." (Let. xviii. p. 197.)

Again, we may be sure that the following quotations are not omitted (Let. xxv. p. 265):—

"But there is not one of the Fathers or Doctors of antiquity who enlarges so copiously or so pointedly on this title of the true Church as the great St. Augustine, who died in the early part of the fifth century. 'Many things,' he says, 'detain me in the bosom of the Catholic Church—the very name of CATHOLIC detains me in it, which she has so happily preserved amidst the different heretics; that whereas they are all desirous of being called *Catholics*, yet, if any stranger were to ask them, *Which is the assembly of the Catholics?* none of them would dare to point out his own place of worship.' To the same purpose he says elsewhere, 'We must hold fast the communion of that Church which is called *Catholic*, not only by her own children but also by all her enemies. For heretics and schismatics, whether they will or not, when they are speaking of the Catholic Church with strangers, or with their own people, call her by the name of *Catholic;* inasmuch as they would not be understood if they did not call her by the name by which all the world calls her.'"

"'The Catholic Church (says St. Augustine) is so called because it is spread throughout the world. If your Church, adds he, addressing certain heretics, is Catholic, show me that it spreads its branches throughout the world; for such is the meaning of the word Catholic." (Let. xxvi. p. 268.)

"In finishing this subject I shall quote a passage from St. Augustine, which is as applicable to the sectaries of this age as it was to those of the age in which he wrote:—'There are heretics everywhere, but not the same heretics everywhere. For there is one sort in Africa, another sort in the East, a third sort in Egypt, and a fourth sort in Mesopotamia, being different in different countries, though all produced by the same mother, namely, pride. Thus also the faithful are all born of one common mother, the Catholic Church; and though they are everywhere dispersed, they are everywhere the same.'" (Let. xxvi. p. 272.)

Now, in not one of these extracts does Augustine give us the slightest indication that he was referring to the Roman branch of the

Christian Church, any more than that he was referring to the Greek Church. I have already shown that the authority of the Bishop of Rome was restricted to the district covered by the Prefecture of that city. That Dr. Milner intended his readers to understand by these extracts that Augustine was in fact alluding to the communion of Christians presided over by the Bishop of Rome is evident from his Letter xxviii., on "Apostolicity," wherein he gives in each successive century the name of each Bishop who presided over that See. Included in each century he gives also the names of eminent Christian Fathers, as if they were all members of the same Roman Church, whether Greeks, or Asiatics, or Africans. Thus, under the fifth century (p. 235), he names Popes " Zosimus, Boniface I., and Celestine I." as contemporaries of Augustine, and adds: "Their zeal was well seconded by some of the brightest ornaments of orthodoxy and literature that ever illustrated the Church "; and among these he names " St. Augustine," who, as we have seen, actually opposed those very three Bishops when they attempted to foist on the African Church a forged canon, in order to usurp an authority over the African Church, and who, as I have shown, were he now alive, preaching and teaching the same doctrines as he then taught, would be condemned as a rank heretic !

I maintain, therefore, without fear of contradiction, that for Dr. Milner to press the name of Augustine before his readers as a member of his Church is the height of dishonesty.

On questions of doctrine I have shown that not only did Augustine not teach one single article of Pope Pius' Creed, but that he in many respects condemned modern Roman theories as heresies, as preached in his day. Not one of these passages do we find attempted to be explained away or in any manner referred to. But a striking feature in this part of the " controversy" is the entire absence of a single quotation to prove that Augustine held any single dogma of the Roman Creed.

In Letter xlviii., p. 462, Dr. Milner says :—

"I have often wondered, in a particular manner, at the confidence with which Bishop Porteus asserts and denies facts of ancient Church history, in opposition to known truth. An instance of this occurs in the conclusion of the chapter before me, where he says: 'The primitive Church did not attempt, for several hundreds of years, to make any *doctrine* necessary, which we do not, as the learned well know from their writings.' The palpable falsehood of this position must strike you, on looking back to the authorities adduced by me from the ancient Fathers and historians, in proof of the several points of controversy which I have maintained."

In p. 267 he has the boldness to tell us that the doctrine taught in the days of Augustine is " as good and certain now as it was in his time." Let us examine the evidence (if any) he has adduced to prove this assertion:—

"*On Supremacy of the Bishop of Rome*" (Letter xlvi.) there is not one single reference to Augustine; but, as a heading to another chapter (Part II.), we have the extract I have elsewhere examined, in which Augustine, opposing the claim of a Donatist Bishop to the See of Rome, traces the descent of the existing Bishop in the "See of Peter" as the lawful Bishop. This is quoted in order to prove that Augustine testified that Peter was the first Bishop of Rome. Independent of the fact that the passage is most probably interpolated, this is a statement professedly of the fifth century, which contradicts the testimony of Irenæus and Tertullian, of the second century, that Peter was not the *first* Bishop of Rome. Alexandria was sometimes called the "See of Peter," though it is not pretended Peter was ever in that city.

"*On Invocation of Saints*" (Letter xxxiii.) there is not one single reference to Augustine.

"*On Image Worship*" (Letter xxxiv.), headed "*On Religious Memorials*," we are informed that Augustine, in dividing the Ten Commandments, included what we call the second commandment in the first (p. 346); but he does not continue to tell us that Augustine reprobated and utterly condemned the use of images in religious exercises, and specially the relative worship as professed by the Roman Church in the present day.

"*Transubstantiation*" (Letter xxxvi.). Not one single reference to Augustine. The like "*The Real Presence*" (Letter xxxvii.). The like "*Communion in One Kind*" (Letter xxxix.). The like "*On the Sacrifice of the Law*" (Letter xl.) The like "*On Absolution from Sin*" (Letter xli.) The like "*On Indulgences*" (Letter xlii.). The like "*On Extreme Unction*" (Letter xliv.).

"*On Purgatory*" (Letter xliii.) Dr. Milner says, in p. 411:—"I claim a right of considering the two Books of Maccabees as an integral part of the Old Testament, because the Catholic Church so considers them, from whose traditions, and not from that of the Jews, as St. Augustine signifies, our *sacred* canon is formed."

The foot references are:—"Council of Carthage (III.), St. Cyprian, St. Augustine (Lib. xviii. De Civ. Dei), and Innocent I."

In Chapter V. I have proved that the "Catholic Church" utterly condemned these two books. I have also proved that the appeal to the Council of Carthage cannot be sustained, and that Cyprian absolutely rejected the whole of the Apocrypha, including the two Books of Maccabees.

The appeal to Innocent I. is one that only a dishonest controversialist would resort to. The list relied on is said to be in a

Decretal of Pope Innocent I., A.D. 405.* No one ever heard of this alleged list of Innocent for 460 years after the date assigned to the decretal letter. We hear of it for the first time in the ninth century, when the mass of forged Decretals appeared. The list stands just at the end, where it was convenient for a forger to add to it; and, to render the difficulty still more oppressing, in the earliest copies of this Letter we do not find the Book of Tobit.†

I have in the former chapter given references as to what Augustine included in the "*Sacred* Canon of Scriptures." But it is fair to Dr. Milner that I should set out the passage in full on which he relies, *but does not quote*, from the "City of God," Lib. xviii. c. 36 :—

"The account of which times *we have not in the Canonical Scriptures, but in others, amongst which the books of the Maccabees* are also, which the Church, indeed, holdeth for canonical because of the vehement and wonderful sufferings of some Martyrs of the law of God before the coming of Christ. Such there were that endured intolerable torments, yet these books are but apocryphal to the Jews."‡

Cardinal Cajetan, as I have shown clearly, warns us not to misunderstand Augustine when he applies the word " canonical " to those Apocryphal books, and that we are to distinguish them from the *Sacred* and *Inspired Canon*. Augustine on this head cannot be mistaken. In another place he said :—

"Although there may something be found in the Books of Maccabees meet for this order of writing, and worthy to be joined with the number of miracles, yet we have intended only to touch a short rehearsal of miracles contained in the *Divine* Canon."§

We have also the authority of Pope Gregory I. (the Great), so late as the beginning of the seventh century, giving direct testimony on this subject :—" We do not amiss if we produce a testimony out of the Books of Maccabees (*licet non Canonicis*), though not canonical, but published for the edification of the Church."‖

There is no subject on which the early Christians agreed more decidedly than in the rejection of the Books of Maccabees from the Sacred Canon of Scripture. The Roman Church professes to adopt their Vulgate from Jerome. Now Jerome is precise on this subject. He said :—" As, therefore, the Church reads the Books of Judith, and Tobias, and of the Maccabees, but does not receive them into the canonical Scriptures, so also she may read these two writings

---

* Ep. ad Exuperium, n. 7, Tom. ii. col. 1265, Lab. Concil. Paris, 1671.
† L. i. Ep. 369, Cyro., p. 96. Paris, 1633.
‡ P. 725. London, 1610.
§ Aug. de Mirab. Sac. Scrip., p. 26, Tom. iii. Ed. 1686. (Authority doubtel.)
‖ See the Vatican Edition, Tom. ii. p. 899. Rome, 1608.

[Ecclesiasticus and Wisdom] for the edification of the people, *not to establish the authority of* Ecclesiastical doctrines."*

In the very edition sanctioned by the Council of Trent as the authorized Vulgate of Jerome, Prefaces appeared at the head of each book which most distinctly excluded the Apocrypha from the canon. These have been subsequently withdrawn from the headings, which otherwise would have warned the reader of their apocryphal character.

Dr. Milner, as a Bishop of the Roman Church, ought to have been aware of the true history of the Apocrypha. If he was not, then he was not qualified to write on the controversy. If he was aware of former protests, then he was guilty of wilful fraud and deception. I leave the reader to judge for himself—" Utrum horum mavis accipe."

But, giving Dr. Milner all the benefit he can derive from the circumstance relied on (2 Macc. xii. 45), he is no nearer the mark. The Roman Purgatory is for those who die in the faith of Christ, the justified, whose sins have been absolved in their (so-called) Sacrament of Penance, and the *eternal* punishment remitted, and who are completing " Satisfaction," or *temporal* punishment. The soldiers in the text died, according to Roman theory, in *mortal sin*, as idols "were found on them." The collection made was, according to the Jewish custom, a sin-offering on behalf of the *living*, that they should not participate in the sins of the dead. Indeed, it is not pretended that there was a Purgatory previous to Christ's mission in this world.

Again, we are informed (p. 412) that Augustine held there was a middle state, citing the narrative of Dives and Abraham. If " Abraham's Bosom" is the Roman Purgatory, very few persons would pay the Priest to free a relative from that happy state; he would conclude that the frightful tales of torments there endured were inconsistent with the happy state of those in " Abraham's Bosom."

Dr. Milner continues (p. 413) :—" I might here add, as a farther proof of a Purgatory, the denunciation of Christ concerning *blasphemy against the Holy Ghost;* namely, that this sin *shall not be forgiven, either in this world or in the world to come* (Matt. xii. 32) : which words clearly imply, that *some sins* are forgiven in the world to come, as the ancient Fathers show." And in a foot-note we are referred to " Aug. De Civit. Dei, lib. xxi. c. 24," being the same passage as cited by Dr. Wiseman (*ante* p. 111). Besides the fact, as I have there shown, of the doubt on the genuineness of the quotation, it is merely necessary to observe that " the world to come," " where (Dr. Milner tells us that) some sins are forgiven," cannot point to the Romish Purgatory, for in their Purgatory sins are there not forgiven,

---

* In Op. Hieron., Ben. Edit., Præf. in Libros Salomonis, Tom. i. pp. 938-9.

but is represented as a place or state of temporal punishment for sins alleged to be already forgiven.

And of course we are reminded of Augustine's prayer for his mother, Monnica (p. 415):—"How affecting is this Saint's account of the death of his mother, St. Monica, when she entreated him to remember her soul at the altar, and when, after her decease, he performed this duty, in order, as he declares, ' to obtain the pardon of her sins!'" And here we again object that Purgatory is not a place where *sin* can be pardoned; and I have elsewhere repeatedly shown how inappropriate is the reference to this incident.

Having now examined every single appeal to Augustine to support the figment of Popish Purgatory, we must admire Dr. Milner's boldness when he adds (p. 415), that "the doctrine of the Church" (naming Augustine as one of his authorities) " was the same that it is now, not only within a thousand but also within four hundred years from the time of Christ, with respect both to prayers for the dead, and an intermediate state which we call Purgatory."

We have no reference to the doctrines of Confession or Penance; and the other Sacraments are not even mentioned!

"*On Miracles,*" we are informed (Letter xxiii. p. 237), that "the great St. Augustine in various passages of his works refers to the miracles wrought in the Catholic Church in *evidence of her veracity;*" and in p. 241 in particular, Dr. Milner refers us to book xxii. cap. 8, of "The City of God," in proof of this claim to miracles as "*evidence* of her veracity"! It is true that in this chapter—if genuine—Augustine cites a series of most absurd tales, to which no intelligent Romanist of the present day would give the slightest credence. As for the debatable argument of *veracity,* we have a very good authority in support of our doubt as to the genuineness of the chapter; for Ludovicus Vives, a learned Roman Catholic commentator on this work, in his notes on this very chapter, says, "that there are many additions in the chapter, I make no question, foisted in by such as make a practice of depraving authors of authority." Dr Milner very briefly quotes one of the series, the case of a man recovering his sight at the tomb of two Martyrs, who were revealed to be Martyrs to Ambrose, Bishop of Milan, *in a dream!* Not one of these marvels does Augustine say he himself performed or even witnessed personally, but that they were related to him. How far such " old wives' fables " assist Dr. Milner in enlisting Augustine in favour of the Roman branch of the " Catholic Church " I fail to discover. They may reveal to us the " mark of the beast," who should develop itself with " signs and lying wonders."*   Augustine opens the chapter with this

---

* If this is the genuine production of Augustine, the entire chapter is a black spot and a blemish in his otherwise glorious productions. It shows how nearly allied is superstition to religion, and that the great mind of Augustine was not free from that

remarkable passage :—" But how cometh it to pass that you have no such miracles now-a-days as you say were done of yore ? I might answer that they were necessary, before the world believed, to induce it to believe, and he that seeketh to be confirmed by miracles now is to be wondered at most of all himself in refusing to believe when all the world believeth besides him."* The Donatists also appealed to their miracles to prove that they alone constituted the Catholic Church. Augustine met them with the following reply :—

" Let them, if they can, demonstrate their Church, not by the talk and rumour of the Africans; not by the Councils of their Bishops; not by the books of their disputes; *not by deceitful miracles, against which we are cautioned by the Word of God;* but in the prescript of the Law, in the predictions of the Prophets, in the verses of the Psalms, in the voice of the Shepherd Himself, in the preaching and works of the Evangelists; that is, in all the canonical authorities of the Sacred Scriptures."†

But, perhaps, the most impudent appeal to Augustine is conveyed by a citation which is selected as a motto, heading the very first Letter, doubtless intending that his readers should believe that the Roman Church has ever followed the precept laid down by Augustine deprecating persecutions for conscience' sake. The following is the passage :—

" ' Let those treat you harshly, who are not acquainted with the difficulty of attaining to truth and avoiding error. Let those treat you harshly who know not how hard it is to get rid of old prejudices. Let those treat you harshly who have not learned how very hard it is to purify the interior eye, and render it capable of contemplating the sun of the soul, truth.—But as to us : we are far from this disposition towards persons who are separated from us, not by errors of their own invention, but by being entangled in those of others. We are so far from this disposition, that we pray to God, that in refuting the false opinions of those whom you follow, not from malice but imprudence, He would bestow upon us that spirit of peace which feels no other sentiment than charity, no other interest than that of Jesus Christ, no other wish but for your salvation.'—St. Augustine, Doctor of the Church, A.D. 400, contra Ep. Fund. l. i. c. ii."

When Augustine wrote this Christians were the persecuted. Times changed when the Roman Church became dominant, and we contrast with the above the language of Pope Pius V. when the Duke of Alva boasted that he had slaughtered 18,000 unoffending Protes-

---

failing. That the reader may form his own judgment in the matter, I have given in Appendix A, almost in the very words of Augustine, each case that Augustine cites. (I quote from Edition of 1610, with Ludovicus Vives' annotations.)
* Ed. London, 1610, p. 882.
† Bened. Edit., Tom. ix. p. 252.

tants in the Netherlands. The Pontiff wrote to the Duke "as his dear son," encouraging him in the course of persecution, and in this way to rise in his progress to everlasting glory.

"Nothing is more glorious (he wrote) to the Church or more acceptable to our paternal mind, than to learn that military men and courageous generals, such as you were always known to be, and proved in the present most dangerous war, seek not their own interest or glory, but serve under the Omnipotent God, who will reward His soldiers fighting for Him, and the glory of His name, not with a corruptible, but with an eternal and imperishable crown."*

From the days of Archbishop Berengarius (A.D. 1059), who was compelled, under pain of being burnt alive, to subscribe to the dogma of Transubstantiation in its grossest and most literal form, until the power of persecution was taken away from her at the Reformation, the Church of Rome has been an essentially persecuting Church. Witness the exterminating decrees of Innocent III.,† Honorius III., Innocent IV., Innocent VIII., Alexander IV., Urban IV., John XXII., Boniface IX., Julius II., Leo X., Pius V., &c., &c., all directed to the extermination of so-called heretics. Witness the

---

* See Mendham's Life of Pius V., pp. 65, 68, 90. London. 1832.

† Innocent III. may be accepted as a pattern of persecuting Popes. His exterminating Bull, which was passed into a law at the Fourth Lateran Council, was directed more especially against the Albigenses (Protestants in the south of France), but in fact extended to "all heretics, under whatever names they may be ranged." Pope Gregory IX. had this law formally included in the Canon Law of the Roman Church, and to the present day it is to be found among the Decretals of Gregory IX., book v. title vii. c. 3, Tom. ii. col. 758. Edit. Lips., 1839. The Bull commences thus :—" We excommunicate and anathematise every heresy exalting itself against that holy, orthodox, and Catholic faith which we have above set forth ; condemning all heretics, under whatever names they may be ranged ; let those persons, when condemned, be abandoned to the secular authorities, in order that they may be duly punished, &c., &c." The nature of that punishment we learn from the " Ecclesiastical Annals" of Bzovius, the Roman Catholic historian, wherein he tells us that " Pope Innocent III. could no longer brook the obstinacy of the erring Albigenses ;" he enlisted the services of Simon Count Montfort, " a most eager adversary of the heretics."—" Much trouble was expended in taking the camp of Minerva, for there were found therein 180 persons *who preferred being burnt alive to adopting a pious creed*." He further tells us that in the year 1209, at Innocent's command, a Crusade was established at Lyons "for the destruction of the Albigenses, so that 500,000 were reckoned in the Catholic army."—" Verum was taken by storm. There also the impious *were delivered to fire*, when they persisted in their madness."— " Louvain being taken, Agmeri, the Lord of Mountroyal, was hanged ; 80 others, who fell from the gibbet, were slain by the Crusaders, who were impatient of the delay, by the orders of Simon, and *innumerable heretics burnt*." . . . " In the same year the Crusaders obtained possession of another great city, by the Divine aid, situated near Toulouse—in which, when, after an examination of the people, all promised to return to the faith, 450 of them, hardened by the devil, persisted in their obstinacy, of whom 400 were burnt, and the rest were hanged. The same was done in the other towns and castles ; these wretches willingly exposing themselves to death." He then tells us that not content with this, he handed over to the " Godlike Dominick " and the Inquisition the task of exterminating the heretics. (Bzovii Annal. Eccl., Tom. xiii. p. 156 ; An. Chr. 1209 : and see An. 1211, An. 1215 ; Innocent III., 12, 14, 19.) Pope Innocent issued a Bull compelling the secular power, under pain of anathema, to exterminate the Albigenses !

decrees of the Fourth Lateran Council and of Constance, which ordered that heretics should be burnt alive; and witness the burning of John Huss and Jerome of Prague, and of our English Reformers, Cranmer, Ridley, Latimer, Hooper, &c., in the reign of Mary. Witness the cruel persecutions of the Waldenses and Albigenses, the massacres of French Protestants, the Dragonades, and the thousands that were tortured and murdered by the "Holy Inquisition"! The same system of persecution of so-called heretics was advocated by Thomas Aquinas, Liguori, Alphonsus à Castro, and others. Even in our own times persecution of heretics is boldly advocated, when it can be enforced, even to imprisonment and death, and religious liberty is declared to be wholly incompatible with the existence of the Roman religion.* "Catholicism," the writer boasts, "is the most intolerant of creeds."

Dr. John Milner, on the authority of St. Augustine, would have us believe that the Roman Church, in the "spirit of peace and charity," would lead us, erring heretics, to the knowledge of the truth by prayer and gentle persuasion. He seems himself to have forgotten his own episcopal oath to "persecute and fight" (persequar impugnabo) heresy wherever he meets it!

I thus dispose of Rome's great champion, the author of "The End of Religious Controversy," in his appeals to Augustine.

CHAPTER XIV.

"THE FAITH OF CATHOLICS" AND AUGUSTINE.

I HAVE now only left for consideration the Commonplace Book of the Fathers, passing under the title "The Faith of Catholics." This work was originally compiled by two Roman Priests, Kirk and Berington. As first presented to us, this compilation was replete with disgraceful misquotations from the "Fathers," which were successfully exposed by the Rev. R. T. Pope in his "Roman Misquotations," and by the Rev. George Stanley Faber in his "Difficulties of Romanism."

The present edition of "The Faith of Catholics," 1846, bearing the name of the Rev. James Waterworth as Editor, while free from such disgraceful blemishes, nevertheless errs in another direction, namely, by a systematic omission of passages from the "Fathers," which, if honestly quoted, would nullify Rome's modern theories.

---

* See the "Rambler," a Romish "Monthly," January, 1854, p. 2; June, 1849; September, 1851 (see Appendix B).

With few exceptions, we in vain search for such passages in this revised edition. Here, again, "Suppressio veri suggestio falsi"—the suppression of the truth is a suggestion of falsehood—is a received maxim; and I may be permitted to quote the words of a recent Lord Chancellor when giving judgment in the famous Overend and Gurney frauds. Referring to some evidence adduced, he said, "The objection is not that it does not state the truth, but that it conceals most material facts, the very concealment of which *gives to the truth the character of falsehood.*"

This systematic suppression of the whole truth we find more especially exercised with regard to the writings of Augustine. I have reckoned up upwards of two hundred and fifty passages quoted from his works, but we in vain search among these for the numerous extracts I have given in the foregoing pages.

The subjects treated of in "The Faith of Catholics" are introduced under different heads, the first being "*Justification through Christ and the merit of good works.*" In the outset we are startled with the "Proposition," boldly advanced as a "Catholic" truth, in the very words of Augustine, placed in inverted commas as a quotation, but without any intimation that they are his:—"God crowns His own gifts when He crowns the good works of His servants" (Vol. i. p. 3). Further, there is not the slightest intimation that this very passage had been solemnly condemned by the Roman Church, being entered in their Expurgatory Index as decidedly heretical! There is no doctrine more clearly taught by the early Christian writers than that FAITH—in derision called "Solifidianism" when applied to Luther's teaching—is our sole justification before God; and yet this is the only quotation given on this important point, made doubly important from the acrimonious discussions that have been raised on the subject, and as being the great question on which the Reformation of the Church in the sixteenth century was based.

I trust I shall be pardoned here if I venture to fill in this glaring omission by citing the testimony of some of the Fathers. I propose to quote only a few of such passages on the "Solifidian" system. The following passages are set out with full text and references in Birckbek's "Protestant Evidence":*—

Justin Martyr, A.D. 130.
"To see God is granted to men by faith only, and what alone we see God by, by that alone we are justified."

Tertullian, A.D. 201.
"The faith by which the just live, is the faith of the same God whose the law is in which he that worketh is not justified."

---
* See Vol. I., reprint. London, 1849.

Clement of Alexandria, A.D. 200.
"Faith alone is the Catholic salvation of mankind."

Origen, A.D. 230.
"The Apostle saith, that justification by faith alone is sufficient."

Ambrose, Bishop of Milan, A.D. 370, or if not Ambrose, some writer, according to Bellarmine, contemporary with him.*
"They are justified by faith alone by the gift of God."—
"Only faith is appointed to salvation."

Basil the Great, Bishop of Cæsarea, A.D. 370.
"As it is written, 'Let him that boasteth, boast in the Lord.' In this is the perfect and complete boasting in God, that no one is extolled on account of his own righteousness, but we know that he, being destitute of real righteousness, is justified by faith only in Christ."

Hilary, Bishop of Poitiers, A.D. 360.
"Wages cannot be considered as a gift, because they are due to work; but God has given free grace to all men by the justification of faith."

Gregory Nazianzen, A.D. 370.
"Confess Jesus Christ, and believe that He has risen from the dead, and thou shalt be saved. For believing only is righteousness."

Chrysostom, Bishop of Constantinople, A.D. 406.
"Thou obtainest righteousness not by thine own labour, but by gift from above, bringing one thing only from within, namely faith."

"And it is reasonable for us to say this at present; let us approach asking with boldness. Let us bring faith alone, and He gives all things."—"For these things are the sustaining means of salvation; not at all by works, not at all by uprightness, but by true faith."

Theodoret, Bishop of Cyrus, A.D. 430.
"We can attain these spiritual good things, not by any laudable works of ours, but by faith alone."

Augustine, Bishop of Hippo, A.D. 420.
"The faith of Christ alone purifieth the heart."—"Faith being absent, what other justice of man remaineth."

Fulgentius, a Bishop of Africa, 520.
"We are freely justified by faith only and not by works."

---

* "Auctor 'Commentariorum in Ep. Pauli,' aqualis sine dubio Ambrosii fuit." Bell., Lib. iv. de Justif., cap. viii.

Primasius, a Bishop of Africa, A.D. 545.
"Not by works, but by faith alone through grace dost thou know that thou hast life."*

And so we might proceed from year to year even to the days of Luther, who was declared a heretic and derided for teaching this very same doctrine, so continually repeated by Augustine.

The above will sufficiently exemplify my accusation against the compilers of "The Faith of Catholics" of the sin of omission, rather than the sin of commission.

We are next presented with elaborate extracts, under the heading "*Authority of the Church.*" Wherever the words "Catholic" or "Catholic Church" are used, the same are pressed into the service of the Romish Church without hesitation as if the peculiar sect represented by the Bishop of Rome, as its head, was pointed out as being exclusively vested with supreme authority, and specially referred to under those titles. Never was such a fallacy. This remark is more pointedly applicable to the extracts from Augustine's works, in which the Church of Rome, or the Church presided over by the Bishop of that See, is never once mentioned in any such exclusive character.

The same remarks apply to the extracts under the headings of "*The Unity of the Church,*" "*The Visibility of the Church,*" and "*Indefectibility of the Church,*" the extracts being principally from Augustine's writings against the Donatists, who, like modern Romanists, had set up their communion as the only "Catholic Church."

Under the title "*Apostolicity of the Church,*" there is an important passage thrice quoted, which is attributed to Augustine.† The Donatists, as we have already noticed, had set up one of their Bishops at Rome in opposition to the legitimate Bishop of that See. Augustine protested against this assumption, pointing out the direct descent of the then presiding Bishop from the Apostles as the title to the legitimate succession. The passage is thus quoted:—"For if the order of Bishops succeeding to each other is to be considered, how much more securely, and really beneficially, do we reckon from Peter himself, to whom bearing a figure of the Church, the Lord says, 'Upon this rock I will build my Church, and the gates of Hell shall not overcome it.' For to Peter succeeded Linus; to Linus, Clement [he gives the whole successors]; to Damasus, Syricius; to Syricius, Anastasius. In this order of suc-

---

* We find in the Madrid edition of Expurgatory Index, 1667 (p. 53, col. 2), quoted in Chapter III., the following:—"Christus dele etiam. Justificat gratia sua, non ex operibus," to be expunged from the works of St. Athanasius, in addition to the passages I have pointed out as expurgated from Augustine's works.
† Vol. i. p. 283, and vol. ii. pp. 41, 85.

cession no Donatist Bishop appears." Again (vol. i. p. 284), "Nay, if all throughout the whole world were such as you most idly slander them, what has the chair of the Roman Church, in which Peter sat, and in which Anastasius now sits?" Here, beyond the assertion of a direct Apostolic descent, there is asserted, as an alleged fact, that Peter sat as *first* Bishop of Rome. As a *historical fact*, however, we have the testimony of the first two writers who ever mentioned the subject, namely, Irenæus, Bishop of Lyons, and Tertullian, his contemporary, who give us another version. Irenæus informs us that while Paul and Peter *were together* journeying, founding and establishing churches, they *together appointed* LINUS as the first Bishop of Rome,* while Tertullian testified that Peter ordained CLEMENT as the *first* Bishop of Rome.† But neither of them asserts that Peter personally was first, or ever Bishop of Rome. Therefore, if the passages inserted in Augustine's works are genuine, they are historically false. When we find a similar admitted forgery in Cyprian's works, it will not be uncharitable to suggest that this is also an interpolation.

Under the title "*Catholicity of the Church*," the extracts prove that Augustine was referring to the Universal Church spread throughout the world. The Roman Church is not once named.

Under the title of "*The Scriptures*," not one single passage which I have quoted in a former chapter is to be found under this heading!

On "*The Church the Expounder of Scriptures*," we are nowhere told by Augustine that we are to appeal to Rome or to her Priests for such exposition. Nor on "*Private Judgment*" is there any authority quoted for asserting that we are to follow the expositions emanating either from Rome or from any private individual.

On "*Apostolic Tradition*" we have here quoted the two passages already noticed as to Infant Baptism, and those relating to the "celebrating with an anniversary solemnity" of the Passion and the Resurrection, and the Ascension of the Lord into heaven, and the coming of the Holy Spirit from heaven. These facts are clearly laid down in Scripture, but Augustine was merely referring to the annual celebration commemorating these facts;‡ he was not treating of doctrine. We are referred to an extract on "Prayers for the Dead," and Augustine's belief that "the Lord may deal with them more mercifully than their sins have deserved." I have admitted that the custom of praying for the dead was a very ancient custom; in fact, it was *the* earliest innovation, introduced into the Church about the beginning of the third century, and we find in the old

---

* See "Faith of Catholics," Vol. i. p. 253.
† Præs. Hæret., Tom. ii. c. 32, p. 470. Wirceb., 1781.
‡ See Vol. i. p. 439, of "Faith of Catholics."

Liturgies that in those prayers were included prayers *for* the Patriarchs, Prophets, Apostles, the Virgin Mary, and Martyrs; all which would be proclaimed heresy in the present day.

These are the only evidences adduced from the writings of Augustine of his acceptance of *Apostolic Tradition*. And under the title of "*Councils*," all that Augustine admitted to be authorized by such tribunals as "Apostolic Traditions" were questions of custom, but not of doctrine.

Confirmation (vol. i. p. 149). There are three quotations given under this head referring to the descent of the Holy Spirit, and that "they upon whom hands are laid should speak with tongues." What that has to do with "Confirmation" is difficult to conceive. Augustine is then quoted as follows:—"Sprinkling with water." "The Chrism is this. For the oil of our fire is the Sacrament of the Holy Ghost."—"Of Christ it is written in the Acts of the Apostles, 'how God anointed Him with the Holy Ghost,' not, indeed, with visible oil, but with the gift of grace which is signified by that visible unction wherewith the Church anoints the baptized." But there is not one word of *Confirmation*, either as a Sacrament or otherwise as a form of the Church, though probably Confirmation was practised.

The Eucharist. I have already observed that we meet in the Fathers most extravagant language as applied to this subject. Indeed, the compilers of "The Faith of Catholics" (vol. ii. p. 317) have given us a striking instance. In quoting from a Homily of Chrysostom, we read:—"Wherefore, then, what ought not he to be more pure who enjoys so great a sacrifice? Purer than any solar ray should that hand be that divides the flesh*; that mouth that is filled with a spiritual fire; that *tongue that is reddened with that most awful blood*. Think how thou hast been honoured. What a table thou enjoyest. That at which when the angels look upon it they tremble, and dare not without dread regard fixedly by reason of the brightness that emanates thence, with that we are nourished, with that commingled, and have become one body and one flesh with Christ." And he says much more to the same effect. When, however, these writers abandon this extravagant style, and in their sober moments, we find them describing the elements as *types, images, representations*, &c., &c., of the body and blood of Christ. It is in this spirit we must read these ancient authors. The real question between us is whether any one single Father of the Church for the first five centuries ever alluded to a *change of substance of the bread and wine* as now taught by the Roman Church. We in vain search for any such passages in the several quotations given as from

---

* By the way, we may note in passing that Priests alone can offer this so-called "Sacrifice," and their being in *mortal* sin does not, they tell us, vitiate their exceptional Sacerdotal powers, nor alter the efficacy of the Sacrament!

Augustine. Among those given* they have quoted as orthodox the passage wherein Augustine referred to the Israelites eating the same *spiritual* meat as Christians, which sentiment, we have seen, was condemned as heretical! (See *ante*, p. 15.)

The passage referring to David's feigned madness, "that he bore himself in his own hands" (vol. ii. p. 337), and that Augustine applied this to Christ at the Last Supper, is also quoted. The compilers, however, have the candour to put the original passage in a note, though not the full translation in the text:—" Et ferebatur in manibus suis . . . *quomodo* ferebatur in manibus suis? Quia cum commendaret ipsum corpus suum et sanguinem suum, accepit in manus quod norunt fideles: et ipse se portabat *quodam modo* cum diceret 'Hoc est corpus meum.'" Augustine does not say that our Lord did *really* carry His own body in His own hand, but only *after a certain manner.* The proposition sought to be established is truly too ridiculous. Augustine's theory was that signs of things represent the things signified. The bread and wine represented a *type* or *figure* of His body and blood, and, therefore, *after a certain manner*, that is, typically or allegorically, He bore Himself in His own hands. Nothing more can be made of this passage. We may rest assured, as is the fact, that the compilers have omitted the striking passages I have quoted:—"You shall not eat this body which you see, nor drink this blood which they shall shed, that will crucify Me. I have commanded a certain sacrament unto you, *that being spiritually understood*, will quicken you. Although it is needful that this be visibly celebrated, *yet it must be spiritually understood.*" Nor, indeed, do we find any of the other important passages on this subject which I have quoted—a clear indication that Augustine's doctrines are not accepted as "the Faith of Catholics" of the present day.

Communion in One Kind (vol. ii. p. 389). We have not one single quotation from the works of Augustine to sanction the refusal of the cup to the laity. The fact being, whenever Augustine mentions the Sacrament, he invariably couples the two—bread and wine—body and blood—in one sentence. Indeed, we have seen that when Augustine says that the *bread* and *wine* are to be administered to infants he is censured. (*Ante*, p. 25, No. 73.)

Sacrifice of the Mass. There is a fallacy which runs through the entire chapter under this heading with reference to Augustine. Wherever the word *Sacrifice* is used it is attributed to the Sacrifice of the Mass; and several times we are referred to Augustine's allusion to the "Clean Sacrifice" offered up by the Priests "according to the order of Melchisedeck," foretold by the Prophet Malachi (i., ii.). This, they state, has reference to their Sacrifice

---

* Vol. i. p. 333; vol. ii. p. 33.

of the Mass. But Augustine distinctly tells us that "by the daily sacrifice spoken of by the Prophet Malachi are meant *the prayers and praises of the Saints*."* This is the same interpretation as given by Justin Martyr, Clement of Alexandria, Eusebius, Hilary, and Chrysostom.† This interpretation we take to be a key to the other references when a Christian Sacrifice is alluded to. I have already noted the important fact that the present Service of the Mass is very different from that which was used by the Church in the days of Augustine, particularly in the notable additions, in, especially that part of the Service which is now esteemed its very essence, namely, its propitiatory character, by offering up the *unconsecrated* elements.‡ And, what is more to the point, I have noted the blundering manner in which they have placed the five prayers offering up the elements as a propitiatory sacrifice *before* the act of consecration, and, therefore, the bare unconsecrated elements, simply *bread* and *wine*, are offered up in the Roman Mass as a propitiatory Sacrifice.

But this by the way. We have, of course, recorded the request of Monnica, Augustine's mother, to her son, "to remember her at the altar of the Lord," and that Augustine informs us that "the sacrifice of ransom was offered up for her." I have already given my views on this incident. They may or may not be correct, but it is very probable that the mourners partook of the Sacrament after the burial ceremony, when they offered up their *prayers* and *praises* according to the custom of the period. Nothing more can be gathered from these extracts, certainly not that Augustine believed in the propitiatory character of the ceremonies.

Penance.§ It may be taken for granted that we do not find in the "Faith of Catholics" any patristic authority for the complicated ecclesiastical machinery for getting rid of our sins and *eternal* and *temporal* punishments, as laid down in their so called Sacrament of "Penance." We have no mention of *Attrition, Confession, Absolution*, and *Satisfaction* under this head as parts of the so-called Sacrament, or that the latter, "*Satisfaction*," is wiped out by Indulgences, Purgatory, or the Mass, or by proxy! We have under this head but one passage from Augustine.‖ This passage refers to the early custom of doing penances, as a discipline prescribed by the Church; but there is no reference to previous confession to a Priest or to the other appointed forms.

* Lib. ii. Cont. Lit., c. 86, p. 272, Tom. ix. Paris, 1688.
† Justin Martyr, Dialog. cum Tryph., p. 219. London, 1722. Clement. Alexand. Strom., Lib. viii. Oper., p. 728, Eusebius, says that the prayers of believers are the unbloody and reasonable sacrifice. De Laud. Const. Orat., p. 659; Demonst. Evang., Lib. i. c. 8; De Vit. Const., Lib. iv. c. 45; Hilary, in Pslm. cxl, Oper., p. 330; Chrysostom, Hom. xi. on Heb. vi.
‡ See *ante*, p. 82.
§ Vol. iii. p. 2. "Faith of Catholics," 1846.
‖ Vol. iii. p. 33. *Ibid.*

On Confession. There are eighteen quotations as from Augustine. Not only does not one of them mention private confession to a Priest, but they all point to a confession to God. "Hope in the Lord, for I will still confess TO HIM," is the recommendation of every single direction as to confession. We do not find among these extracts Augustine's direct repudiation of confession to his fellow-man.* And as to *Satisfaction*, all they can tell us is that Augustine exclaimed:—"A sacrifice to God is a contrite spirit; a contrite heart God does not despise." But we fail to see in all this the instrumentality of the Priest or a Sacrament!

On Indulgences Augustine is judiciously passed over in silence!†

Purgatory. By the usual artifice this subject is coupled with *prayers for the dead*, an admittedly ancient custom, but, as we have seen, Augustine had no fixed notions as to this third state, and those passages expressing his doubts on the subject are characteristically omitted.‡

On Extreme Unction. We have here again no reference to Augustine!§

Orders.‖ There is one only reference from Augustine on "Orders," and that is on a Donatist Priest "going over to the Church from their party," Augustine adds:—"And when it is judged expedient for the Church that such Prelates, in returning to Catholic fellowship should not exercise therein their hands, the Sacraments themselves of ordination are not taken away from them, but remain with them."¶ But as Augustine referred to many other ceremonies, even signing with the Cross, as Sacraments, this cannot be cited as any evidence that "Orders" were held by him as a Sacrament, such as Baptism and the Lord's Supper, otherwise he would have mentioned "Orders" specially with those two. Although "Orders" was not authoritatively declared to be a Sacrament until A.D. 1439, by the Council of Florence, it is not at all to be wondered at that a Priest should attach great importance to his own office, and even impart to it a Sacramental character, though it will be difficult for them to state when such a Sacrament was ordained by Christ, a necessary antecedent to be proved.

On Celibacy of the Clergy. Here Augustine is again silent!**

On Images.†† Not one of the numerous passages in condemnation of the use of images in religious exercises is given, nor is there a single passage quoted from Augustine's works on this important subject, although the present Roman Creed makes the use of images in religious worship imperative, especially in Churches!

Invocation of Angels and Saints.‡‡ On this we have thirteen passages quoted; all, save one, refer to the departed praying *for*

---

* See *ante*, p. 94. † Vol. iii. p. 131. ‡ Vol. iii. p. 140.
§ Vol. iii. p. 208. ‖ Vol. iii. p. 213. ¶ Vol. iii. p. 225.
** Vol. iii. p. 233. †† Vol. iii. p. 317. ‡‡ Vol. iii. p. 322.

those on earth. Even in this view Augustine expresses a doubt.*
" The question is indeed a great one, not to be discussed at present
. . . whether, or how far, or in what way, the spirits of the dead
know the things which happen in our regard." That is a very
different question from praying *to* them for their help and assistance,
and our pleading their supposed superabundant merits on our
behalf. True, the compilers cite the case alleged to be recorded by
Augustine (p. 377), of " a certain woman, who seeing that her child
was dead and irreparably lost," ran with the dead body to a place
dedicated to "the blessed Martyr Stephen, and began demanding
her son from him," and to " restore her son." And accordingly we
are told that her son came to life! Well! if such was the genuine
production of Augustine, all we can add is, that it is very different
from his other sentiments expressed on the subject of prayers; and I
venture to assert that no lay Roman Catholic of the present day will
believe that such a circumstance ever took place. Modern Romanists
under similar circumstances, if they offered up any prayer at all,
would invoke the Virgin Mary, not Stephen!

It is evident that the compilers of Patristic authority, purported to
be collected in their commonplace book of the Fathers, "The
Faith of Catholics," have utterly failed to vindicate Rome's peculiar
dogmas, as having received any sanction from the writings of Augustine. The genuine works of Augustine are triumphantly cleared of
all taint of Romanism. Augustine nowhere acknowledged the
Supremacy or Infallibility of the Bishop of Rome. He proclaimed
the Canonical Scriptures as his sole guide in matters of faith,
rejecting the Apocrypha from the Sacred Canon. There is no
trace in his writings of the modern theological enigma passing under
the name of "Transubstantiation," nor of the worship of the consecrated elements, nor of any propitiatory character in the celebration of the Lord's Supper. He nowhere maintained Sacerdotal
Sacramentalism, the essence of Rome's present theological system.
Sacramental Confession and Priestly Absolution were formally rejected
by him. The theory of Purgatory, though then germinating, was
not developed until many years after Augustine's day, and the use
and application of Indulgences were unknown to him. His teaching
on the doctrine of Justification and Meritorious Works has been
formally repudiated, and he knew nothing of Works of Supererogation
and the bank of " Celestial Treasure," forming an alleged inexhaustible fund of superabundant merits of departed Saints, nor of
their application for the relief of others. He recognised one sole
Mediator between God and Man, CHRIST JESUS. The Invocation
of Saints, and use of Images in religious worship, were practices
wholly foreign to his system of Theology. And Rome's Immaculate

---

* Vol. iii. p. 374. "Faith of Catholics," 1846.

Virgin, though held by Augustine as a being highly favoured, was, in his estimation, like every other son or daughter of Adam, a being born in sin.

In fact Rome has built up for herself a system of her own, a Sacerdotal Sacramental system, by which the PRIEST is made the instrument of salvation through the Sacraments, and the Mother of Christ's humanity is raised to the rank of a Goddess in heaven, " as the only hope of sinners," " for to her," they tell us, " belongs dominion and power," " the Eternal Father having given the office of *judge and avenger* to the Son, and that of showing *mercy* and *relieving the necessitous* to the Mother;" and " AT THE COMMAND OF MARY ALL OBEY, EVEN GOD."*

CONCLUSION.

HAVING thus carefully and critically examined every important passage in the works of Augustine, which bears in any way on the doctrines and teachings of the Roman Church, as now professed in her Creed, we cannot sufficiently admire the boldness of professors of that system of worship when they claim Augustine as a Doctor and canonized Saint of their Church, whose teaching is to be followed in approaching our God in prayer, and whose example is placed before us as to the manner and means of obtaining salvation.

For a striking example of the more modern appeal to Augustine, in the manner above indicated, I cannot better conclude than by quoting the words of Cardinal Focaccetti, Bishop of Lystra, in his " Apostolic Notification," issued 12th June, 1873, on the occasion of the success attending the Evangelical Mission of Signor Borelli, in Italy. In this document he appeals to Augustine as proof that there is only one Church, out of which there can be no salvation, and that one Church is exclusively *the* Church over which the Bishop of Rome presides. After lamenting the spread of what he is pleased to designate as heresy, that is the preaching of the pure Gospel of Christ, the Cardinal proceeds as follows:—

"My sons, be on your guard, and take care that no one come and ensnare you with foolish discourses. By the grace of God, you belong to the only true Church of Jesus Christ,—the holy, Catholic, Apostolic, Roman Church; and whosoever shall try to separate you therefrom, is not only a deceiver, but a vile satellite of Antichrist. The Apostle Paul declared to the Galatians, 'If an angel from

---

* Cardinal Manning's Edition of Liguori's " Glories of Mary," pp. 102, 12, 14, 115. London, 1868.

heaven came and preached any other Gospel to you than that which we have preached unto you, let him be accursed!' *Now the doctrine preached to the world by Paul himself and the other Apostles, is the same as that inviolably transmitted to us through the Infallible Ruler of the Church;* and whosoever shall gainsay it is a heretic. Because, as says the same Apostle, 'There is one Lord, one faith, one baptism': therefore, as the great AUGUSTINE explains it, there is one incorruptible Catholic Church, out of which there is no salvation. Bear always in mind that he who attacks the Church, attacks its visible head, the Roman Pontifex Maximus, for *ubi Petrus, ibi Ecclesia* [where Peter is, there is the Church]; and the edifice cannot be separated from the foundation on which it is based. Wherefore, he who shall endeavour to withdraw you from submission to the Vicar of Jesus Christ, intends to seduce you to schism and heresy; and thereby not only exposes you in every way to the most cruel shame, but will plunge you into the abyss of unbelief and eternal perdition."

If it were possible for Augustine to return to this earth, with what astonishment would he behold the Roman Priesthood of the present day, in witnessing their eccentric ceremonies and complicated services, their vestments, lights, incense, images; and, on listening to their strange doctrines, he would assuredly exclaim, "Who are ye? I know not whence ye are"!

APPENDICES.

APPENDIX A. (P. 124.)

From Augustine's "City of God," Book xxii. c. viii. pp. 882-890. Lud. Vives' Translation. London, 1610.

1. A blind man obtained his sight at the shrine of two Martyrs:— "Their bodies lay long unknown until Ambrose the Bishop had notice of them by relation in a dream."

2. Innocentius was operated on for fistula. Two painful but unsuccessful operations had been made. Another skilled surgeon was called in. The patient was visited by "Holy Men," who prayed with him. They advised him "to trust in God and be patient." After prayers the Bishop gave a blessing. The next day they returned with the surgeon. When, however, the third operation was about to be performed, lo! they found the patient already cured.

3. A devout woman had a cancer in her breast, which was pronounced incurable. She was advised to have the parts cut away. She prayed; and in a dream she was told at Easter, then close on, she would meet with a woman at the Baptismal font, and that she should entreat that woman to sign her with the sign of the cross. She acted up to her instructions, and was cured. However, Augustine tells us that when he inquired about this alleged miracle, none of her fellow-matrons had heard of it!

4. A physician, troubled with the gout, gave in his name to be baptized. The night before he was forbidden "by a crew of curly-headed negro boys, whom he knew to be devils, but he refusing to obey them, they stamped on his feet so that he was put to extreme pain"; nevertheless, he was baptized next day, and was cured of the gout.

5. Another was freed of palsy by baptism.

6. A captain was haunted by evil spirits. A priest "prayed with him and he was cured. Now he had a little of the earth whereon the Sepulchre of Christ standeth, bestowed on him by a friend, which he had hung up in his chamber for the better avoidance of these wicked illusions from his own person."

7. Another case of palsy cured by prayer.

8. A young man was brought to a martyr's memorial possessed with the devil. He was aroused from a stupor by women singing psalms. He woke up in a fright and seized hold of the altar, whereupon "the devil within him began mournfully to cry for mercy,

relating how he entered the man, and how he would leave him. He named the parts of him he would spoil at his departure; so saying these words he departed. But one of the young man's eyes fell down on his cheek, and hung only by a little string." The people helped him with their prayers. They advised a surgeon, but "his sister's husband said that God, who had delivered him from the devil, had power to restore his eye." He replaced the eye, bound it up, and the young man was cured.

9. A virgin was freed from the devil which possessed her "only by anointing with oil mixed with the tears of the Priest that prayed for her."

10. A Bishop is said to have ejected the devil from a youth he had never seen.

11. "A poor and godly man," a cobbler, lost his upper garment, and not being able to buy another he came to the shrine of the "Twenty Martyrs," and prayed to them to "help him to regarments," where he was jeered by the street boys. He afterwards "spied a great fish newly cast up by the sea." This he took "to a cook, a good Christian," and sold the fish to him "for 300 halfpence, intending to buy wool for his wife to spin a garment for him." The cook, cutting up the fish, "found a ring of gold in its belly which amazed him; his conscience made him send for the poor man, and gave him the ring, saying to him, 'Behold how the Twenty Martyrs have apparelled you!'"

12. A Bishop carrying the reliques of Saint Stephen, among the people who flocked to see them was a blind woman, who recovered her sight by having flowers, given her by the same Bishop, which she applied to her eyes.

13. Another Bishop also bearing the reliques was absolutely cured of fistula.

14. Another was cured of stone by the same reliques. Being laid out for dead of another disease, he was brought to the shrine of Stephen and was restored to life.

15. A certain "son-in-law" at the shrine of Stephen prayed "with showers of tears and storms of religious sighs" for the conversion of his father-in-law. He took some of the flowers from the shrine of Stephen, and laid them on his father-in-law's head while asleep; when he awoke he believed, and, to the amazement of all, was baptized."

16. Two others were cured of the gout at the same shrine.

17. A child, run over by a cart, and so crushed as to pass all hope of recovery, was made whole on being presented at the shrine of St. Stephen.

18. A woman sick, past recovery, had her garments sent to the same shrine; before they were brought back she died. The parents covered her with the garments, and she came to life.

19, 20, 21. A similar case is recorded of one Bassus, and one Irenus; and the son of one Elusius was brought to life by being taken to the same shrine. And here Augustine is made to excuse himself for being tedious, and adds that he might fill volumes with the narration of all the miracles done at the shrine of St. Stephen. He adds, that although the shrine had been there only two years, "there are almost seventy volumes written of those that have been recorded since that time to this." But at Calama, he says, "the shrine is more ancient, the miracles more often, and the books far more in number," and regrets that a more careful record is not made of these facts.

22. Another case was so extraordinary that he feels himself forced to relate it. Under the advice of a Jew, a noble woman who had found a ring, in which was a peculiar stone, from the inside of an ox, sewed it in a girdle of hair, which she was told she must wear next to her skin. Thus arrayed, she visited the Martyr's shrine. On her way, however, "she spied the ring lie at her feet," notwithstanding she felt the ring in her girdle. "She took this as a good presage of her recovery, and loosing her girdle she cast both it and the ring into the river." She was accordingly cured of her disease. "Now they that will not believe that Jesus Christ was born without interruption of the virginal parts, nor passed in to his Apostles when the doors were shut, neither will they believe this." Augustine is then made to admit that these miracles are not so famous as those wrought by God!

23. But he cannot resist, he says, mentioning one other case. There were seven sons and three daughters of noble parents. The father died. The children gave cause of anger to the mother, whereupon she cursed them. "They were all taken with horrible trembling of all their whole bodies." They were dispersed. Two came to the shrine of Stephen and were cured.

I have given every single case recorded in this chapter. There are two remarkable facts to be noted. The first is that Augustine himself does not seem to have personally witnessed any of these so-called miracles, and, secondly, the *Virgin Mary* does not appear to have been an agent in any of them, contrary to the practice of more modern times.

Ludovicus Vives, who has elaborately illustrated this work with notes, says:—" There are many additions in that chapter (chap. 8, book 22), without question, foisted in by such as make practice of depraving authors of great authority."

If, however, this chapter is a genuine production of the pen of Augustine, which I cannot bring myself to believe, it will be a striking example how a mind so gifted as was Augustine's can nevertheless have a strange corner in it—superstition and religion being often too nearly allied. It is a blemish which we must lament—

> " Since the more fair and crystal is the sky,
> The uglier seem the clouds that in it fly."

I will, however, venture to assert that there is not one educated Romanist of the present day who will give credence to any of these " old wives' fables."

APPENDIX B. (P. 126.)

(Extracted from the Romish Magazine, "The Rambler.")

"The Church has persecuted, and on principle—there is no denying the fact;—but the principle is one of policy and prudence, not of dogma, and in the present state of the world, she rarely acts upon it; not that, in itself, the principle is indefensible even on modern grounds, for the punishment of a religious offence by *imprisonment and* DEATH is in itself no more incompatible with reason, or with the Christian spirit, than the infliction of the same punishment on the thief and murderer."—*Jan.*, 1854; p. 2.

"For our own selves, we are prepared to maintain that it is no more morally wrong to put a man to death for *heresy* than for *murder!*—that in many cases *persecution* for *religious opinions* is not only permissible, but highly advisable and necessary."—*June*, 1849.

"It is difficult to say in which of the two popular expressions—'the rights of *civil* liberty,' or 'the rights of *religious* liberty'—is embodied the greatest amount of nonsense and falsehood. As these phrases are perpetually uttered both by Protestants and by some Catholics, they contain about as much truth and good sense as would be found in a cry for the inalienable right to suicide. * * * Let this pass, then, in the case of Protestants and politicians. But how can it be justified in the case of Catholics, who are the children of a Church which has ever avowed the deepest hostility to the *principle* of '*religious liberty*,' and which never has given the shadow of a sanction to the theory that 'civil liberty,' as such, is *necessarily* a blessing at all? How intolerable is it to see this miserable device for deceiving the Protestant world still so widely popular amongst us! * * * Believe us not, Protestants of England and Ireland, for an instant, when you see us pouring forth our liberalisms. When you hear a Catholic orator at some public assemblage declaring solemnly that 'this is the most humiliating day in his life when he is called upon to defend once more the glorious principle of *religious freedom*—(especially if he says anything about the Emancipation Act, and the 'toleration' it *conceded* to Catholics)—be not too simple in your credulity. These are brave words, but they mean nothing. No; nothing more than the promises of a Parliamentary candidate to his constituents on the hustings. * * * Shall I, therefore, fall in with this abominable delusion. * * * Shall I foster that damnable doctrine that Socinianism, and Calvinism, and Anglicanism, and Judaism are not every one of them mortal sins, like MURDER and ADULTERY? Shall I lend my countenance to this unhappy persuasion of my brother, that he is not flying in the face of ALMIGHTY GOD every day that he remains a Protestant? Shall I hold out hopes to him that I will not meddle with his creed, if he will not meddle with mine? Shall I lead him to think that religion is a matter for private opinion, and tempt him to forget that *he has no more right to his religious views than he has to my purse, or to my house, or my life-blood?* No! Catholicism is the most intolerant of creeds. It is intolerance itself, for it is truth itself. We might as rationally maintain that a sane man has a right to believe that two and two do not make four, as this theory of *religious liberty*. Its impiety is only equalled by its absurdity."—*Sept.*, 1851.

WORKS BY MR. C. H. COLLETTE.

MONSIG. CAPEL ON ANGLICAN ORDERS:

"A ROLAND FOR AN OLIVER."

Price 1s.

THE ROMAN BREVIARY;

A

CRITICAL AND HISTORICAL REVIEW,

WITH

COPIOUS CLASSIFIED EXTRACTS.

SECOND EDITION, REVISED AND ENLARGED.

Per ambages et ministeria deorum
Præcipitandus est liber spiritus.—PETRON.

By Fable's aid ungovern'd fancy soars,
And claims the ministry of heavenly powers.

Price 5s.

LONDON:
W. H. ALLEN & CO., 13, WATERLOO PLACE, S.W.

April, 1882.

BOOKS, &c.,

ISSUED BY

MESSRS. W. H. ALLEN & Co.,

Publishers & Literary Agents to the India Office,

COMPRISING

MISCELLANEOUS PUBLICATIONS IN GENERAL LITERATURE.

DICTIONARIES, GRAMMARS, AND TEXT BOOKS IN EASTERN LANGUAGES.

MILITARY WORKS, INCLUDING THOSE ISSUED BY THE GOVERNMENT.

INDIAN AND MILITARY LAW.

MAPS OF INDIA, &c.

13, WATERLOO PLACE, LONDON, S.W.

Works issued from the India Office, and Sold by Wm. H. ALLEN & Co.

Tree and Serpent Worship;
Or, Illustrations of Mythology and Art in India in the First and Fourth Centuries after Christ, from the Sculptures of the Buddhist Topes at Sanchi and Amravati. Prepared at the India Museum, under the authority of the Secretary of State for India in Council. Second edition, Revised, Corrected, and in great part Re-written. By JAMES FERGUSSON, Esq , F.R.S.. F.R.A.S. Super-royal 4to. 100 plates and 31 engravings, pp. 270. Price £5 5s.

Illustrations of Ancient Buildings in Kashmir.
Prepared at the Indian Museum under the authority of the Secretary of State for India in Council. From Photographs, Plans, and Drawings taken by Order of the Government of India. By HENRY HARDY COLE, LIEUT. R.E., Superintendent Archæological Survey of India, North-West Provinces. In One vol.; half-bound, Quarto. Fifty-eight plates. £3 10s.

The Illustrations in this work have been produced in Carbon from the original negatives, and are therefore permanent.

Pharmacopœia of India.
Prepared under the Authority of the Secretary of State for India. By EDWARD JOHN WARING, M.D. Assisted by a Committee appointed for the Purpose. 8vo. 6s.

The Stupa of Bharhut. A Buddhist Monument.
Ornamented with numerous Sculptures illustrative of Buddhist Legend and History in the Third Century B.C. By ALEXANDER CUNNINGHAM. C.S.I., C.I.E., Major-General, Royal Engineers (Bengal Retired); Director-General Archæological Survey of India. 4to. Fifty-seven Plates. Cloth gilt. £3 3s.

Archælogical Survey of Western India.
Report of the First Season's Operations in the Belgâm and Kaladgi Districts. January to May, 1874 Prepared at the India Museum and Published under the Authority of the Secretary of State for India in Council. By JAMES BURGESS, Author of the "Rock Temples of Elephanta," &c , &c., and Editor of "The Indian Antiquary." Half-bound Quarto. 58 Plates and Woodcuts. £2 2s.

Archæological Survey of Western India. Vol. II.
Report on the Antiquities of Kâthiâwâd and Kachh, being the result of the Second Season's Operations of the Archæological Survey of Western India. 1874-75. By JAMES BURGESS, F.R.G S , M.R.A.S., &c., Archæological Surveyor and Reporter to Government, Western India. 1876. Half-bound. Quarto. Seventy-four Plates and Woodcuts. £3 3s.

Archæological Survey of Western India. Vol. III.
Report on the Antiquities in the Bidar and Aurungabad Districts in the Territory of H.H. the Nizam of Haidarabad, being the result of the Third Season's Operations of the Archæological Survey of Western India. 1875-1876. By JAMES BURGESS, F.R.G.S., M.R.A.S., Membre de la Societé Asiatique, &c., Archæological Surveyor and Reporter to Government, Western India. Half-bound. Quarto. Sixty six Plates and Woodcuts. £2 2s.

Illustrations of Buildings near Muttra and Agra,
Showing the Mixed Hindu-Mahomedan Style of Upper India Prepared at the India Museum under the authority of the Secretary of State for India in Council, from Photographs, Plans, and Drawings taken by Order of the Government of India. By HENRY HARDY COLE, Lieut. R.E., late Superintendent Archæological Survey of India, North West Provinces 4to. With Photographs and Plates. £3 10s.

The Cave Temples of India.
By JAMES FERGUSON, D.C.L., F.R.A.S., V.P.R A.S,, and JAMES BURGESS, F.R.G.S., M.R.A.S., &c. Printed nd Published by Order of Her Majesty's Secretary of State, &c. Royal 8vo. With Photographs and Woodcuts. £2 2s.

Aberigh-Mackay (G.) Twenty-one Days in India.
Being the Tour of Sir ALI BABA, K.C.B. By GEORGE
ABERIGH-MACKAY. Post 8vo. 4s.

Adam W. (late of Calcutta) Theories of History.
An Inquiry into the Theories of History,—Chance,—Law,—
Will. With Special Reference to the Principle of Positive
Philosophy. By WILLIAM ADAM. 8vo. 15s.

Æsop, the Fables of, and other Eminent Mythologists.
With Morals and Reflections. By Sir ROGER L'ESTRANGE, kt.
A facsimile reprint of the Edition of 1669. Folio, antique,
sheep. 21s.

Akbar. An Eastern Romance
By Dr. P. A. S. VAN LIMBURG-BROUWER. Translated from
the Dutch by M. M. With Notes and Introductory Life of
the Emperor Akbar, by CLEMENTS R. MARKHAM, C.B., F.R.S.
Crown 8vo. 10s. 6d.

Alberg (A.) Snowdrops: Idylls for Children.
From the Swedish of Zach Topelius. By ALBERT ALBERG,
Author of "Whisperings in the Wood." 3s. 6d.

—— **Whisperings in the Wood**: Finland Idylls for Children.
From the Swedish of Zach Topelius. By ALBERT ALBERG,
Author of "Fabled Stories from the Zoo," and Editor of
"Chit-Chat by Puck," "Rose Leaves," and "Woodland
Notes." 3s. 6d.

Allen's Series.
1.—Ansted's World We Live In. 2s.
2.—Ansted's Earth's History. 2s.
3.—Ansted's 2000 Examination Questions in Physical Geography. 2s.
4.—Geography of India. (See page 10.) 2s.
5.—Ansted's Elements of Physiography. 1s. 4d.
6.—Hall's Trigonometry. (See page 11.) 2s.
7.—Wollaston's Elementary Indian Reader. 1s. (See p. 36.)

Ameer Ali. The Personal Law of the Mahommedans (according to all the Schools). Together with a Comparative
Sketch of the Law of Inheritance among the Sunnis and
Shiahs. By SYED AMEER ALI, Moulvi, M.A., LL.B., Barrister-
at-Law, and Presidency Magistrate at Calcutta. 8vo. 15s.

Anderson (Ed. L.) How to Ride and School a Horse.
With a System of Horse Gymnastics. By EDWARD L.
ANDERSON. Cr. 8vo. 2s. 6d.

Anderson (P.) The English in Western India. 8vo. 14s.

Anderson (T.) History of Shorthand.
With an analysis and review of its present condition and prospects at Home and Abroad. By THOMAS ANDERSON, Parliamentary Reporter, &c. With Portraits. Crown 8vo. 12s. 6d.

Andrew (W. P.) India and Her Neighbours.
By W. P. ANDREW, Author of "Our Scientific Frontier," "The Indus and Its Provinces," "Memoir of the Euphrates Route." With Two Maps. 8vo. 15s.

—— **Our Scientific Frontier.**
With Sketch-Map and Appendix. 8vo. 6s.

Ansted (D. T.) Physical Geography.
By Professor D. T. ANSTED, M.A., F.R.S., &c. Fifth Edition. Post 8vo., with Illustrative Maps. 7s.
CONTENTS:—PART I.—INTRODUCTION.—The Earth as a Planet.—Physical Forces.—The Succession of Rocks. PART II.—EARTH—Land.—Mountains.—Hills and Valleys.—Plateaux and Low Plains. PART III.—WATER.—The Ocean.—Rivers.—Lakes and Waterfalls.—The Phenomena of Ice.—Springs PART IV.—AIR.—The Atmosphere. Winds and Storms.—Dew, Clouds, and Rain.—Climate and Weather. PART V.—FIRE.—Volcanoes and Volcanic Phenomena.—Earthquakes. PART VI.—LIFE.—The Distribution of Plants in the different Countries of the Earth.—The Distribution of Animals on the Earth.—The Distribution of Plants and Animals in Time.—Effects of Human Agency on Inanimate Nature.

"The Book is both valuable and comprehensive, and deserves a wide circulation."—*Observer.*

—— **Elements of Physiography.**
For the use of Science Schools. Fcap. 8vo. 1s. 4d.

—— **and Latham (R. G.) Channel Islands. Jersey, Guernsey,** Alderney, Sark, &c.
THE CHANNEL ISLANDS. Containing: PART I.—Physical Geography. PART II.—Natural History. PART III.—Civil History. PART IV.—Economics and Trade. By DAVID THOMAS ANSTED, M.A., F.R.S., and ROBERT GORDON LATHAM, M.A., M.D., F.R.S. New and Cheaper Edition in one handsome 8vo. Volume, with 72 Illustrations on Wood by Vizetelly, Loudon, Nicholls, and Hart; with Map. 8vo. 16s.

"This is a really valuable work. A book which will long remain the standard authority on the subject. No one who has been to the Channel Islands, or who purposes going there will be insensible of its value."—*Saturday Review.*

"It is the produce of many hands and every hand a good one."

Ansted (D. T.) The World We Live In.
Or First Lessons in Physical Geography. For the use of Schools and Students. By D. T. ANSTED, M.A., F.R S., &c. Fcap 2s. 25th Thousand, with Illustrations.

—— **The Earth's History.**
Or, First Lessons in Geology. For the use of Schools and Students. By D. T. ANSTED. Third Thousand. Fcap. 2s.

—— **Two Thousand Examination Questions** in Physical Geography. pp. 180. Price 2s.

—— **Water, and Water Supply.**
Chiefly with reference to the British Islands. Part I.— Surface Waters. 8vo. With Maps. 18s.

Archer (Capt. J. H. Laurence) Commentaries on the Punjaub Campaign—1848-49, including some additions to the History of the Second Sikh War, from original sources. By Capt. J. H. LAWRENCE-ARCHER, Bengal H. P. Cr. 8vo. 8s.

Army and Navy Calendar for the Financial Year 1882-83.
Being a Compendium of General Information relating to the Army, Navy, Militia, and Volunteers, and containing Maps, Plans, Tabulated Statements, Abstracts, &c. Compiled from authentic sources 2s. 6d.

Army and Navy Magazine.
Vols. I. and II. are issued, each containing Six Cabinet Photographs of Celebrated Officers. Volumes 7s. 6d. each.

Aynsley (Mrs.) Our Visit to Hindustan, Kashmir, and Ladakh.
By Mrs. J. C. MURRAY AYNSLEY. 8vo 14s.

Bellew (Capt.) Memoirs of a Griffin; or, A Cadet's First Year in India. By Captain BELLEW. Illustrated from Designs by the Author. A New Edition. Cr. 8vo. 10s. 6d.

Bernay (Dr. A. J.) Students' Chemistry.
Being the Seventh Edition of Household Chemistry, or the Science of Home Life. By ALBERT J. BERNAYS, PH. DR. F.C.S., Prof. of Chemistry and Practical Chemistry at St. Thomas' Hospital, Medical, and Surgical College. Crown 8vo. 5s. 6d.

Blanchard (S.) Yesterday and To-day in India.
By SIDNEY LAMAN BLANCHARD. Post 8vo. 6s.

CONTENTS.—Outward Bound.—The Old Times and the New.—Domestic Life.—Houses and Bungalows.—Indian Servants.—The Great Shoe Question.—The Garrison Hack.—The Long Bow in India.—Mrs. Dulcimer's Shipwreck.—A Traveller's Tale, told in a Dark Bungalow.—Punch in India.—Anglo-Indian Literature.—Christmas in India.—The Seasons in Calcutta.—Farmers in Muslin.—Homeward Bound.—India as it Is.

Blenkinsopp (Rev. E. L.) Doctrine of Development in the Bible and in the Church. By REV. E. L. BLENKINSOPP, M.A., Rector of Springthorp. 2nd edition. 12mo. 6s.

Boileau (Major-General J. T.)
A New and Complete Set of Traverse Tables, showing the Differences of Latitude and the Departures to every Minute of the Quadrant and to Five Places of Decimals. Together with a Table of the lengths of each Degree of Latitude and corresponding Degree of Longitude from the Equator to the Poles; with other Tables useful to the Surveyor and Engineer. Fourth Edition, thoroughly revised and corrected by the Author. Royal 8vo. 12s. London, 1876.

Boulger (D. C.) History of China. By DEMETRIUS CHARLES BOULGER, Author of "England and Russia in Central Asia," &c. 8vo. vol. I. With Portrait. 18s. Vol. II. 18s.

—— **England and Russia in Central Asia.** With Appendices and Two Maps, one being the latest Russian Official Map of Central Asia. 2 vols. 8vo. 36s.

—— **Central Asian Portraits;** or the Celebrities of the Khanates and the Neighbouring States. By DEMETRIUS CHARLES BOULGER, M.R.A.S. Crown 8vo. 7s. 6d.

—— **The Life of Yakoob Beg,** Athalik Ghazi and Badaulet, Ameer of Kashgar. By DEMETRIUS CHARLES BOULGER, M R.A.S. 8vo. With Map and Appendix. 16s.

Bowring (Sir J.) Flowery Scroll.
A Chinese Novel. Translated and Illustrated with Notes by SIR J. BOWRING, late H.B.M. Plenipo. China. Post 8vo. 10s. 6d.

Boyd (R. Nelson) Chili and the Chilians, during the War 1879-80. By R. NELSON BOYD, F.R.G.S., F.G.S., Author of Coal Mines Inspection. Cloth, Illustrated. Cr. 8vo. 10s. 6d.

—— **Coal Mines Inspection:** Its History and Results. 8vo. 14s.

Bradshaw (John) The Poetical Works of John Milton, with Notes, explanatory and philological. By JOHN BRADSHAW, LL.D., Inspector of Schools, Madras. 2 vols., post 8vo. 12s. 6d

Brandis' Forest Flora of North-Western and Central India. By DR. BRANDIS, Inspector General of Forests to the Government of India. Text and Plates. £2 18s.

Briggs (Gen. J.) India and Europe Compared.
Post 8vo. 7s.

Bright (W.) Red Book for Sergeants.
Fifth and Revised Edition, 1880. By W. BRIGHT, late Colour-Sergeant, 19th Middlesex R.V. Fcap. interleaved. 1s.

Browne (J. W.) Hardware; How to Buy it for Foreign Markets. 8vo. 10s. 6d.

Buckle (the late Capt. E.) Bengal Artillery.
A Memoir of the Services of the Bengal Artillery from the formation of the Corps. By the late CAPT. E. BUCKLE, Assist.-Adjut. Gen. Ben. Art. Edit. by SIR J. W. KAYE. 8vo. Lond, 1852. 10s.

Buckley (R. B.) The Irrigation Works of India, and their Financial Results. Being a brief History and Description of the Irrigation Works of India, and of the Profits and Losses they have caused to the State. By ROBERT B. BUCKLEY, A M.I.C.E., Executive Engineer of the Public Works Department of India. 8vo. With Map and Appendix. 9s.

Burke (P.) Celebrated Naval and Military Trials.
By PETER BURKE, Serjeant-at-Law. Author of "Celebrated Trials connected with the Aristocracy." Post 8vo. 10s. 6d.

By the Tiber.
By the Author of "Signor Monaldini's Niece." 2 vols. 21s.

Carlyle (Thomas), Memoirs of the Life and Writings of,
With Personal Reminiscences and Selections from his Private Letters to numerous Correspondents. Edited by RICHARD HERNE SHEPHERD, Assisted by CHARLES N. WILLIAMSON. 2 Vols. With Portrait and Illustrations. Crown 8vo. 21s.

Challenge of Barletta (The).
By MASSIMO D'AZEGLIO. Rendered into English by Lady LOUISA MAGENIS. 2 vols. Crown 8vo. 21s.

Collette (C. H.) The Roman Breviary.
A Critical and Historical Review, with Copious Classified Extracts. By CHARLES HASTINGS COLLETTE. 2nd Edition. Revised and enlarged. 8vo. 5s.

—— **Henry VIII.**
An Historical Sketch as affecting the Reformation in England. By CHARLES HASTINGS COLLETTE. Post 8vo. 6s.

Colquhoun (Major J. A. S.) With the Kurrum Force in the Caubul Campaign of 1878-79. By Major J. A. S. COLQUHOUN. R.A. With Illustrations from the Author's Drawings, and two Maps. 8vo. 16s.

Cooper's Hill College. Calendar of the Royal Indian Engineering College, Cooper's Hill. Published by authority in January each year. 5s.
CONTENTS.—Staff of the College; Prospectus for the Year; Table of Marks; Syllabus of Course of Study; Leave and Pension Rules of Indian Service; Class and Prize Lists; Past Students serving in India; Entrance Examination Papers, &c.

Corbet (M. E.) A Pleasure Trip to India, during the Visit of H.R.H. the Prince of Wales, and afterwards to Ceylon. By Mrs. CORBET. Illustrated with Photos. Crown 8vo. 7s. 6d.

Crosland (Mrs. N.) Stories of the City of London; Retold for Youthful Readers. By Mrs. NEWTON CROSLAND. With ten Illustrations. Cr. 8vo. 6s.
These Stories range from the early days of Old London Bridge and the Settlement of the Knights Templars in England to the time of the Gordon Riots; with incidents in the Life of Brunel in relation to the Thames Tunnel; narrated from Personal recollections.

Cruise of H.M.S. "Galatea,"
Captain H.R.H. the Duke of Edinburgh, K.G., in 1867—1868. By the REV. JOHN MILNER, B.A., Chaplain; and OSWALD W. BRIERLY. Illustrated by a Photograph of H.R.H. the Duke of Edinburgh; and by Chromo-Lithographs and Graphotypes from Sketches taken on the spot by O. W. BRIERLY. 8vo. 16s.

Cunningham (H. S.) British India, and its Rulers.
By H. S. CUNNINGHAM, M.A., one of the Judges of the High Court of Calcutta, and late Member of the Famine Commission. 10s. 6d.

Daumas (E.) Horses of the Sahara, and the Manners of the Desert. By E. DAUMAS, General of the Division Commanding at Bordeaux, Senator, &c., &c. With Commentaries by the Emir Abd-el-Kadir (Authorized Edition). 8vo. 6s.
"We have rarely read a work giving a more picturesque and, at the same time, practical account of the manners and customs of a people, than this book on the Arabs and their horses."—*Edinburgh Courant.*

Deighton (K.) Shakespeare's King Henry the Fifth.
With Notes and an Introduction. By K. DEIGHTON, Principal of Agra College. Crown 8vo. 5s.

Destruction of Life by Snakes, Hydrophobia, &c., in Western India. By an EX-COMMISSIONER. Fcap. 2s. 6d.

Dickins, (F. V.) Chiushingura: or the Loyal League.
A Japanese Romance. Translated by FREDERICK V. DICKINS, Sc.B., of the Middle Temple, Barrister-at-Law. With Notes

and an Appendix containing a Metrical Version of the Ballad of Takasako, and a specimen of the Original Text in Japanese character. Illustrated by numerous Engravings on Wood, drawn and executed by Japanese artists and printed on Japanese paper. 8vo. 10s. 6d.

Doran (Dr. J.) "Their Majesties Servants":
Annals of the English Stage. Actors, Authors, and Audiences From Thomas Betterton to Edmund Kean. By Dr. DORAN, F.S.A., Author of "Table Traits," "Lives of the Queens of England of the House of Hanover." &c. Post 8vo. 6s.

"Every page of the work is barbed with wit, and will make its way point foremost. . . . . . provides entertainment for the most diverse tastes."—*Daily News.*

Drury (Col. H.) The Useful Plants of India,
With Notices of their chief value in Commerce, Medicine, and the Arts. By COLONEL HEBER DRURY. Second Edition, with Additions and Corrections. Royal 8vo. 16s.

Dwight (H. O.) Turkish Life in War Time.
By HENRY O. DWIGHT. Crown 8vo. 12s.

Edwards (G. Sutherland) A Female Nihilist.
By ERNEST LAVIGNE. Translated from the French by G. SUTHERLAND EDWARDS. Crown 8vo. 9s.

Edwards (H. S.) The Lyrical Drama: Essays on Subjects, Composers, and Executants of Modern Opera. By H. SUTHERLAND EDWARDS, Author of "The Russians at Home and Abroad," &c. Two vols. Crown 8vo. 21s.

—— **The Russians At Home and the Russians Abroad.**
Sketches, Unpolitical and Political, of Russian Life under Alexander II. By H. SUTHERLAND EDWARDS. 2 vols. Crown 8vo. 21s.

Ensor (F. Sydney) Incidents of a Journey through Nubia to Darfoor. By F. SYDNEY ENSOR, C.E. 10s. 6d.

—— **The Queen's Speeches in Parliament.**
Edited by F. SYDNEY ENSOR, Author of "From Nubia to Darfoor." Crown 8vo. 7s. 6d.

Eyre, (Major-General Sir V.), K.C.S.I., C.B. The Kabul Insurrection of 1841-42. Revised and corrected from Lieut. Eyre's Original Manuscript. Edited by Colonel G. B. MALLESON, C.S.I. Crown 8vo., with Map and Illustrations. 9s.

Fearon (A.) Kenneth Trelawny.
By ALEC FEARON. Author of "Touch not the Nettle."
2 vols. Crown 8vo. 21s.

Forbes (Capt. C. J. F. S.) Comparative Grammar of the
Languages of Further India. A Fragment; and other Essays, the Literary Remains of Captain C. J. F. S. FORBES, of the British Burma Commission. Author of "British Burma and its People: Sketches of Native Manners, Customs, and Religion." 6s.

Fraser (Lieut.-Col. G. T.) Records of Sport and Military
Life in Western India. By the late Lieut.-Colonel G. T. Fraser, formerly of the 1st Bombay Fusiliers, and more recently attached to the Staff of H.M.'s Indian Army. With an Introduction by Colonel G. B. MALLESON, C.S.I. 7s. 6d.

Garrick (H. B. W.) Mansukhi and Sundar Singh.
A Hindu Tale. Hindustani and English. With 24 Illustrations. By H. B. W. GARRICK. 4to. 1s. 6d.

Gazetteers of India.
Thornton, 4 vols., 8vo. £2 16s.
,, 8vo. 21s.
,, (N.W.P., &c.) 2 vols., 8vo. 25s.

Gazetteer of Southern India.
With the Tenasserim Provinces and Singapore. Compiled from original and authentic sources. Accompanied by an Atlas, including plans of all the principal towns and cantonments. Royal 8vo. with 4to. Atlas. £3 3s.

Geography of India.
Comprising an account of British India, and the various states enclosed and adjoining. Fcap. pp. 250. 2s.

Geological Papers on Western India.
Including Cutch, Scinde, and the south-east coast of Arabia. To which is added a Summary of the Geology of India generally. Edited for the Government by HENRY J. CARTER, Assistant Surgeon, Bombay Army. Royal 8vo. with folio Atlas of maps and plates; half-bound. £2 2s.

Gillmore (Parker) Encounters with Wild Beasts.
By PARKER GILLMORE, Author of "The Great Thirst Land," "A Ride Through Hostile Africa," &c. With Ten full-page Illustrations. Cr. 8vo. 7s. 6d.

—— **Prairie and Forest.** A description of the Game of North America, with Personal Adventures in its Pursuit. By PARKER GILLMORE (Ubique). With Thirty-Seven Illustrations. Crown 8vo. 7s. 6d.

Glyn (A. C.) History of Civilization in the Fifth Century.
Translated by permission from the French of A. Frederic Ozanam, late Professor of Foreign Literature to the Faculty of Letters at Paris. By ASHBY C. GLYN, B.A., of the Inner Temple, Barrister-at-Law. 2 vols., post 8vo. £1 1s.

Goldstucker (Prof. Theodore), The late. The Literary Remains of. With a Memoir. 2 vols. 8vo. 21s.

Graham (Alex.) Genealogical and Chronological Tables, illustrative of Indian History. 4to. 5s.

Grant (Jas.) Derval Hampton: A Story of the Sea.
By JAMES GRANT, Author of the "Romance of War," &c. 2 vls. Crown 8vo. 21s.

Greene (F. V.) The Russian Army and its Campaigns in Turkey in 1877–1878. By F V. GREENE, First Lieutenant in the Corps of Engineers, U.S. Army, and lately Military Attaché to the United States Legation at St. Petersburg. 8vo. With Atlas. 32s. Second Edition.

—— **Sketches of Army Life in Russia.**
Crown 8vo. 9s.

Griffith (Ralph T. H.) Birth of the War God.
A Poem. By KALIDASA. Translated from the Sanscrit into English Verse. By RALPH T. H. GRIFFITH. 8vo. 5s.

Hall (E. H.) Lands of Plenty, for Health, Sport, and Profit
British North America. A Book for all Travellers and Settlers. By E. HEPPLE HALL, F.S.S. Crown 8vo., with Maps. 6s.

Hall's Trigonometry.
The Elements of Plane and Spherical Trigonometry. With an Appendix, containing the solution of the Problems in Nautical Astronomy. For the use of Schools. By the REV. T. G. HALL, M.A., Professor of Mathematics in King's College, London. 12mo. 2s.

Hancock (E. C.) The Amateur Pottery and Glass Painter.
With Directions for Gilding, Chasing, Burnishing, Bronzing, and Groundlaying. By E. CAMPBELL HANCOCK. Illustrated with Chromo-Lithographs and numerous Woodcuts. Fourth Edition. 8vo. 6s.

—— **Copies for China Painters.**
By E. CAMPBELL HANCOCK. With Fourteen Chromo-Lithographs and other Illustrations. 8vo. 10s.

Handbook of Reference to the Maps of India.
Giving the Lat. and Long. of places of note. 18mo. 3s. 6d.
* *This will be found a valuable Companion to Messrs. Allen & Cos.' Maps of India.*

Harcourt (Maj. A. F. P.) Down by the Drawle.
By MAJOR A. F. P. HARCOURT, Bengal Staff Corps, author of "Kooloo, Lahoul, and Spiti," "The Shakespeare Argosy," &c. 2 Vols. in one, crown 8vo. 6s.

Helmes (Ludwig Verner) Pioneering in the Far East, and Journeys to California in 1849, and to the White Sea in 1878. By LUDWIG VERNER HELMES. With Illustrations from original Sketches and Photographs, and Maps. 8vo. 18s.

Hensman (Howard) The Afghan War, 1879–80.
Being a complete Narrative of the Capture of Cabul, the Siege of Sherpur, the Battle of Ahmed Khel, the brilliant March to Candahar, and the Defeat of Ayub Khan, with the Operations on the Helmund, and the Settlement with Abdur Rahman Khan. By HOWARD HENSMAN, Special Correspondent of the "Pioneer" (Allahabad) and the "Daily News" (London). 8vo. With Maps. 21s.

General Sir Frederick Roberts writes in regard to the letters now re-published:—

"Allow me to congratulate you most cordially on the admirable manner in which you have placed before the public the account of our march from Cabul, and the operations of 31st August and 1st September around Candahar. *Nothing could be more accurate or graphic.* I thought your description of the fight at Charasai was one that any soldier might have been proud of writing; but your recent letters are, if possible, even better."

Holden (E. S.) Sir William Herschel. His Life and Works. By EDWARD S. HOLDEN, United States Naval Observatory Washington. Cr. 8vo. 6s.

Holland.
By Edmondo de Amicis. Translated from the Italian by CAROLINE TILTON. Crown 8vo. 10s. 6d.

Hough (Lieut.-Col. W.) Precedents in Military Law.
8vo. cloth. 25s.

Hughes (Rev. T. P.) Notes on Muhammadanism.
Second Edition, Revised and Enlarged. Fcap. 8vo. 6s.

Hutton (J.) Thugs and Dacoits of India.
A Popular Account of the Thugs and Dacoits, the Hereditary Garotters and Gang Robbers of India. By JAMES HUTTON. Post 8vo. 5s.

India Directory (The).
For the Guidance of Commanders of Steamers and Sailing Vessels. Founded upon the Work of the late CAPTAIN JAMES HORSBURGH, F.R.S.

PART I.—The East Indies, and Interjacent Ports of Africa and South America. Revised, Extended, and Illustrated with Charts of Winds, Currents, Passages, Variation, and Tides. By COMMANDER ALFRED DUNDAS TAYLOR, F.R.G.S., Superintendent of Marine Surveys to the Government of India. £1 18s.

PART II.—The China Sea, with the Ports of Java, Australia and Japan and the Indian Archipelago Harbours, as well as those of New Zealand. Illustrated with Charts of the Winds, Currents, Passages, &c. By the same. (*In preparation.*)

Indian and Military Law.

Mahommedan Law of Inheritance, &c. A Manual of the Mahommedan Law of Inheritance and Contract; comprising the Doctrine of the Soonee and Sheea Schools, and based upon the text of Sir H. W. MACNAGHTEN's Principles and Precedents, together with the Decisions of the Privy Council and High Courts of the Presidencies in India. For the use of Schools and Students. By STANDISH GROVE GRADY, Barrister-at-Law, Reader of Hindoo, Mahommedan, and Indian Law to the Inns of Court. 8vo. 14s.

Hedaya, or Guide, a Commentary on the Mussulman Laws, translated by order of the Governor-General and Council of Bengal. By CHARLES HAMILTON. Second Edition, with Preface and Index by STANDISH GROVE GRADY. 8vo. £1 15s.

Institutes of Menu in English. The Institutes of Hindu Law or the Ordinances of Menu, according to Gloss of Collucca. Comprising the Indian System of Duties, Religious and Civil, verbally translated from the Original, with a Preface by SIR WILLIAM JONES, and collated with the Sanscrit Text by GRAVES CHAMNEY HAUGHTON, M.A., F.R.S., Professor of Hindu Literature in the East India College. New edition, with Preface and Index by STANDISH G. GRADY, Barrister-at-Law, and Reader of Hindu, Mahommedan, and Indian Law to the Inns of Court. 8vo., cloth. 12s.

Indian Code of Criminal Procedure. Being Act X. of 1872, Passed by the Governor-General of India in Council on the 25th of April, 1872. 8vo. 12s.

Indian Code of Civil Procedure. Being Act X. of 1877. 8vo. 6s.

Indian Code of Civil Procedure. In the form of Questions and Answers, with Explanatory and Illustrative Notes. By ANGELO J. LEWIS, Barrister-at-law. 12mo. 12s. 6d.

Indian Penal Code. In the Form of Questions and Answers. With Explanatory and Illustrative Notes. BY ANGELO J. LEWIS, Barrister-at-Law. Post 8vo. 7s. 6d.

Hindu Law. Defence of the Daya Bhaga. Notice of the Case on Prosoono Coomar Tajore's Will. Judgment of the Judicial Committee of the Privy Council. Examination of such Judgment. By JOHN COCHRANE, Barrister-at-Law. Royal 8vo. 20s.

Law and Customs of Hindu Castes, within the Dekhan Provinces subject to the Presidency of Bombay, chiefly affecting Civil Suits. By ARTHUR STEELE. Royal 8vo. £1 1s.

Moohummudan Law of Inheritance. (See page 29.)

Chart of Hindu Inheritance. With an Explanatory Treatise, By ALMARIO RUMSEY. 8vo. 6s. 6d.

Manual of Military Law. For all ranks of the Army, Militia and Volunteer Services. By Colonel J. K. PIPON, Assist. Adjutant General at Head Quarters, & J. F. COLLIER, Esq., of the Inner Temple, Barrister-at-Law. Third and Revised Edition. Pocket size. 5s.

Precedents in Military Law; including the Practice of Courts-Martial; the Mode of Conducting Trials; the Duties of Officers at Military Courts of Inquests, Courts of Inquiry, Courts of Requests, &c., &c. The following are a portion of the Contents:—
1. Military Law. 2. Martial Law. 3. Courts-Martial. 4. Courts of Inquiry. 5. Courts of Inquest. 6. Courts of Request. 7. Forms of Courts-Martial. 8. Precedents of Military Law. 9. Trials of Arson to Rape (Alphabetically arranged.) 10. Rebellions. 11. Riots. 12. Miscellaneous. By Lieut.-Col. W. HOUGH, late Deputy Judge-Advocate-General, Bengal Army, and Author of several Works on Courts-Martial. One thick 8vo. vol. 25s.

The Practice of Courts Martial. By HOUGH & LONG. Thick 8vo. London, 1825. 26s.

Indian Criminal Law and Procedure,
Including the Procedure in the High Courts, as well as that in the Courts not established by Royal Charter; with Forms of Charges and Notes on Evidence, illustrated by a large number of English Cases, and Cases decided in the High Courts of India; and an APPENDIX of selected Acts passed by the Legislative Council relating to Criminal matters. By M. H. STARLING, ESQ., LL.B. & F. B. CONSTABLE, M.A. Third edition. 8vo. £2 2s.

Indian Infanticide.
Its Origin, Progress, and Suppression. By JOHN CAVE-BROWN, M.A. 8vo. 5s.

Irwin (H. C.) The Garden of India; or, Chapters on Oudh History and Affairs. By H. C. IRWIN, B.A. Oxon., Bengal Civil Service. 8vo. 12s.

Jackson (Lt.-Col. B.) Military Surveying, &c. 8vo. 14s. (See page 24).

**Jackson (Lowis D'A.) Hydraulic Manual and Working
Tables,** Hydraulic and Indian Meteorological Statistics.
Published under the patronage of the Right Honourable the
Secretary of State for India. By LOWIS D'A. JACKSON. 8vo. 28s.

—— **Canal and Culvert Tables.**
Based on the Formula of Kutter, under a Modified Classi-
fication, with Explanatory Text and Examples. By LOWIS
D'A. JACKSON, A.M.I.C.E., author of " Hydraulic Manual
and Statistics." &c. Roy. 8vo. 28s.

—— **Pocket Logarithms and other Tables for Ordinary**
Calculations of Quantity, Cost, Interest, Annuities, Assurance, and Angular Functions, obtaining Results correct in the
Fourth figure. By LOWIS D'A. JACKSON. Cloth, 2s. 6d.;
leather, 3s. 6d.

—— **Accented Four-Figure Logarithms, and other Tables.**
For purposes both of Ordinary and of Trigonometrical Calcu-
lation, and for the Correction of Altitudes and Lunar Distances.
Arranged and accented by LOWIS D'A. JACKSON, A.M.I.C.E.,
Author of " Canal and Culvert Tables," " Hydraulic Manual,"
&c. Crown 8vo. 9s.

James (A. G. F. Eliot) Indian Industries.
By A. G. F. ELIOT JAMES, Author of " A Guide to Indian
Household Management," &c. Crown 8vo. 9s.
CONTENTS :—Indian Agriculture ; Beer ; Cacao ; Carpets ; Cereals ;
Chemicals ; Cinchona ; Coffee ; Cotton ; Drugs ; Dyeing and Colouring
Materials ; Fibrous Substances ; Forestry ; Hides ; Skins and Horns ;
Gums and Resins ; Irrigation ; Ivory ; Mining ; Oils ; Opium ; Paper ;
Pottery ; Ryots ; Seeds ; Silk ; Spices ; Sugar ; Tea ; Tobacco ; Wood ;
Wool. Table of Exports. Index.

Jerrold (Blanchard) at Home in Paris.
2 Vols. Post 8vo. 16s.

Joyner (Mrs.) Cyprus: Historical and Descriptive.
Adapted from the German of Herr FRANZ VON LÖHER. With
much additional matter. By Mrs. A. BATSON JOYNER.
Crown 8vo. With 2 Maps. 10s. 6d.

Kaye (Sir J. W.) The Sepoy War in India.
A History of the Sepoy War in India, 1857—1858. By Sir
JOHN WILLIAM KAYE, Author of " The History of the War in
Afghanistan." Vol. I., 8vo. 18s. Vol. II. £1. Vol. III. £1.
CONTENTS OF VOL. I. :—BOOK I.—INTRODUCTORY.—The Con-
quest of the Punjab and Pegu.—The " Right of Lapse."—The
Annexation of Oude.—Progress of Englishism. BOOK II.—The
SEPOY ARMY : ITS RISE, PROGRESS, AND DECLINE.—Early His-

tory of the Native Army.—Deteriorating Influences.—The Sindh Mutinies.—The Punjaub Mutinies. Discipline of the Bengal Army. BOOK III.—THE OUTBREAK OF THE MUTINY.—Lord Canning and his Council.—The Oude Administration and the Persian War.—The Rising of the Storm.—The First Mutiny.—Progress of Mutiny.—Excitement in Upper India — Bursting of the Storm.—APPENDIX.

CONTENTS OF VOL II.:—BOOK IV.—THE RISING IN THE NORTH-WEST. The Delhi History.—The Outbreak at Meerut.—The Seizure of Delhi.—Calcutta in May.—Last Days of General Anson.—The March upon Delhi BOOK V.—PROGRESS OF REBELLION IN UPPER INDIA—Benares and Allahabad.—Cawnpore.—The March to Cawnpore.—Re-occupation of Cawnpore. BOOK VI.—THE PUNJAB AND DELHI.—First Conflicts in the Punjab.—Peshawur and Rawul Pinder.—Progress of Events in the Punjab.—Delhi.—First Weeks of the Siege.—Progress of the Siege.—The Last Succours from the Punjab.

CONTENTS OF VOL III.:—BOOK VII.—BENGAL, BEHAR, AND THE NORTH-WEST PROVINCES.—At the Seat of Government.—The Insurrection in Behar.—The Siege of Arrah.—Behar and Bengal. BOOK VIII.—MUTINY AND REBELLION IN THE NORTH-WEST PROVINCES.—Agra in May.—Insurrection in the Districts.—Bearing of the Native Chiefs.—Agra in June, July, August and September. BOOK IX.—LUCKNOW AND DELHI.—Rebellion in Oude.—Revolt in the Districts.—Lucknow in June and July.—The siege and Capture of Delhi.

(For continuation, see " History of the Indian Mutiny," by Colonel G. B. MALLESON, p. 19.)

Kaye (Sir J. W.) History of the War in Afghanistan.
New edition. 3 Vols. Crown 8vo. £1. 0s.
—— **H. St. G. Tucker's Life and Correspondence.** 8vo. 10s
—— **Memorials of Indian Governments.**
By H. ST. GEORGE TUCKER. 8vo. 10s.

Keatinge (Mrs.) English Homes in India.
By MRS. KEATINGE. Part I.—The Three Loves. Part II.—The Wrong Turning Two vols., Post 8vo. 16s.

Keene (H. G.) Mogul Empire.
From the death of Aurungzeb to the overthrow of the Mahratta Power, by HENRY GEORGE KEENE. B.C.S. Second edition. With Map. 8vo. 10s. 6d.
This Work fills up a blank between the ending of Elphinstone's and the commencement of Thornton's Histories.

Keene (H. G.). Administration in India.
Post 8vo. 5s.

—— **Peepul Leaves.**
Poems written in India. Post 8vo 5s.

—— **The Turks in India.**
Historical Chapters on the Administration of Hindostan by the Chugtai Tartar, Babar, and his Descendants. 12s. 6d.

Latham (Dr. R. G.) Russian and Turk,
From a Geographical, Ethnological, and Historical Point of View. 8vo 18s.

Laurie (Col. W. F. B.) Our Burmese Wars and Relations
with Burma. With a Summary of Events from 1826 to 1879, including a Sketch of King Theebau's Progress. With various Local, Statistical, and Commercial Information. By Colonel W. F. B. LAURIE, Author of "Rangoon," "Narrative of the Second Burmese War," &c. 8vo. With Plans and Map. 16s.

—— **Ashe Pyee, the Superior Country;** or the great attractions of Burma to British Enterprise and Commerce. By Col. W. F. B. LAURIE, Author of "Our Burmese Wars and Relations with Burma." Crown 8vo. 5s.

Lee (F. G.) The Church under Queen Elizabeth.
An Historical Sketch. By the Rev. F. G. LEE, D.D. Two Vols., Crown 8vo. 21s.

—— **Reginald Barentyne;** or Liberty Without Limit. A Tale of the Times. By FREDERICK GEORGE LEE. With Portrait of the Author. Crown 8vo. 10s. 6d.

—— **The Words from the Cross:** Seven Sermons for Lent, Passion-Tide, and Holy Week. By the Rev. F. G. LEE, D.D. Third Edition revised. Fcap. 3s. 6d.

—— **Order Out of Chaos.** Two Sermons.
By the Rev. FREDERICK GEORGE LEE, D.D. Fcap. 2s. 6d.

Lee's (Dr. W. N.) Drain of Silver to the East.
Post 8vo. 8s.

Le Messurier (Maj. A.) Kandahar in 1879.
Being the Diary of Major A. LE MESSURIER, R.E., Brigade Major R.E. with the Quetta Column. Crown 8vo. 8s.

Lewin (T. H.) Wild Races of the South Eastern Frontier of
India. Including an Account of the Loshai Country. By Capt. T. H. LEWIN, Dep. Comm. of Hill Tracts. Post 8vo. 10s. 6d.

Lewis (A. J.) Indian Penal Code
In the Form of Questions and Answers. With Explanatory and Illustrative Notes. By ANGELO J. LEWIS. Post 8vo. 7s. 6d.
—— **Indian Code of Civil Procedure.**
In the Form of Questions and Answers. With Explanatory and Illustrative Notes. By ANGELO J. LEWIS. Post 8vo. 12s. 6d.

Liancourt's and Pincott's Primitive and Universal Laws of the Formation and development of language; a Rational and Inductive System founded on the Natural Basis of Onomatops. 8vo. 12s. 6d.

Lloyd (J. S.) Shadows of the Past.
Being the Autobiography of General Kenyon. Edited by J. S. LLOYD, Authoress of "Ruth Everingham," "The Silent Shadow," &c. Crown 8vo. 9s.

Lockwood (Ed.) Natural History, Sport and Travel.
By EDWARD LOCKWOOD, Bengal Civil Service, late Magistrate of Monghyr. Crown 8vo. With numerous Illustrations. 9s.

Lovell (Vice-Adm.) Personal Narrative of Events from 1799 to 1815. With Anecdotes. By the late Vice-Adm. WM. STANHOPE LOVELL, R.N., K H. Second edition. Crown 8vo. 4s.

Lupton (J. I.) The Horse, as he Was, as he Is, and as he Ought to Be. By JAMES IRVINE LUPTON, F.R.C.V.S., Author of "The External Anatomy of the Horse," &c. &c. Illustrated. 3s 6d.

MacGregor (Col. C. M.) Narrative of a Journey through the Province of Khorassan and on the N. W. Frontier of Afghanistan in 1875. By Colonel C. M. MACGREGOR, C.S.I., C.I.E., Bengal Staff Corps. 2 vols. 8vo. With map and numerous illustrations. 30s.

Mackay (C.) Luck, and what came of it. A Tale of our Times. By CHARLES MACKAY, LL.D. Three vols. 31s. 6d.

Maggs (J.) Round Europe with the Crowd.
Crown 8vo. 5s.

Magenis (Lady Louisa) The Challenge of Barletta. By Massimo D'Azeglio. Rendered into English by Lady LOUISA MAGENIS. 2 vols., crown 8vo. 21s.

Malleson (Col. G. B.) Final French Struggles in India and on the Indian Seas. Including an Account of the Capture of the Isles of France and Bourbon, and Sketches of the most eminent Foreign Adventurers in India up to the period of that Capture. With an Appendix containing an Account of the Expedition from India to Egypt in 1801. By Colonel G. B. MALLESON, C.S.I. Crown 8vo. 10s. 6d.

Malleson (Col. G. B.) History of the Indian Mutiny, 1857–1858, commencing from the close of the Second Volume of Sir John Kaye's History of the Sepoy War. Vol. I. 8vo. With Map. 20s.

CONTENTS.—Calcutta in May and June.—William Tayler and Vincent Eyre.—How Bihar and Calcutta were saved.—Mr. Colvin and Agra.—Jhansi and Bandalkhand.—Colonel Durand and Holkar.—Sir George Lawrence and Rajputana.—Brigadier Polwhele's great battle and its results.—Bareli, Rohilkhand, and Farakhabad.—The relation of the annexation of Oudh to the Mutiny.—Sir Henry Lawrence and the Mutiny in Oudh.—The siege of Lakhnao.—The first relief of Lakhnao.

VOL. II.—The Storming of Delhi, the Relief of Lucknow, the Two Battles of Cawnpore, the Campaign in Rohilkhand, and the movements of the several Columns in the N.W. Provinces, the Azimgurh District, and on the Eastern and South-Eastern Frontiers. 8vo. With 4 Plans. 20s.

VOL. III.—Bombay in 1857. Lord Elphinstone. March of Woodburn's Column. Mr. Seton-Karr and the Southern Maratha Country. Mr. Forjett and Bombay. Asirgarh. Sir Henry Durand. March of Stuart's Column. Holkar and Durand. Malwa Campaign. Haidarabad. Major C. Davidson and Salar Jang Sagar and Narbadi Territory. Sir Robert Hamilton and Sir Hugh Rose. Central India Campaign. Whitlock and Kirwi. Sir Hugh Rose and Gwaliar. Le Grand Jacob and Western India. Lord Canning's Oudh policy. Last Campaign in, and pacification of, Oudh. Sir Robert Napier, Smith, Michell, and Tantia Topi. Civil Districts during the Mutiny. Minor Actions at Out-stations. Conclusion. 8vo. With Plans. 20s.

—— **History of Afghanistan,** from the Earliest Period to the Outbreak of the War of 1878. 8vo. Second Edition. With Map. 18s.

—— **Herat: The Garden and Granary of Central Asia.** With Map and Index. 8vo. 8s

Manning (Mrs.) Ancient and Mediæval India.
Being the History, Religion, Laws, Caste, Manners and Customs, Language, Literature, Poetry, Philosophy, Astronomy, Algebra, Medicine, Architecture, Manufactures, Commerce, &c., of the Hindus, taken from their writings. Amongst the works consulted and gleaned from may be named the Rig Veda,

Sama Veda, Yajur Veda, Sathapatha Brahmana, Bhagavat Gita, The Puranas, Code of Manu, Code of Yajnavalkya, Mitakshara, Daya Bhaga, Mahabharata, Atriya, Charaka, Susruta, Ramayana, Raghu Vansa, Bhattikavya. Sakuntala, Vikramorvasi, Malati and Madhava, Mudra Rakshasa, Ratnavali. Kumara Sambhava, Prabodha, Chandrodaya, Megha Duta, Gita Govinda. Panchatantra, Hitopadesa, Katha Sarit, Sagara, Ketala, Pancaavinsati, Dasa Kumara Charita, &c. By Mrs. MANNING, with Illustrations. 2 vols., 8vo. 30s.

Marvin (Chas.) Merv, the Queen of the World and the Scourge of the Men-stealing Turcomans. By CHARLES MARVIN, author of "The Disastrous Turcoman Campaign," and "Grodekoff's Ride to Herat." With Portraits and Maps. 8vo. 18s.

—— **Colonel Grodekoff's Ride from Samarcand to Herat,** through Balkh and the Uzbek States of Afghan Turkestan. With his own March-route from the Oxus to Herat. By CHARLES MARVIN. Crown 8vo. With Portrait. 8s.

—— **The Eye-Witnesses' Account of the Disastrous Russian** Campaign against the Akhal Tekke Turcomans: Describing the March across the Burning Desert, the Storming of Dengeel Tepe, and the Disastrous Retreat to the Caspian. By CHARLES MARVIN. With numerous Maps and Plans. 8vo. 18s.

Matson (Nellie) Hilda Desmond, or Riches and Poverty. Crown 8vo. 10s. 6d.

Mayhew (Edward) Illustrated Horse Doctor. Being an Accurate and Detailed Account, accompanied by more than 400 Pictorial Representations, characteristic of the various Diseases to which the Equine Race are subjected; together with the latest Mode of Treatment, and all the requisite Prescriptions written in Plain English By EDWARD MAYHEW, M.R.C.V.S. 8vo. 18s. 6d.

CONTENTS.—The Brain and Nervous System.—The Eyes.—The Mouth.—The Nostrils.—The Throat.—The Chest and its contents.—The Stomach, Liver, &c.—The Abdomen.—The Urinary Organs.—The Skin.—Specific Diseases.—Limbs.—The Feet.—Injuries.—Operations.

"The book contains nearly 600 pages of valuable matter, which reflects great credit on its author, and, owing to its practical details, the result of deep scientific research, deserves a place in the library of medical, veterinary, and non-professional readers."—*Field.*

"The book furnishes at once the bane and the antidote, as the drawings show the horse not only suffering from every kind of disease, but in the different stages of it, while the alphabetical summary at the end gives the cause, symptoms and treatment of each."—*Illustrated London News.*

Mayhew (Edward) Illustrated Horse Management.
Containing descriptive remarks upon Anatomy, Medicine, Shoeing, Teeth, Food, Vices, Stables; likewise a plain account of the situation, nature, and value of the various points; together with comments on grooms, dealers, breeders, breakers, and trainers; Embellished with more than 400 engravings from original designs made expressly for this work. By E. MAYHEW. A new Edition, revised and improved by J 1. LUPTON. M.R.C.V.S. 8vo. 12s

CONTENTS.— The body of the horse anatomically considered. PHYSIC.— The mode of administering it, and minor operations. SHOEING.— Its origin, its uses, and its varieties. THE TEETH. — Their natural growth, and the abuses to which they are liable.

FOOD.— The fittest time for feeding, and the kind of food which the horse naturally consumes. The evils which are occasioned by modern stables. The faults inseparable from stables. The so-called "incapacitating vices," which are the results of injury or of disease. Stables as they should be. GROOMS.— Their prejudices, their injuries, and their duties. POINTS.— Their relative importance and where to look for their development BREEDING.— Its inconsistencies and its disappointments BREAKING AND TRAINING.— Their errors and their results

Mayhew (Henry) German Life and Manners.
As seen in Saxony. With an account of Town Life—Village Life—Fashionable Life—Married Life—School and University Life, &c. Illustrated with Songs and Pictures of the Student Customs at the University of Jena. By HENRY MAYHEW, 2 vols., 8vo., with numerous illustrations. 18s.

A Popular Edition of the above. With illustrations. Cr. 8vo. 7s
"Full of original thought and observation, and may be studied with profit by both German and English—especially by the German."*Athenæum.*

McCarthy (T. A.) An Easy System of Calisthenics and Drilling. Including Light Dumb-Bell and Indian Club Exercises. By T. A. MCCARTHY, Chief Instructor at Mr. Moss's Gymnasium, Brighton. Fcap. 1s. 6d.

McCosh (J.) Advice to Officers in India.
By JOHN MCCOSH, M.D. Post 8vo. 8s.

Meadow (T.) Notes on China.
Desultory Notes on the Government and People of China and on the Chinese Language. By T. T. MEADOWS. 8vo. 9s.

Menzies (S.) Turkey Old and New: Historical, Geographical, and Statistical. By SUTHERLAND MENZIES. With Map and numerous Illustrations. 2 vols., 8vo. 32s.

Military Works—chiefly issued by the Government.

Field Exercises and Evolutions of Infantry. Pocket edition, 1s.
Queen's Regulations and Orders for the Army. Corrected to 1881. 8vo. 3s. 6d. Interleaved, 5s. 6d. Pocket Edition, 1s. 6d.
Musketry Regulations, as used at Hythe. 1s.
Dress Regulations for the Army. (Reprinting.)
Infantry Sword Exercise. 1875. 6d.
Infantry Bugle Sounds. 6d.
Handbook of Battalion Drill. By Lieut. H. C. SLACK 2s; or with Company Drill, 2s. 6d.
Handbook of Brigade Drill. By Lieut. H. C. SLACK. 3s.
Red Book for Sergeants. By WILLIAM BRIGHT, Colour-Sergeant, 19th Middlesex R.V. 1s.
Handbook of Company Drill; also of Skirmishing, Battalion, and Shelter Trench Drill. By Lieut. CHARLES SLACK. 1s.
Elementary and Battalion Drill. Condensed and Illustrated, together with duties of Company Officers, Markers, &c., in Battalion. By Captain MALTON. 2s. 6d.
Cavalry Regulations. For the Instruction, Formations, and Movements of Cavalry. Royal 8vo. 4s. 6d.
Manual of Artillery Exercises, 1873. 8vo. 5s.
Manual of Field Artillery Exercises. 1877. 3s.
Standing Orders for Royal Artillery. 8vo, 3s.
Principles and Practice of Modern Artillery. By Lt.-Col. C. H. OWEN, R.A. 8vo. Illustrated. 15s.
Artillerist's Manual and British Soldiers' Compendium. By Major F. A. GRIFFITHS. 11th Edition. 5s.
Compendium of Artillery Exercises—Smooth Bore, Field, and Garrison Artillery for Reserve Forces. By Captain J. M. McKenzie. 3s. 6d.
Principles of Gunnery. By JOHN T. HYDE, M.A., late Professor of Fortification and Artillery, Royal Indian Military College, Addiscombe. Second edition, revised and enlarged. With many Plates and Cuts, and Photograph of Armstrong Gun. Royal 8vo. 14s.
Notes on Gunnery. By Captain Goodeve. Revised Edition. 1s.
Text Book of the Construction and Manufacture of Rifled Ordnance in the British Service. By STONEY & JONES. Second Edition. Paper, 3s. 6d., Cloth, 4s. 6d.
Treatise on Fortification and Artillery. By Major HECTOR STRAITH. Revised and re-arranged by THOMAS COOK, R.N., by JOHN T. HYDE, M.A. 7th Edition. Royal 8vo. Illustrated and Four Hundred Plans, Cuts, &c. £2 2s.
Elementary Principles of Fortification. A Text-Book for Military Examinations. By J. T. HYDE, M.A. Royal 8vo. With numerous Plans and Illustrations. 10s. 6d.

Military Surveying and Field Sketching. The Various Methods of Contouring, Levelling, Sketching without Instruments, Scale of Shade, Examples in Military Drawing, &c., &c., &c. As at present taught in the Military Colleges. By Major W. H. RICHARDS, 55th Regiment, Chief Garrison Instructor in India, Late Instructor in Military Surveying, Royal Military College, Sandhurst. Second Edition, Revised and Corrected. 12s.

Treatise on Military Surveying; including Sketching in the Field, Plan-Drawing, Levelling, Military Reconnaissance, &c. By Lieut.-Col. BASIL JACKSON, late of the Royal Staff Corps. The Fifth Edition. 8vo. Illustrated by Plans, &c. 14s.

Instruction in Military Engineering. Vol. I., Part III. 4s

Military Train Manual. 1s.

The Sappers' Manual. Compiled for the use of Engineer Volunteer Corps. By Col. W. A. FRANKLAND, R.E. With numerous Illustrations. 2s.

Ammunition. A descriptive treatise on the different Projectiles Charges, Fuzes, Rockets, &c., at present in use for Land and Sea Service, and on other war stores manufactured in the Royal Laboratory. 6s.

Hand-book on the Manufacture and Proof of Gunpowder. as carried on at the Royal Gunpowder Factory, Waltham Abbey. 5s.

Regulations for the Training of Troops for service in the Field and for the conduct of Peace Manœuvres. 2s.

Hand-book Dictionary for the Militia and Volunteer Services, Containing a variety of useful information, Alphabetically arranged. Pocket size, 3s. 6d.; by post, 3s. 8d.

Gymnastic Exercises, System of Fencing, and Exercises for the Regulation Clubs. In one volume. Crown 8vo. 1877. 2s.

Text-Book on the Theory and Motion of Projectiles; the History, Manufacture, and Explosive Force of Gunpowder; the History of Small Arms. For Officers sent to School of Musketry. 1s. 6d.

Notes on Ammunition. 4th Edition. 1877. 2s. 6d.

Regulations and Instructions for Encampments. 6d.

Rules for the Conduct of the War Game. 2s.

Medical Regulations for the Army, Instructions for the Army, Comprising duties of Officers, Attendants, and Nurses, &c. 1s. 6d.

Purveyors' Regulations and Instructions, for Guidance of Officers of Purveyors' Department of the Army. 3s.

Priced Vocabulary of Stores used in Her Majesty's Service. 4s.

Lectures on Tactics for Officers of the Army, Militia, and Volunteers. By Major F. H. DYKE, Garrison Instructor, E.D. 3s. 6d.

Transport of Sick and Wounded Troops. By DR. LONGMORE. 5s.

Precedents in Military Law. By LT-COL. W. HOUGH. 8vo. 25s.

The Practice of Courts-Martial, by HOUGH & LONG. 8vo. 26s.

Manual of Military Law. For all ranks of the Army, Militia, and Volunteer Services. By Colonel J. K. PIPON, and J. F. COLLIER, Esq. Third and Revised Edition. Pocket size. 5s.
Regulations applicable to the European Officer in India. Containing Staff Corps Rules, Staff Salaries, Commands, Furlough and Retirement Regulations, &c. By GEORGE E. COCHRANE late Assistant Military Secretary, India Office. 1 vol., post 8vo. 7s. 6d.
Reserve Force; Guide to Examinations, for the use of Captains and Subalterns of Infantry, Militia, and Rifle Volunteers, and for Serjeants of Volunteers. By Capt. G. H. GREAVES. 2nd edit. 2s.
The Military Encyclopædia; referring exclusively to the Military Sciences, Memoirs of distinguished Soldiers, and the Narratives of Remarkable Battles. By J. H. STOCQUELER. 8vo. 12s.
The Operations of War Explained and Illustrated. By Col. HAMLEY. New Edition Revised, with Plates. Royal 8vo. 30s.
Lessons of War. As taught by the Great Masters and Others; Selected and Arranged from the various operations in War. By FRANCE JAMES SOADY, Lieut.-Col., R.A. Royal 8vo. 21s.
The Surgeon's Pocket Book, an Essay on the best Treatment of Wounded in War. By Surgeon Major J. H. PORTER. 7s. 6d.
A Precis of Modern Tactics. By COLONEL HOME. 8vo. 8s. 6d.
Armed Strength of Austria. By Capt. COOKE. 2 pts. £1 2s.
Armed Strength of Denmark. 3s.
Armed Strength of Russia. Translated from the German. 7s.
Armed Strength of Sweden and Norway. 3s. 6d.
Armed Strength of Italy. 5s. 6d.
Armed Strength of Germany. Part I. 8s. 6d.
The Franco-German War of 1870—71. By CAPT. C. H. CLARKE. Vol. I. £1 6s. Sixth Section. 5s. Seventh Section 6s. Eighth Section. 3s. Ninth Section. 4s. 6d. Tenth Section. 6s. Eleventh Section. 5s. 3d. Twelfth Section. 4s. 6d.
The Campaign of 1866 in Germany. Royal 8vo. With Atlas, 21s.
Celebrated Naval and Military Trials By PETER BURKE. Post 8vo., cloth. 10s. 6d.
Military Sketches. By SIR LASCELLES WRAXALL. Post 8vo. 6s.
Military Life of the Duke of Wellington. By JACKSON and SCOTT. 2 Vols. 8vo. Maps, Plans, &c. 12s.
Single Stick Exercise of the Aldershot Gymnasium. 6d.
Treatise on Military Carriages, and other Manufactures of the Royal Carriage Department. 5s.
Steppe Campaign Lectures. 2s.
Manual of Instructions for Army Surgeons. 1s.
Regulations for Army Hospital Corps. 9d.
Manual of Instructions for Non-Commissioned Officers, Army Hospital Corps. 2s.
Handbook for Military Artificers. 3s.

Instructions for the use of Auxiliary Cavalry. 2s. 6d.
Equipment Regulations for the Army. 5s. 6d.
Statute Law relating to the Army. 1s. 3d.
Regulations for Commissariat and Ordnance Department 2s.
Regulations for the Commissariat Department. 1s. 6d.
Regulations for the Ordnance Department. 1s. 6d.
Artillerist's Handbook of Reference for the use of the Royal and Reserve Artillery, by WILL and DALTON. 5s.
An Essay on the Principles and Construction of Military Bridges, by SIR HOWARD DOUGLAS. 1853. 15s.

Mill's History of British India,
With Notes and Continuation. By H. H. WILSON. 9 vols. cr. 8vo. £2 10s.

Mitchinson (A. W.) The Expiring Continent; A Narrative of Travel in Senegambia, with Observations on Native Character; Present Condition and Future Prospects of Africa and Colonisation. By ALEX. WILL. MITCHINSON. With Sixteen full-page Illustrations and Map. 8vo. 18s.

Mitford (Maj. R. C. W.) To Caubul with the Cavalry Brigade. A Narrative of Personal Experiences with the Force under General Sir F. S. Roberts, G.C.B. With Map and Illustrations from Sketches by the Author. By Major R. C. W. MITFORD, 14th Beng. Lancers. 8vo. Second Edit. 9s.

Muller's (Max) Rig-Veda-Sanhita.
The Sacred Hymns of the Brahmins; together with the Commentary of Sayanacharya. Published under the Patronage of the Right Honourable the Secretary of State for India in Council. 6 vols., 4to. £2 10s. per volume.

Mysteries of the Vatican;
Or Crimes of the Papacy. From the German of DR. THEODORE GREISENGER. 2 Vols. post 8vo. 21s.

Neville (Ralph) The Squire's Heir.
By RALPH NEVILLE, Author of "Lloyd Pennant." Two Vols. 21s.

Nicholson (Capt. H. W.) From Sword to Share; or, a Fortune in Five Years at Hawaii. By Capt. H. WHALLEY NICHOLSON. Crown 8vo. With Map and Photographs. 12s. 6d.

Nirgis and Bismillah.
NIRGIS; a Tale of the Indian Mutiny, from the Diary of a Slave Girl: and BISMILLAH; or, Happy Days in Cashmere. By HAFIZ ALLARD. Post 8vo. 10s. 6d.

Norris-Newman (C. L.) In Zululand with the British, throughout the War of 1879. By CHARLES L. NORRIS-NEWMAN, Special Correspondent of the London "Standard," Cape Town "Standard and Mail," and the "Times" of Natal. With Plans and Four Portraits. 8vo. 16s.

—— **With the Boers in the Transvaal and Orange Free State** in 1880-81. By C. L. NORRIS-NEWMAN, Special War Correspondent, Author of "In Zululand with the British." 8vo. With Maps. 14s.

Notes on the North Western Provinces of India. By a District Officer. 2nd Edition. Post 8vo., cloth. 5s.
CONTENTS.—Area and Population.—Soils.—Crops.—Irrigation.—Rent.—Rates.—Land Tenures.

O'Donoghue (Mrs. P.) Ladies on Horseback. Learning, Park Riding, and Hunting. With Notes upon Costume, and numerous Anecdotes. By Mrs. POWER O'DONOGHUE, Authoress of "The Knave of Clubs," "Horses and Horsemen," "Grandfather's Hunter," "One in Ten Thousand," &c. &c. Cr. 8vo. With Portrait. 5s.

Oldfield (H. A.) Sketches from Nipal, Historical and Descriptive; with Anecdotes of the Court Life and Wild Sports of the Country in the time of Maharaja Jang Bahadur, G.C.B.; to which is added an Essay on Nipalese Buddhism, and Illustrations of Religious Monuments, Architecture, and Scenery, from the Author's own Drawings. By the late HENRY AMBROSE OLDFIELD, M.D., of H. M.'s Indian Army, many years Resident at Khatmandu. Two vols. 8vo. 36s.

Old Stager (An) Private Theatricals. Being a Practical Guide for the Home Stage, both before and behind the Curtain. By AN OLD STAGER. Illustrated with Suggestions for Scenes after designs by Shirley Hodson.

Oliver (Capt. S. P.) On and Off Duty. Being Leaves from an Officer's Note Book. Part I.—Turania; Part II.—Lemuria; Part III.—Columbia. By Captain S. P. OLIVER. Crown 4to. With 38 Illustrations. 14s.

—— **On Board a Union Steamer.** A compilation. By Captain S. P. OLIVER. To which is added "A Sketch Abroad," by MISS DORETON. 8vo. With Frontispiece. 8s.

Osborne (Mrs. W.) Pilgrimage to Mecca (A).
By the Nawab Sikandar Begum of Bhopal. Translated from the Original Urdu. By Mrs. WILLOUGHBY OSBORNE. Followed by a Sketch of the History of Bhopal. By Col. WILLOUGHBY-OSBORNE, C.B. With Photographs, and dedicated, by permission, to HER MAJESTY, QUEEN VICTORIA. Post 8vo. £1. 1s.
 This is a highly important book, not only for its literary merit, and the information it contains, but also from the fact of its being the first work written by an Indian lady, and that lady a Queen.

Owen (Sidney) India on the Eve of the British Conquest.
A Historical Sketch. By SIDNEY OWEN, M.A. Reader in Indian Law and History in the University of Oxford. Formerly Professor of History in the Elphinstone College. Bombay. Post 8vo. 8s.

Oxenham (Rev. H. N.) Catholic Eschatology and Universalism. An Essay on the Doctrine of Future Retribution. Second Edition, revised and enlarged. Crown 8vo. 7s. 6d.

—— **Catholic Doctrine of the Atonement.** An Historical Inquiry into its Development in the Church, with an Introduction on the Principle of Theological Development. By H. NUTCOMBE OXENHAM, M.A. 3rd Edition and Enlarged. 8vo. 14s.
 "It is one of the ablest and probably one of the most charmingly written treatises on the subject which exists in our language."—*Times*.

—— **The First Age of Christianity and the Church.**
By JOHN IGNATIUS DÖLLINGER, D.D., Professor of Ecclesiastical History in the University of Munich, &c., &c. Translated from the German by HENRY NUTCOMBE OXENHAM, M.A., late Scholar of Baliol College, Oxford. Third Edition. 2 vols. Crown 8vo. 18s.

Ozanam's (A. F.) Civilisation in the Fifth Century. From the French. By The Hon. A. C. GLYN. 2 Vols., post 8vo. 21s

Pebody (Charles) Authors at Work.
Francis Jeffrey—Sir Walter Scott—Robert Burns—Charles Lamb—R. B. Sheridan—Sydney Smith—Macaulay—Byron Wordsworth—Tom Moore—Sir James Mackintosh. Post 8vo 10s. 6d.

Pelly (Sir Lewis). The Miracle Play of Hasan and Husain.
Collected from Oral Tradition by Colonel Sir LEWIS PELLY, K.C.B., K.C.S.I., formerly serving in Persia as Secretary of Legation, and Political Resident in the Persian Gulf. Revised, with Explanatory Notes, by ARTHUR N. WOLLASTON, H.M. Indian (Home) Service, Translator of Anwar-i-Suhaili, &c. 2 Vols. royal 8vo. 32s.

Pincott (F.) Analytical Index to Sir JOHN KAYE's History of the Sepoy War, and Col. G. B. MALLESON's History of the Indian Mutiny. (Combined in one volume.) By FREDERIC PINCOTT, M.R.A.S. 8vo. 10s. 6d.

Pipon and Collier's Manual of Military Law.
By Colonel J. K. PIPON, and J. F. COLLIER, Esq., of the Inner Temple, Barrister-at-Law. 5s.

Pollock (Field Marshal Sir George) Life & Correspondence.
By C. R. Low. 8vo. With portrait. 18s.

Pope (G. U.) Text-book of Indian History; with Geographical Notes, Genealogical Tables, Examination Questions, and Chronological, Biographical, Geographical, and General Indexes. For the use of Schools, Colleges, and Private Students. By the Rev. G. U. POPE, D D., Principal of Bishop Cotton's Grammar School and College, Bangalore; Fellow of the Madras University. Third Edition, thoroughly revised. Fcap. 4to. 12s.

Practice of Courts Martial.
By HOUGH & LONG. 8vo. London. 1825. 26s.

Prichard's Chronicles of Budgepore, &c.
Or Sketches of Life in Upper India. 2 Vols., Foolscap 8vo. 12s.

Prinsep (H. T.) Historical Results.
Deducible from Recent Discoveries in Affghanistan. By H. T. PRINSEP. 8vo. Lond. 1844. 15s.

—— **Tibet, Tartary, and Mongolia.**
By HENRY T. PRINSEP. Esq. Second edition. Post 8vo. 5s.

—— **Political and Military Transactions in India.**
2 Vols. 8vo. London, 1825. 18s.

Richards (Major W. H.) Military Surveying, &c.
12s. (See page 22.)

Rowe (R.) Picked up in the Streets; or, Struggles for Life among the London Poor. By RICHARD ROWE, "Good Words" Commissioner, Author of "Jack Afloat and Ashore," &c. Crown 8vo. Illustrated. 6s.

Rumsey (Almaric) Moohummudan Law of Inheritance, and Rights and Relations affecting it. Sunni Doctrine. Comprising, together with much collateral information, the substance, greatly expanded, of the author's "Chart of Family Inheritance." By ALMARIC RUMSEY, of Lincoln's Inn, Barrister-at-Law, Professor of Indian Jurisprudence at King's College, London. Author of "A Chart of Hindu Family Inheritance." 8vo. 12s.

Rumsey (Almaric) A Chart of Hindu Family Inheritance.
Second Edition, much enlarged. 8vo. 6s. 6d.

Sachau (Dr. C. Ed.) The Chronology of Ancient Nations. An English Version of the Arabic Text of the Athar-ut Bâkiya of Albîrûnî, or "Vestiges of the Past." Collected and reduced to writing by the Author in A.H. 390–1, A.D. 1,000. Translated and Edited, with Notes and Index, by Dr. C. EDWARD SACHAU, Professor in the Royal University of Berlin. Published for the Oriental Translation Fund of Great Britain and Ireland. Royal 8vo. 42s.

Sanderson (G. P.) Thirteen Years among the Wild Beasts of India; their Haunts and Habits, from Personal Observation; with an account of the Modes of Capturing and Taming Wild Elephants. By G. P. SANDERSON, Officer in Charge of the Government Elephant Keddahs at Mysore. With 21 full page Illustrations and three Maps. Second Edition. Fcp. 4to. £1 5s.

Sewell (R.) Analytical History of India.
From the earliest times to the Abolition of the East India Company in 1858. By ROBERT SEWELL, Madras Civil Service. Post 8vo. 8s.

₊ The object of this work is to supply the want which has been felt by students for a condensed outline of Indian History which would serve at once to recall the memory and guide the eye, while at the same time it has been attempted to render it interesting to the general reader by preserving a medium between a bare analysis and a complete history.

Shadow of a Life (The) A Girl's Story.
By BERYL HOPE. 3 vols., post 8vo. 31s. 6d.

Sherer (J. W.) The Conjuror's Daughter.
A Tale. By J. W. SHERER, C.S.I. With Illustrations by Alf. T. Elwes and J. Jellicoe. Cr. 8vo. 6s.

—— **Who is Mary?**
A Cabinet Novel, in one volume. By J. W. SHERER, Esq., C.S.I. 10s. 6d.

Signor Monaldini's Niece.
A Novel of Italian Life. Crown 8vo. 6s.

Simpson (H. T.) Archæologia Adelensis; or, a History of the
Parish of Adel, in the West Riding of Yorkshire. Being
an attempt to delineate its Past and Present Associations,
Archæological, Topographical, and Scriptural. By HENRY
TRAILL SIMPSON, M.A., late Rector of Adel. With nu-
merous etchings by W. LLOYD FERGUSON. Roy. 8vo. 21s.

Small (Rev. G.) A Dictionary of Naval Terms, English and
Hindustani. For the use of Nautical Men trading to India,
&c. By Rev. G. SMALL, Interpreter to the Strangers' Home
for Asiatics. Fcap. 2s. 6d.

Solymos (B.) Desert Life. Recollections of an Expedition
in the Soudan. By B. SOLYMOS (B. E. FALKONBERG), Civil
Engineer. 8vo. 15s.

Starling (M. H.) Indian Criminal Law and Procedure.
Third edition. 8vo. £2 2s. See page 15.

Steele (A.) Law and Customs of Hindu Castes.
By ARTHUR STEELE. Royal 8vo. £1. 1s. (See page 14)

Stent (G. C.) Entombed Alive,
And other Songs and Ballads. (From the Chinese.) By
GEORGE CARTER STENT, M.R.A.S., of the Chinese Imperial
Maritime Customs Service, author of " Chinese and English
Vocabulary," " Chinese and English Pocket Dictionary," " The
Jade Chaplet," &c. Crown 8vo. With four Illustrations. 9s.

Stothard (R. T.) The A B C of Art.
Being a system of delineating forms and objects in nature ne-
cessary for the attainments of a draughtsman. By ROBERT T.
STOTHARD, F.S.A., late H.D.S.A. Fcap. 4s.

Swinnerton (Rev. C.) The Afghan War. Gough's Action at
Futtehabad By the Rev. C. SWINNERTON, Chaplain in the
Field with the First Division, Peshawur Valley Field Force.
With Frontispiece and Two Plans. Crown 8vo. 5s.

Tayler (W.) Thirty-eight Years in India, from Juganath
to the Himalaya Mountains. By WILLIAM TAYLER, Esq.,
Retired B.C.S., late Commissioner of Patna. In 2 vols.
Contains a memoir of the life of Mr. William Tayler, from
1829 to 1867—during the Government of eight Governors
General—from Lord William Bentinck to Lord Lawrence,
comprising numerous incidents and adventures, official, personal, tragic, and comic, " from grave to gay, from lively to
severe " throughout that period. The first volume contains
a hundred illustrations, reproduced by Mr. Tayler himself,

from original sketches taken by him on the spot, in Bengal, Behar, N.W. Provinces, Darjeeling, Nipal, and Simla. Vol. I. 25s. (Vol. II. in the press).

Thomson's Lunar and Horary Tables.
For New and Concise Methods of Performing the Calculations necessary for ascertaining the Longitude by Lunar Observations, or Chronometers; with directions for acquiring a knowledge of the Principal Fixed Stars and finding the Latitude of them. By DAVID THOMSON. Sixty-fifth edit. Royal 8vo 10s.

Thornton (P. M.) Foreign Secretaries of the Nineteenth Century. By PERCY M. THORNTON.

Contains—Memoirs of Lord Grenville, Lord Hawkesbury, Lord Harrowby, Lord Mulgrave, C. J. Fox, Lord Howick, George Canning, Lord Bathurst, Lord Wellesley (together with estimate of his Indian Rule by Col. G. B. Malleson, C.S.I.), Lord Castlereagh, Lord Dudley, Lord Aberdeen, and Lord Palmerston. Also, Extracts from Lord Bexley's Papers, including lithographed letters of Lords Castlereagh and Canning, which, bearing on important points of public policy, have never yet been published; together with other important information culled from private and other sources. With Ten Portraits, and a View shewing Interior of the old House of Lords. (Second Edition.) 2 vols. 8vo. 32s. 6d.

Thornton's Gazetteer of India.
Compiled chiefly from the records at the India Office. By EDWARD THORNTON. 1 vol., 8vo., pp. 1015. With Map. 21s.

** *The chief objects in view in compiling this Gazetteer are:—*
1st. *To fix the relative position of the various cities, towns, and villages with as much precision as possible, and to exhibit with the greatest practicable brevity all that is known respecting them; and*
2ndly. *To note the various countries, provinces, or territorial divisions, and to describe the physical characteristics of each, together with their statistical, social, and political circumstances.*

To these are added minute descriptions of the principal rivers and chains of mountains; thus presenting to the reader, within a brief compass, a mass of information which cannot otherwise be obtained, except from a multiplicity of volumes and manuscript records.

The Library Edition.
4 vols., 8vo. Notes, Marginal References, and Map. £2 16s.

—— **Gazetteer of the Punjaub, Affghanistan, &c.**
Gazetteer of the Countries adjacent to India, on the northwest, including Scinde, Affghanistan, Beloochistan, the Punjaub, and the neighbouring States. By EDWARD THORNTON, Esq. 2 vols. 8vo. £1 5s.

Thornton's History of India.
The History of the British Empire in India, by Edward Thornton, Esq. Containing a Copious Glossary of Indian Terms, and a Complete Chronological Index of Events, to aid the Aspirant for Public Examinations. Third edition. 1 vol. 8vo. With Map. 12s.

* *The Library Edition of the above in 6 volumes, 8vo., may be had, price £2 8s.*

Thornton (T.) East India Calculator.
By T. Thornton. 8vo. London, 1825. 10s.

—— **History of the Punjaub,**
And of the Rise, Progress, and Present Condition of the Sikhs. By T. Thornton. 2 Vols. Post 8vo. 8s.

Tilley (H. A.) Japan, the Amoor and the Pacific.
With notices of other Places, comprised in a Voyage of Circumnavigation in the Imperial Russian Corvette *Rynda*, in 1858–1860. By Henry A. Tilley. Eight Illustrations. 8vo. 16s.

Tod (Col. Jas.) Travels in Western India.
Embracing a visit to the Sacred Mounts of the Jains, and the most Celebrated Shrines of Hindu Faith between Rajpootana and the Indus, with an account of the Ancient City of Nehrwalla. By the late Lieut.-Col. James Tod, Illustrations. Royal 4to. £3 3s.

* *This is a companion volume to Colonel Tod's Rajasthan.*

Torrens (W. T. McC.) Reform of Procedure in Parliament
to Clear the Block of Public Business. By W. T. McCullagh Torrens, M.P. Crown 8vo. 6s.

Trimen (Capt. R.) Regiments of the British Army,
Chronologically arranged. Showing their History, Services, Uniform, &c. By Captain R. Trimen, late 35th Regiment. 8vo. 10s. 6d.

Trotter (L. J.) History of India.
The History of the British Empire in India, from the Appointment of Lord Hardinge to the Death of Lord Canning (1844 to 1862). By Captain Lionel James Trotter, late Bengal Fusiliers. 2 vols. 8vo. 16s. each.

—— **Lord Lawrence.**
A Sketch of his Career. Fcap. 1s. 6d.

—— **Warren Hastings, a Biography.**
By Captain Lionel James Trotter, Bengal H. P., author of a "History of India," "Studies in Biography," &c. Crown 8vo. 9s.

Underwood (A. S.) Surgery for Dental Students.
By ARTHUR S. UNDERWOOD, M.R.C.S., L.D.S.E., Assistant Surgeon to the Dental Hospital of London. 5s.

Vambery (A.) Sketches of Central Asia.
Additional Chapters on My Travels and Adventures, and of the Ethnology of Central Asia. By Armenius Vambery. 8vo. 16s.
" A valuable guide on almost untrodden ground."--*Athenæum.*

Vibart (Major H. M.) The Military History of the Madras
Engineers and Pioneers. By Major H. M. VIBART, Royal (late Madras) Engineers. In 2 vols., with numerous Maps and Plans. Vol. I. 8vo. 32s. (Vol. II. in the Press.)

Victoria Cross (The) An Official Chronicle of Deeds of Per-
sonal Valour achieved in the presence of the Enemy during the Crimean and Baltic Campaigns and the Indian, Chinese, New Zealand, and African Wars. From the Institution of the Order in 1856 to 1880. Edited by ROBERT W. O'BYRNE. Crown 8vo. With Plate. 5s.

Vyse (G. W.) Egypt: Political, Financial, and Strategical.
Together with an Account of its Engineering Capabilities and Agricultural Resources. By GRIFFIN W. VYSE, late on special duty in Egypt and Afghanistan for H.M.'s Government. Crown 8vo. With Maps. 6s.

Waring (E. J.) Pharmacopœia of India.
By EDWARD JOHN WARING, M.D., &c. 8vo. 6s. (See page 2.)

Watson (M.) Money.
By JULES TARDIEU. Translated from the French by MARGARET WATSON. Crown 8vo. 7s. 6d.

Watson (Dr. J. F.) and J. W. Kaye, Races and Tribes of
Hindostan. The People of India. A series of Photographic Illustrations of the Races and Tribes of Hindustan. Prepared under the Authority of the Government of India, by J. FORBES WATSON, and JOHN WILLIAM KAYE. The Work contains about 450 Photographs on mounts, in Eight Volumes, super royal 4to. £2. 5s. per volume.

Webb (Dr. A.) Pathologia Indica.
Based upon Morbid Specimens from all parts of the Indian Empire. By ALLAN WEBB, B.M.S. Second Edit. 8vo. 14s.

Wellesley's Despatches.
The Despatches, Minutes, and Correspondence of the Marquis Wellesley, K.G., during his Administration in India. 5 vols. 8vo. With Portrait, Map, &c. £6. 10s.
This work should be perused by all who proceed to India in the Civil Services.

Wellington in India.
Military History of the Duke of Wellington in India. 1s.

Wilberforce (E.) Franz Schubert.
A Musical Biography, from the German of Dr. Heinrich Kreisle von Hellborn. By EDWARD WILBERFORCE, Esq., Author of "Social Life in Munich." Post 8vo. 6s.

Wilk's South of India.
3 vols. 4to. £5. 5s.

Wilkins (W. N.) Visual Art; or Nature through the Healthy Eye. With some remarks on Originality and Free Trade, Artistic Copyright, and Durability. By WM. NOY WILKINS, Author of "Art Impressions of Dresden," &c. 8vo. 6s.

Williams (F.) Lives of the English Cardinals.
The Lives of the English Cardinals, from Nicholas Breakspeare (Pope Adrien IV.) to Thomas Wolsey, Cardinal Legate. With Historical Notices of the Papal Court. By FOLKESTONE WILLIAMS. 2 vols., 8vo. 14s.

—— **Life, &c., of Bishop Atterbury.**
The Memoir and Correspondence of Francis Atterbury, Bishop of Rochester, with his distinguished contemporaries. Compiled chiefly from the Atterbury and Stuart Papers. By FOLKESTONE WILLIAMS, Author of "Lives of the English Cardinals," &c., 2 vols. 8vo. 14s.

Williams (Monier) Indian Wisdom.
Or Examples of the Religious, Philosophical and Ethical Doctrines of the Hindus. With a brief History of the Chief Departments of Sanscrit Literature, and some account of the Past and Present Condition of India, Moral and Intellectual. By MONIER WILLIAMS, M.A., Boden Professor of Sanscrit in in the University of Oxford. Third Edition. 8vo. 15s.

Wilson (H. H.) Glossary of Judicial and Revenue Terms, and of useful Words occurring in Official Documents relating to the Administration of the Government of British India. From the Arabic, Persian, Hindustani, Sanskrit, Hindi, Bengali, Uriya, Marathi, Guzarathi, Telugu, Karnata, Tamil, Malayalam, and other Languages. Compiled and published under the authority of the Hon. the Court of Directors of the E. I. Company. 4to., cloth. £1 10s.

White (S. D.) Indian Reminiscences.
By Colonel S. DEWE' WHITE, late Bengal Staff Corps. 8vo. With 10 Photographs. 14s.

Wollaston (Arthur N.) Anwari Suhaili, or Lights of Canopus. Commonly known as Kalilah and Damnah, being an adaptation of the Fables of Bidpai. Translated from the Persian. Royal 8vo., 42s.; also in royal 4to., with illuminated borders, designed specially for the work, cloth, extra gilt. £3 13s. 6d.

—— **Elementary Indian Reader.**
Designed for the use of Students in the Anglo-Vernacular Schools in India. Fcap. 1s.

Woolrych (Serjeant W. H.)
Lives of Eminent Serjeants-at-Law of the English Bar. By HUMPHRY W. WOOLRYCH, Serjeant-at-Law. 2 vols. 8vo. 30s.

Wraxall (Sir L., Bart.) Caroline Matilda.
Queen of Denmark, Sister of George 3rd. From Family and State Papers. By SIR LASCELLES WRAXALL, Bart. 3 vols., 8vo. 18s.

Young (J. R.) Course of Mathematics.
A Course of Elementary Mathematics for the use of candidates for admission into either of the Military Colleges; of applicants for appointments in the Home or Indian Civil Services; and of mathematical students generally. By Professor J. R. YOUNG. In one closely-printed volume. 8vo., pp. 648. 12s.

"In the work before us he has digested a complete Elementary Course, by aid of his long experience as a teacher and writer; and he has produced a very useful book. Mr. Young has not allowed his own taste to rule the distribution, but has adjusted his parts with the skill of a veteran."—*Athenæum.*

Young (M.) and Trent (R.) A Home Ruler.
A Story for Girls. By MINNIE YOUNG and RACHEL TRENT, Illustrated by C. P. Colnaghi. Crown 8vo. 3s. 6d.

Works in the Press.

THE HISTORY OF INDIA, AS TOLD BY ITS OWN HISTORIANS; the Local Muhammadan Dynasties. Vol. I. Guzerat. By John Dowson, M.R.A.S., late Professor of the Staff College. Forming a Sequel in two or more volumes to Sir H. M. Elliott's Original work on the Muhammadan period of the History of India; already edited, annotated, and amplified by the same Author. Published under the Patronage of H.M.'s Secretary of State for India.

AN INTEGRAL CALCULUS. Simplified for Schools. By W. P. Lynam, Indian Public Works Department.

WANDERINGS IN BALUCHISTAN. By General Sir C. M. MacGregor, C.S.I., &c., Author of "Narrative of a Journey through Khorassan," &c.

THE TRUTH ABOUT OPIUM. A Defence of the Indo-China Opium Trade, and a Refutation of the Allegations of the "Anglo-Oriental Society for the Suppression of the Opium Trade," being the Substance of Three Lectures delivered at St. James's Hall on the 9th, 16th, and 23rd February, 1882. By Wm. E. Brereton, late of Hong Kong, Solicitor.

THE BELGIUM OF THE EAST. By the Author of "Egypt under Ismail Pasha," "Egypt for the Egyptians," &c. Edited by Blanchard Jerrold.

THREE PLAYS AND TWELVE DRAMATIC SCENES. Suitable for Private Theatricals. By Martin F. Tupper, D.C.L., F.R.S., Author of "Proverbial Philosophy."

THIRTY-EIGHT YEARS IN INDIA, from Jugunath to the Himalayan Mountains. Vol. II.

THE PLAYS AND POEMS OF CHARLES DICKENS. Collected and Edited by Richard Herne Shepherd. 2 vols.

THE ENGLISH IN INDIA. New Sketches. By E. de Valbezen, late Consul-General at Calcutta, Minister Plenipotentiary. Translated from the French, with the Author's permission, by a Diplomat.

DIPLOMATIC STUDY OF THE CRIMEAN WAR. Translated from the original as published by the Russian Foreign Office. 2 vols.

AN ILLUSTRATED EDITION OF TWENTY-ONE DAYS IN INDIA. Being the Tour of Sir Ali Baba, K.C.B. By George Aberigh Mackay.

QUEER PEOPLE. From the Swedish of "Leah." By Albert Alberg. 2 vols.

THE JESUITS. A Complete History of public and private proceedings from the foundation of the Order to the present time. By Theodor Greussinger.

FRANZ LISZT, ARTIST AND MAN. By L. Ramann, Translated from the German.

"ON DUTY." A Novel.

FOREIGN SECRETARIES OF THE XIXTH CENTURY. By Percy M. Thornton. Vol. III.

SCHOOL RIDING. By Edward L. Anderson, Author of "How to Ride and School a Horse."

ACCENTED FIVE-FIGURE LOGARITHMS of the numbers from 1 to 99999 without Differences. Arranged and Accented by Lowis D'A. Jackson.

GUJARÁT AND THE GUJARÁTÍS: Pictures of Men and Manners taken from Life. By Behrámjí M. Malabárí, Author of "The Indian Muse in English Garb," "Pleasures of Morality," "Wilson-Virah," &c., and Editor of the "Indian Spectator."

Oriental Works in the Press.

A Hindi Manual. By FREDERIC PINCOTT, M.R.A.S.
An English-Arabic Dictionary. By DR. STEINGASS.
An Arabic-English Dictionary. By DR. STEINGASS.
An English-Hindi Dictionary. By FREDERIC PINCOTT, M.R.A.S.
A Malay, Achinese, French, and English Vocabulary. Prepared by Dr. A. J. W. BIKKERS.

A SELECTION FROM

MESSRS. ALLEN'S CATALOGUE
OF BOOKS IN THE EASTERN LANGUAGES, &c.

HINDUSTANI, HINDI, &c.

[*Dr. Forbes's Works are used as Class Books in the Colleges and Schools in India.*]

Forbes's Hindustani-English Dictionary in the Persian Character, with the Hindi words in Nagari also; and an English Hindustani Dictionary in the English Character; both in one volume. By DUNCAN FORBES, LL.D. Royal 8vo. 42s.

Forbes's Hindustani-English and English Hindustani Dictionary, in the English Character. Royal 8vo. 36s.

Forbes's Smaller Dictionary, Hindustani and English, in the English Character. 12s.

Forbes's Hindustani Grammar, with Specimens of Writing in the Persian and Nagari Characters, Reading Lessons, and Vocabulary. 8vo. 10s. 6d.

Forbes's Hindustani Manual, containing a Compendious Grammar, Exercises for Translation, Dialogues, and Vocabulary, in the Roman Character. New Edition, entirely revised. By J. T. PLATTS. 18mo. 3s. 6d.

Forbes's Bagh o Bahar, in the Persian Character, with a complete Vocabulary. Royal 8vo. 12s. 6d.

Forbes's Bagh o Bahar in English, with Explanatory Notes, illustrative of Eastern Character. 8vo. 8s.

Forbes's Bagh o Bahar, with Vocaby., English Character. 5s.

Forbes's Tota Kahani ; or, " Tales of a Parrot," in the Persian Character, with a complete Vocabulary. Royal 8vo. 8s.

Forbes's Baital Pachisi ; or, " Twenty-five Tales of a Demon," in the Nagari Character, with a complete Vocabulary. Royal 8vo. 9s.

Forbes's Ikhwanu s Safa; or, " Brothers of Purity," in the Persian Character. Royal 8vo. 12s. 6d.

[*For the higher standard for military officers' examinations.*]

Forbes's Oriental Penmanship ; a Guide to Writing Hindustani in the Persian Character. 4to. 8s.

Platts' Grammar of the Urdu or Hindustani-Language. 8vo. 12s.

Eastwick (Edward B.) The Bagh-o-Bahar—literally translated into English, with copious explanatory notes. 8vo. 10s. 6d.

Small's (Rev. G.) Tota Kahani; or, "Tales of a Parrot." Translated into English. 8vo. 8s.

Small's (Rev. G.) Dictionary of Naval Terms, English and Hindustani. For the use of Nautical Men Trading to India," &c. Fcap. 2s. 6d.

Platts' J. T., Baital Pachisi; translated into English. 8vo. 8s.

Platts' Ikhwanu S Safa; translated into English. 8vo. 10s. 6d.

Platt's (J. T.), A Hindustani Dictionary. Part I. Royal 8vo. 10s. 6d.

Hindustani Selections, with a Vocabulary of the Words. By JAMES R. BALLANTYNE. Second Edition. 1845. 5s.

Singhasan Battisi. Translated into Hindi from the Sanscrit. A New Edition. Revised, Corrected, and Accompanied with Copious Notes. By SYED ABDOOLAH. Royal 8vo. 12s. 6d.

Akhlaki Hindi, translated into Urdu, with an Introduction and Notes. By SYED ABDOOLAH. Royal 8vo. 12s. 6d.

Sakuntala. Translated into Hindi from the Bengali recension of the Sanskrit. Critically edited, with grammatical, idiomatical, and exegetical notes, by FREDERIC PINCOTT. 4to. 12s. 6d.

Alif Laila, ba-Zubán-i-Urdú (The Arabian Nights in Hindustani). Roman Character. Edited by F. PINCOTT, M.R.A.S.

Principles of Persian Caligraphy. Illustrated by Lithographic Plates of the Ta"lik Character, the one usually employed in writing the Persian and the Hindustani. Prepared for the use of the Scottish Naval and Military Academy by JAMES R. BALLANTYNE. Second Edition. 4to. 3s. 6d.

SANSCRIT.

Haughton's Sanscrit and Bengali Dictionary, in the Bengali Character, with Index, serving as a reversed dictionary. 4to. 30s.

Williams's English-Sanscrit Dictionary. 4to., cloth. £3. 3s.

Williams's Sanskrit-English Dictionary. 4to. £4 14s. 6d.

Wilkin's (Sir Charles) Sanscrit Grammar. 4to. 15s.

Williams's (Monier) Sanscrit Grammar. 8vo. 15s.

Williams's (Monier) Sanscrit Manual; to which is added, a Vocabulary, by A. E. GOUGH. 18mo. 7s. 6d.

Gough's (A. E.) Key to the Exercises in Williams's Sanscrit Manual. 18mo. 4s.

Williams's (Monier) Sakuntala, with Literal English Translation of all the Metrical Passages, Schemes of the Metres, and copious Critical and Explanatory Notes. Royal 8vo. 21s.

Williams's (Monier) Sakuntala. Translated into English Prose and Verse. Fourth Edition. 8s.

Williams's (Monier) Vikramorvasi. The Text. 8vo. 5s

Cowell's (E. B.) Translation of the Vikramorvasi. 8vo. 3s 6d.

Thompson's (J. C.) Bhagavat Gita. Sanscrit Text. 5s.
Haughton's Menu, with English Translation. 2 vols. 4to. 24s.
Johnson's Hitopadesa, with Vocabulary. 15s.
Hitopadesa. A new literal translation from the Sanskrit Text of Prof. F. Johnson. For the use of Students. By FREDERIC PINCOTT, M.R.A.S. 6s.
Hitopadesa, Sanscrit, with Bengali and English Trans. 10s. 6d.
Wilson's Megha Duta, with Translation into English Verse, Notes, Illustrations, and a Vocabulary. Royal 8vo. 6s.

PERSIAN.

Richardson's Persian, Arabic, and English Dictionary. Edition of 1852. By F. JOHNSON. 4to. £4.
Forbes's Persian Grammar, Reading Lessons, and Vocabulary. Royal 8vo. 12s. 6d.
Ibraheem's Persian Grammar, Dialogues, &c. Royal 8vo. 12s. 6d.
Gulistan. Carefully collated with the original MS., with a full Vocabulary. By JOHN PLATTS, late Inspector of Schools, Central Provinces, India. Royal 8vo. 12s. 6d.
Gulistan. Translated from a revised Text, with Copious Notes. By JOHN PLATTS. 8vo. 12s. 6d.
Ouseley's Anwari Soheili. 4to. 42s.
Wollaston's (Arthur N.) Translation of the Anvari Soheili. Royal 8vo. £2 2s.
Wollaston's (Arthur N.) English-Persian Dictionary. Compiled from Original Sources. 8vo. 25s.
Keene's (Rev. H. G.) First Book of The Anwari Soheili. Persian Text. 8vo. 5s.
Ouseley's (Col.) Akhlaki Mushini. Persian Text. 8vo. 5s
Keene's (Rev. H. G.) Akhlaki Mushini. Translated into English. 8vo. 3s. 6d.
Clarke's (Captain H. Wilberforce, R.E.) The Persian Manual. A Pocket Companion.
PART I.—A CONCISE GRAMMAR OF THE LANGUAGE, with Exercises on its more Prominent Peculiarities, together with a Selection of Useful Phrases, Dialogues, and Subjects for Translation into Persian.
PART II.—A VOCABULARY OF USEFUL WORDS, ENGLISH AND PERSIAN, showing at the same time the difference of idiom between the two Languages. 18mo. 7s. 6d.
The Bústán. By Shaikh Muslihu-d-Dín Sa'di Shírází. Translated for the first time into Prose, with Explanatory Notes and Index. By Captain H. WILBERFORCE CLARKE, R.E. 8vo. With Portrait. 30s.
A Translation of Robinson Crusoe into the Persian Language. Roman Character. Edited by T. W. H. TOLBORT, Bengal Civil Service. Cr. 8vo. 7s.

BENGALI.

Haughton's Bengali, Sanscrit, and English Dictionary, adapted for Students in either language; to which is added an Index, serving as a reversed dictionary. 4to. 30s.

Forbes's Bengali Grammar, with Phrases and dialogues. Royal 8vo. 12s. 6d.

Forbes's Bengali Reader, with a Translation and Vocabulary Royal 8vo. 12s. 6d.

Nabo Nari. 12mo. 7s.

ARABIC.

Richardson's Arabic, Persian and English Dictionary. Edition of 1852. By F. Johnson. 4to., cloth. £4.

Forbes's Arabic Grammar, intended more especially for the use of young men preparing for the East India Civil Service, and also for the use of self instructing students in general. Royal 8vo., cloth. 18s.

Palmer's Arabic Grammar. 8vo. 18s.

Forbes's Arabic Reading Lessons, consisting of Easy Extracts from the best Authors, with Vocabulary. Royal 8vo., cloth. 15s.

The Arabic Manual. Comprising a condensed Grammar of both Classical and Modern Arabic; Reading Lessons and Exercises, with Analyses and a Vocabulary of useful Words. By Prof. E. H. Palmer, M.A., &c., Author of "A Grammar of the Arabic Language." Fcap. 7s. 6d.

TELOOGOO.

Brown's Dictionary, reversed; with a Dictionary of the Mixed Dialects used in Teloogoo. 3 vols. in 2, royal 8vo. £5.

Campbell's Dictionary. Royal 8vo. 30s.

Brown's Reader. 8vo. 2 vols. 14s.

Brown's Dialogues, Teloogoo and English. 8vo. 5s. 6d.

Pancha Tantra. 8s.

Percival's English-Teloogoo Dictionary. 10s. 6d.

TAMIL.

Rottler's Dictionary, Tamil and English. 4to. 42s

Babington's Grammar (High Dialect). 4to. 12s.

Percival's Tamil Dictionary. 2 vols. 10s. 6d.

GUZRATTEE.

Mavor's Spelling, Guzrattee and English. 7s, 6d.
Shapuaji Edalji's Dictionary, Guzrattee and English. 21s.

MAHRATTA.

Molesworth's Dictionary, Mahratta and English. 4to. 42s.
Molesworth's Dictionary, English and Mahratta. 4to. 42s.
Esop's Fables. 12mo. 2s. 6d.
A Grammar of the Mahratta Language. For the use of the East India College at Hayleybury. By JAMES R. BALLANTYNE, of the Scottish Naval and Military Academy. 4to. 5s.

MALAY.

Marsden's Grammar. 4to. £1 1s.

CHINESE.

Morrison's Dictionary. 6 vols. 4to. £10.
Marshman's—Clavis Sinica, a Chinese Grammar. 4to. £2 2s.
Morrison's View of China, for Philological purposes; containing a Sketch of Chinese Chronology, Geography, Government, Religion and Customs, designed for those who study the Chinese language. 4to. 6s.

PUS'HTO.

The Pushto Manual. Comprising a Concise Grammar; Exercises and Dialogues; Familiar Phrases, Proverbs, and Vocabulary. By Major H. G. RAVERTY, Bombay Infantry (Retired). Author of the Pus'hto Grammar, Dictionary, Selections Prose and Poetical, Selections from the Poetry of the Afgháns (English Translation), Æsop's Fables, &c. &c. Fcap. 5s.

MISCELLANEOUS.

Reeve's English-Carnatica and Carnatica-English Dictionary. 2 vols. (Very slightly damaged). £8.
Collett's Malayalam Reader. 8vo. 12s. 6d.
Esop's Fables in Carnatica. 8vo. bound. 12s. 6d.
A Turkish Manual, comprising a Condensed Grammar with Idiomatic Phrases, Exercises and Dialogues, and Vocabulary. By Captain C. F. MACKENZIE, late of H.M.'s Consular Service. 6s.

W. H. ALLEN & CO'S ORIENTAL MANUALS.

Forbes's Hindustani Manual, containing a Compendious Grammar, Exercises for Translation, Dialogues, and Vocabulary, in the Roman Character. New edition, entirely revised. By J. T. PLATTS, 18mo. 3s. 6d.

Williams's (Monier) Sanskrit Manual; to which is added, a Vocabulary, by A. E. GOUGH. 18mo. 7s. 6d.

Gough's (A. E.) Key to the Exercises in Williams's Sanscrit Manual. 18mo. 4s.

The Arabic Manual. Comprising a condensed Grammar of both Classical and Modern Arabic; Reading Lessons and Exercises, with Analyses and a Vocabulary of useful Words. By Prof. E. H. PALMER, M.A., &c., Author of "A Grammar of the Arabic Language." Fcap. 7s. 6d.

A Turkish Manual, comprising a Condensed Grammar with Idiomatic Phrases, Exercises and Dialogues, and Vocabulary. By Captain C. F. MACKENZIE, late of H.M.'s Consular Service. 6s.

Clarke's (Capt. H. W., R.E.) The Persian Manual, containing a concise Grammar, with Exercises, useful Phrases, Dialogues, and Subjects for Translation into Persian; also a Vocabulary of Useful Words, English and Persian. 18mo. 7s. 6d.

The Pushto Manual. Comprising a Concise Grammar; Exercises and Dialogues; Familiar Phrases, Proverbs, and Vocabulary. By Major H. G. RAVERTY, Bombay Infantry (Retired). Fcap. 5s.

A RELIEVO MAP OF INDIA.
BY HENRY F. BRION.
In Frame, 21s.

"A map of this kind brings before us such a picture of the surface of a given country as no ordinary map could ever do. To the mind's eye of the average Englishman, India consists of 'the plains' and 'the hills,' chiefly of the former, the hills being limited to the Himalayas and the Nilgiris. The new map will at least enable him to correct his notions of Indian geography. It combines the usual features of a good plain map of the country on a scale of 150 miles to the inch, with a faithful representation of all the uneven surfaces, modelled on a scale thirty-two times the horizontal one; thus bringing out into clear relief the comparative heights and outlines of all the hill-ranges, and showing broad tracts of uneven ground, of intermingled hill and valley, which a common map of the same size would hardly indicate, except to a very practised eye. The plains of Upper India are reduced to their true proportions; the Central Provinces, Malwa, and Western Bengal reveal their actual ruggedness at a glance; and Southern India, from the Vindhyas to Cape Comorin, proclaims its real height above the sea-level. To the historical as well as the geographical student such a map is an obvious and important aid in tracing the course of past campaigns, in realising the conditions under which successive races carried their arms or settlements through the Peninsula, and in comprehending the difference of race, climate, and physical surroundings which make up our Indian Empire. Set in a neat frame of maplewood, the map seems to attract the eye like a prettily-coloured picture, and its price, a guinea, should place it within the reach of all who care to combine the useful with the ornamental."—*Home News.*

MAPS OF INDIA, etc.

Messrs. Allen & Co.'s Maps of India were revised and much improved during 1876, with especial reference to the existing Administrative Divisions, Railways, &c.

District Map of India; corrected to 1876;
Divided into Collectorates with the Telegraphs and Railways from Government surveys. On six sheets—size, 5ft. 6in. high; 5ft. 8in. wide, £2; in a case, £2 12s. 6d.; or, rollers, varn., £3 3s.

A General Map of India; corrected to 1876;
Compiled chiefly from surveys executed by order of the Government of India. On six sheets—size, 5 ft. 3 in. wide; 5 ft. 4 in. high, £2; or, on cloth, in case, £2 12s. 6d.; or, rollers, varn., £3 3s.

Map of India; corrected to 1876;
From the most recent Authorities. On two sheets—size, 2 ft. 10in. wide; 3 ft. 3 in. high, 16s.; or, on cloth, in a case, £1 1s.

Map of the Routes in India; corrected to 1874;
With Tables of Distances between the principal Towns and Military Stations On one sheet—size, 2 ft. 3 in. wide; 2 ft. 9 in. high, 9s.; or, on cloth, in a case, 12s.

Map of the Western Provinces of Hindoostan,
The Punjab, Cabool, Scinde, Bhawulpore, &c., including all the States between Cundahar and Allahabad. On four sheets—size, 4 ft. 4in. wide; 4 ft. 2 in. high, 30s.; or, in case, £2; rollers, varnished, £2 10s.

Map of India and China, Burmah, Siam, the Malay Peninsula, and the Empire of Anam. On two sheets—size, 4 ft. 3 in. wide; 3 ft. 4 in. high, 16s.; or, on cloth, in a case, £1 5s.

Map of the Steam Communication and Overland Routes between England, India, China, and Australia. In a case, 14s.; on rollers, and varnished, 18s.

Map of China,
From the most Authentic Sources of Information. One large sheet—size, 2 ft. 7 in. wide; 2 ft. 2 in. high, 6s.; or, on cloth, in case, 8s.

Map of the World;
On Mercator's Projection, showing the Tracts of the Early Navigators, the Currents of the Ocean, the Principal Lines of great Circle Sailing, and the most recent discoveries. On four sheets—size, 6ft. 2 in. wide; 4 ft. 3 in. high, £2; on cloth, in a case, £2 10s; or, with rollers, and varnished, £3.

Handbook of Reference to the Maps of India.
Giving the Latitude and Longitude of places of note. 18mo. 3s. 6d.

Russian Official Map of Central Asia. Compiled in accordance with the Discoveries and Surveys of Russian Staff Officers up to the close of the year 1877. In 2 Sheets. 10s. 6d., or in cloth case, 14s.

In January and July of each year is published in 8vo., price 10s. 6d.,

THE INDIA LIST, CIVIL & MILITARY,
BY PERMISSION OF THE SECRETARY OF STATE FOR INDIA IN COUNCIL.

CONTENTS.

CIVIL.—Gradation Lists of Civil Service, Bengal, Madras and Bombay. Civil Annuitants. Legislative Council, Ecclesiastical Establishments, Educational, Public Works, Judicial, Marine, Medical, Land Revenue, Political, Postal, Police, Customs and Salt, Forest, Registration and Railway and Telegraph Departments, Law Courts, Surveys, &c., &c.

MILITARY.—Gradation List of the General and Field Officers (British and Local) of the three Presidencies, Staff Corps, Adjutants-General's and Quartermasters-General's Offices, Army Commissariat Departments, British Troops Serving in India (including Royal Artillery, Royal Engineers, Cavalry, Infantry, and Medical Department), List of Native Regiments, Commander-in-Chief and Staff, Garrison Instruction Staff, Indian Medical Department, Ordnance Departments, Punjab Frontier Force, Military Departments of the three Presidencies, Veterinary Departments, Tables showing the Distribution of the Army in India, Lists of Retired Officers of the three Presidencies.

HOME.—Departments of the Office of the Secretary of State, Coopers Hill College, List of Selected Candidates for the Civil and Forest Services, Indian Troop Service.

MISCELLANEOUS.—Orders of the Bath, Star of India, and St. Michael and St. George. Order of Precedence in India. Regulations for Admission to Civil Service. Regulations for Admission of Chaplains. Civil Leave Code and Supplements. Civil Service Pension Code—relating to the Covenanted and Uncovenanted Services. Rules for the Indian Medical Service. Furlough and Retirement Regulations of the Indian Army. Family Pension Fund. Staff Corps Regulations. Salaries of Staff Officers. Regulations for Promotion. English Furlough Pay.

THE
ROYAL KALENDAR,
AND COURT AND CITY REGISTER,
FOR ENGLAND, IRELAND, SCOTLAND, AND THE COLONIES,

For the Year 1882.

CONTAINING A CORRECT LIST OF THE TWENTY-FIRST IMPERIAL PARLIAMENT, SUMMONED TO MEET FOR THEIR FIRST SESSION—MARCH 5TH, 1874.

House of Peers—House of Commons—Sovereigns and Rulers of States of Europe—Orders of Knighthood—Science and Art Department—Queen's Household—Government Offices—Mint—Customs—Inland Revenue—Post Office—Foreign Ministers and Consuls—Queen's Consuls Abroad—Naval Department—Navy List—Army Department—Army List—Law Courts—Police—Ecclesiastical Department—Clergy List—Foundation Schools—Literary Institutions—City of London.—Banks—Railway Companies—Hospitals and Institutions—Charities—Miscellaneous Institutions—Scotland, Ireland, India, and the Colonies; and other useful information.

Price with Index, 7s.; without Index, 5s

Published on the arrival of every Mail from India. Subscription 26s. per annum, post free, specimen copy, 6d.

ALLEN'S INDIAN MAIL,
AND
Official Gazette
FROM
INDIA, CHINA, AND ALL PARTS OF THE EAST.

ALLEN'S INDIAN MAIL contains the fullest and most authentic Reports of all important Occurrences in the Countries to which it is devoted, compiled chiefly from private and exclusive sources. It has been pronounced by the Press in general to be *indispensable* to all who have Friends or Relatives in the East, as affording the only *correct* information regarding the Services, Movements of Troops, Shipping, and all events of Domestic and individual interest.

The subjoined list of the usual Contents will show the importance and variety of the information concentrated in ALLEN'S INDIAN MAIL.

Summary and Review of Eastern News.

Precis of Public Intelligence	Shipping—Arrival of Ships
Selections from the Indian Press	,, ,, Passengers
Movements of Troops	,, Departure of Ships
The Government Gazette	,, ,, Passengers
Courts Martial	Commercial—State of the Markets
Domestic Intelligence—Births	,, Indian Securities
,, ,, Marriages	,, Freights
,, ,, Deaths	&c. &c. &c.

Home Intelligence relating to India, &c.

Original Articles	Arrival reported in England
Miscellaneous Information	Departures ,, ,,
Appointments, List of Furloughs, Extensions, &c.	Shipping—Arrival of Ships
	,, ,, Passengers
,, Civil	,, Departure of Ships
,, Military	,, ,, Passengers
,, Ecclesiastical and	,, Vessel spoken with
,, Marine	&c. &c. &c.

Review of Works on the East.—and Notices of all affairs connected with India and the Services.

Each year an INDEX is furnished, to enable Subscribers to bind up the Volume which forms a complete

ASIATIC ANNUAL REGISTER AND LIBRARY OF REFERENCE.

LONDON: WM. H. ALLEN & Co., 13, WATERLOO PLACE, S.W.

(PUBLISHERS TO THE INDIA OFFICE),

To whom Communications for the Editor, and Advertisements are requested to be addressed.

Subscription, 32s. per annum. Postage Free. Or in Monthly Parts, price 3s.

PRÉCIS OF OFFICIAL PAPERS,

BEING

ABSTRACTS OF ALL PARLIAMENTARY RETURNS

DIRECTED TO BE PRINTED BY

BOTH HOUSES OF PARLIAMENT.

"Messrs. Allen have commenced the publication of a most useful work, the need of which has been felt for a long time, though until now no one has had the courage to attempt it. . . . . . The *précis* is very well done."—*Journal of the Statistical Society*, June, 1890.

"There is no doubt as to the value of most parliamentary publications, but few persons have the time or inclination to wade through them, and thus much valuable matter is missed, but in this *précis* Messrs. Allen and Co. give an outline of just what is required."—*Iron Trade Review.*

"Messrs. Allen & Co.'s book is composed of abstracts of all returns directed to be printed by either or both of the Houses of Parliament, and the work has evidently been done by practised *précis* writers who understand how to reach the important features of Government papers."—*Liverpool Daily Courier.*

"This is a publication which supplies a great want. We gladly welcome this work, both for reading and for reference."—*United Service Gazette.*

"The papers are carefully condensed."—*British Mail.*

"In the case of statistical returns it is especially good."—*Cambridge Chronicle.*

"This is not a Blue-book; but none of them can exceed it in value. Every business man will have it upon the desk corner for reference, and it should be found on the table of every public reading room and private library."—*Western Times.*

"A most useful work of reference."—*The Railway News.*

"This is a very important work, and its perusal will place readers on a far higher intellectual level and acquaintance with the parliamentary papers than most embryo members of Parliament possess."—*Finance Chronicle and Insurance Circular.*

"This serial is calculated to be of much service."—*Iron.*

"The above contains a vast amount of valuable information and statistics."—*Sunday Times.*

"We scarcely need add that it is a valuable work."—*Herapath's Railway Journal.*

"As a book of reference, promises to be of inestimable value to public men, journalists, economists, historical students, and, indeed, all who are interested in national progress and contemporary politics."—*The Statist.*

"The difficult work of summarising is extremely well executed. Both paper and type are good."—*Broad Arrow.*

"An excellent publication."—*The Farmer.*

"Messrs. Allen & Co. earn the gratitude of all who require to keep themselves acquainted with the contents of parliamentary papers by the publication of this *précis*. The compilation has been made with discretion, and will be found extremely valuable and useful for reference."—*Dundee Advertiser.*

"As a handy work of reference, and a means of saving time and labour, it will be highly appreciated."—*Allen's Indian Mail.*

"The utility of the *précis* is very considerably heightened by an admirable table of contents numerically and alphabetically arranged."—*The Railway News and Joint Stock Journal.*

"The *précis* of official papers will give new value to the parliamentary returns."—*Liverpool Courier.*

"Nous croyons rendre service au public et à ceux de nos confreres qui ne la connaitraient pas, en leur signalent cette publication nouvelle."—*Moniteur des Intérêts Materiels, Brussels.*

LONDON: W. H. ALLEN & CO., 13, WATERLOO-PLACE.

www.ingramcontent.com/pod-product-compliance
Lightning Source LLC
Chambersburg PA
CBHW020926230426
43666CB00008B/1582